A Republic— If We Can Keep It

Lawrence W. Reed
Burton W. Folsom, Jr.

D1508003

FOUNDATION FOR
ECONOMIC EDUCATION

ISBN-10: 1572460318

ISBN-13: 978-1-57246-031-7

Also available in Kindle and ePub formats, ISBN 9781572460171 .

Cover design by Courtney Hechler

Original versions of the included articles can be found on the website of *The Freeman*, www.TheFreemanOnline.org, or that of the Mackinac Center for Public Policy, www.Mackinac.org.

Find us online at:

Facebook.com/FEEonline

Twitter.com/FEEonline (@feeonline)

Contact us directly at:

1-800-960-4FEE (4333)

Foundation for Economic Education

30 S. Broadway

Irvington, New York 10533

260 Peachtree St. NW

Suite 2200

Atlanta GA 30303

FEE.org

To those many young people whom we've been blessed to teach over the years and who are helping to keep the torch of liberty lit.

Preface

Economics as it is taught today is replete with fallacies. So is History. Combine the two into Economic History and you frequently get a witch's brew of mumbo jumbo.

The Industrial Revolution was a setback for workers. Free markets caused monopoly and exploitation. Government intervention was required for economic growth and for economic recovery. These are but a few of the many misconceptions that constantly need revisiting, and are addressed within this volume.

The authors recognize that both economics and history must be about much more than numbers. That's why many of the offerings here focus on the interesting contributions of people who changed the course of events. One of the essential points we hope readers of this anthology will come away with is the critical importance of specific individuals in shaping the course of the amorphous collective known as "society."

Almost all of the chapters herein first appeared in *The Freeman*, the journal of the Foundation for Economic Education (FEE). We invite readers to visit FEE's website, fee.org, and also our Facebook pages.

Our original intent in assembling this anthology was to provide teachers of history, economics and economic history with a companion text of readings. We hope this collection will be of interest to a wider audience as well, especially to those who support the ideas and philosophy of the free society.

We thank our friend Doug Bandow of the Cato Institute for his assistance in organizing the chapters and devising the unit headings. We also thank Michael Nolan of FEE for his assistance in editing and layout.

We give special thanks to the Earhart Foundation of Ann Arbor, Michigan for its support of this volume.

Table of Contents

I. Principles of Limited Government

II. The Trials of Unlimited Government

III. Our Cousins Stand for Liberty

IV. The Positive Power of the Entrepreneur

V. The Negative Power of the Bureaucrat

VI. Depressions, Poverty and Inequality

VII. Individuals Against Government Injustice

VIII. The Big Government Warfare State

Part I

Principles of Limited Government

1

Chapter **One**

The Holiday That Isn't

By October, most people have already begun to think of the holidays just around the corner. We each observe the traditional ones according to our personal wishes—a precious right won for us by past and present patriots.

Allow me to advise you, however, not to let this year end without taking note of "the holiday that isn't." It's not recognized officially, and few Americans really know of it. I had to be reminded of it by a friend from Arizona, Roy Miller, one of the founders of the Goldwater Institute.

The day is December 15. It was on that date in 1791 that the fledgling United States of America formally adopted what we know as the Bill of Rights, the first ten amendments to the Constitution. Miller says, "Few days in American history were more critical to securing or proclaiming the principles behind the nation's founding."

A "Bill of Rights Day" is not on the calendar, but a free people don't have to wait for Congress to declare a holiday to celebrate one. On December 15, take a moment to reread the Bill of Rights and reflect on its importance. Call it to the attention of friends and family. Without an agreement that a Bill of Rights would be added or without a consensus of what they would do, the Constitution itself would probably not have been accepted. The ten amendments ultimately adopted guarantee freedoms of religion, speech, the press, peaceful assembly and petition; the rights of the people to keep and bear arms, and to hold private property; rights to fair treatment for people accused of crimes, protection from unreasonable search and seizure and self-incrimination; and rights to a speedy and impartial jury trial and representation by counsel.

In this modern and supposedly enlightened age, not many people among the world's 7 billion can honestly say they enjoy many of these rights to their fullest—or at all. Even in America we have to work hard to educate fellow citizens about the liberties the Bill of Rights is meant to protect. There are plenty in our midst who would sacrifice one or more liberties for the temporary and dubious security of a government program. In June 2008 the Supreme Court affirmed the right to keep and bear arms but only by a 5–4 vote. No wonder Benjamin Franklin said the Constitution gave us "a republic, madam, if you can keep it."

In the grand scheme of American liberty, how important is the Bill of Rights? It's fundamental and foundational, and about as bedrock as it gets. In fewer than 500 words, many of our most cherished liberties are expressed as rights and unequivocally protected. It's a roster of instructions to government to keep out of where it doesn't belong. It bears the heavy imprint of a giant of republican government, James Madison.

Why did such critical protections end up as amendments instead of as core elements of the primary document? Here's the background:

The Second Continental Congress, originally convened in 1775 at the outbreak of hostilities with the mother country, adopted the Articles of Confederation as the new nation's first formal, national government. Some Americans came to believe by the late 1780s, however, that the Articles were weak and inadequate. The Constitutional Convention of 1787 produced a draft Constitution to replace them, subject to ratification by the states. A great debate ensued and people lined up in one camp or the other—the Federalists or the Antifederalists. The former favored the Constitution and in most cases, at least at first, without any amendments. The latter either opposed it altogether or conditioned their approval on adoption of stronger protections for individual liberties.

Keep in mind that virtually all the leading figures in this great debate were libertarians by today's standards. They believed in liberty and limited government. Even the least libertarian among them would be horrified if he could see how later generations have ballooned the size and intrusiveness of the federal establishment. It never occurred to the most ardent Federalist that government should rob Peter to pay Paul for his health care, art work, alternative energy, prescription drugs, hurricane relief, or his notions of regime change in Somalia.

The Constitution and Centralization

So even without the Bill of Rights, the Constitution represented a huge advance for civilization. But during the ratification debate, enough citizens were wary of any centralization of power that they wanted to go further. I think they instinctively understood something that Thomas Jefferson once so aptly expressed, "The natural progress of things is for liberty to yield and government to gain ground." When the Massachusetts legislature made it clear it would not ratify the Constitution unless language was added to strengthen individual rights, it triggered a movement among the states to do just that.

Madison is regarded as the "Father of the Constitution" because he was its primary author and, along with Alexander Hamilton and John Jay, part of the trio that wrote the Federalist Papers in its defense. On the matter of amending it with a Bill of Rights, he was at first opposed, being of the view that enumerating some rights in the form of amendments would open the door to government violations of any that were not listed. He eventually met that very objection by devising what became the Ninth Amendment: "The enumeration in the Constitution, of certain rights, shall not be construed to deny or disparage others retained by the people." Madison became one of the most eloquent defenders of the Bill of Rights, and it is unlikely the Constitution would have been ratified without him or them.

In 1789 New Jersey was the first state to adopt the ten amendments that would become the Bill of Rights. When Virginia did so on December 15, 1791, they became part of the supreme law of the land. (Actually, 12 amendments were sent to the states, but two failed to win enough states to be ratified. The unratified amendments, originally numbers 1 and 2, set the ratio of House representative to population and forbade congressional pay raises to take effect "until an election of Representatives shall have intervened." The latter was ratified as the 27th amendment in 1992.)

If you want to bone up on the Bill of Rights before December 15, check out the website of the Bill of Rights Institute (billofrightsinstitute.org), which produces instructional materials and sponsors seminars about America's foundational documents. Some excellent books to consult on the subject include *We the People* by Forrest McDonald, *Fighting for Liberty and Virtue* by Marvin Olasky, *Simple Rules for a Complex World* by Richard Epstein, and *Restoring the Lost Constitution: The Presumption of Liberty* by Randy Barnett.

—LWR, October 2008

2

Chapter **Two**

The Founders, the Constitution, and the Historians

The first step in getting Americans to disregard the Constitution is to get them to distrust the men who wrote it. This assault on the Founders, subtle at first, began in earnest almost 100 years ago. The first historian to challenge the motives of the Founders was Charles Beard in *An Economic Interpretation of the Constitution of the United States* (1913).

In this landmark book, Beard, a professor of history at Columbia University, argued that the Constitution was "an economic document drawn with superb skill by men whose property interests were immediately at stake." The Founders, then, rather than being patriots, wise lawmakers, or thoughtful students of government, were primarily in the Constitution-writing business to protect their "property interests."

Conflicts of Interest

The Founders' economic motives, according to Beard, were straightforward—they were owed money from their support of the

Revolution, and those "public securities" (receipts for loans made to support American independence) were not being repaid under the weak Articles of Confederation. A stronger governing document was needed to ease the transfer of tax dollars from ordinary citizens into the pockets of the more affluent Founders.

Thus, according to Beard, the constitutional convention in Philadelphia in 1787 was promoted by "a small and active group of men immediately interested through their personal possessions in the outcome of their labors. . . . The propertyless masses were . . . excluded at the outset from participation. . . ."

Beard, who was among the first generation of professionally trained historians, gathered evidence on the Founders: "Many leaders in the movement for ratification were large [public] security holders," he argued. Those who opposed the Constitution owned fewer public securities.

Each state had to vote on ratifying the Constitution, and Beard offered evidence that "the leaders who supported the Constitution in the ratifying conventions represented the same economic groups as the members of the Philadelphia convention." The Founders, Beard conceded, did not write the Constitution merely to make money, but nonetheless, "The Constitution was essentially an economic document."

Beard's thesis, seemingly well researched, was presented in a tentative way, but it soon swept the historical profession and became gospel in college classrooms by the 1920s. The Constitution, professors suggested to their students, was not a document worthy of special respect. It was a product of self-interest that should be interpreted loosely and changed as the Progressives saw fit.

The constitutional separation of powers, for example, according to Woodrow Wilson—a friend of Beard's and a fellow Ph.D. in history—was a "grievous mistake" by the Founders. More centralization of power was needed—especially in the executive branch—to change society through needed reforms, such as the progressive income tax.

Beard made his reputation with his book and went on to an illustrious career: He authored or coauthored 49 books that had sold more than 11 million copies by 1952.

Questionable Scholarship

During the 1950s, historian Forrest McDonald did a more thorough study of the Founders and discovered what can most generously be described as errors in research and, less generously, as fraudulent research. McDonald traveled to archives throughout the original 13 states and meticulously compiled data on thousands of men involved in the debate over the Constitution. After systematically studying the lives of the Founders and the state convention delegates, McDonald wrote *We the People*, which debunked Beard completely. "No correlation" exists, McDonald discovered, "between their economic interests and their votes on issues in general or on key economic issues." In fact, McDonald emphasized that in Pennsylvania, South Carolina, and New York "most [public] security holders opposed ratification."

How could Beard have erred so badly? In part Beard missed the mark because he was trying to hit something else—a Progressive agenda for reform, the excuse to transfer wealth from the haves to the have-nots. If the Founders were merely protecting their economic interests, Beard and his progressive friends were justified in supporting the redistribution of wealth.

How can we be sure that Beard was blinded by his ideology? One indication is that he seems to have willfully distorted his evidence to suggest that certain signers of the Constitution owned more public securities (and other forms of wealth) than they actually did. For example, Daniel Jenifer of Maryland, who signed the Constitution in Philadelphia, held no public securities—a point against Beard's view that the signers were self-interested. But Beard classified Jenifer among the large security holders because his son Daniel Jenifer, Jr., held several thousand dollars' worth of them.

But alas, as McDonald shows, "Jenifer had no children—at least no legitimate ones—for in both of the sources Beard used to gather data on Jenifer, it is expressly stated that Jenifer was a bachelor." Beard also classified Gunning Bedford, Jr., a delegate from Delaware, as a security holder, but, as Beard admits, there were two Gunning Bedfords in Delaware, and the one who didn't sign the Constitution was the one who owned the public securities. Furthermore, Beard places delegates Nicholas Gilman, William Samuel Johnson, Charles Pinckney, and others as holders of public securities, but they did not acquire these securities until long after they signed the Constitution.

Some of Beard's mistakes are more subtle. He classifies delegate William Few as a security holder because Few funded a "certificate of 1779" with a "nominal" value of $2,170. True, but what Beard neglects to say is that Few's "nominal" value was scaled down to a mere $114.80, a sum hardly worth motivating Few to sign the Constitution to redeem.

No doubt all the Founders were concerned about their own finances as well as those of the nation. But in writing the Constitution, they were above all trying to apply principles of natural rights and limited government to create a durable nation that would be a bastion of freedom in an unfree world. James Madison and other Founders diligently studied ancient and modern republics to learn from their mistakes what safeguards to employ to protect liberty while allowing elected politicians enough authority to effectively lead the nation.

The Sacrifices Made

What Beard omits from his history is the wisdom and dedication of the Founders in overcoming narrow self-interest to produce a masterful guiding document for the country. The actions of Robert Morris of Pennsylvania and Nathaniel Gorham of Massachusetts, for example, are remarkable. Both men signed the Constitution and supported it vigorously even though they ultimately lost money doing so.

Both men had committed to buy land with public securities—which were trading at only about 15 percent of par value before the Constitution was ratified. When the Constitution was ratified and the public securities were redeemed, both Morris and Gorham had to buy the securities at par value, so they both lost fortunes. Morris, in fact, went from being the wealthiest merchant in the United States in 1787 to being tossed into debtors' prison in the 1790s. Contrary to Beard, Morris had voted against his own economic self-interest, and for his country's financial integrity.

—BWF, July 2009

3

Chapter **Three**

Madison's Veto Sets a Precedent

Today, when a president looks at a spending bill that has passed Congress, he typically asks, "How will this help my party gain votes?" and "What interest groups will this bring to my side?" Sometimes, when modern presidents are more philosophical, they ask, "Will this spending help the economy, or advance the nation's interests?"

Our first presidents approached spending bills very differently. The first question they usually asked was, "Is this spending constitutional?" Only if the answer was yes would they then ask if it was wise, if it would benefit the nation, or if it would gain votes.

These early presidents viewed the Constitution as a binding document that separated the powers of government for a purpose. Only if power were decentralized, they argued, could tyranny, high taxes, and government oppression be avoided. Thus Article 1, Section 8, of the Constitution restricted the power of Congress to spend taxpayer dollars to a limited number of items, mainly national defense.

An example of how early presidents adhered to the Constitution—even when it would have been politically expedient to do otherwise—is the issue of federal aid for internal improvements, the building and improving of roads, canals, and waterways in our new nation. The

Constitution does not grant Congress the right to appropriate funds for roads and canals. The Founders did recognize that improving our highways was essential for economic development, but they believed that states or private companies should do the work; neither good government nor just results occurred when the people in Georgia could be taxed to build a canal in New York.

The problem, of course, is that congressmen in New York had incentives to argue that federal funds could be used profitably and in the national interest to build the Erie Canal. Since votes in the large state of New York were pivotal in many presidential elections, our early presidents had to decide whether to chase votes or follow the Constitution. Sometimes our presidents failed the test. For example, President Thomas Jefferson supported the construction of the inefficient National Road from Maryland to Illinois.

James Madison, who followed Jefferson as president, seems to have supported the National Road, but he learned from the experience. He directly confronted the issue of federal aid to internal improvements in his next-to-last day as president. Congress had passed what was labeled the Bonus Bill of 1817, which would have used federal funds to build roads and canals across the nation. Madison responded with a thundering veto. "I am constrained," he said, "by the insuperable difficulty I feel in reconciling the bill with the Constitution."

Madison admitted the bill would probably help his country, but then he observed that "such a power is not expressly given by the Constitution . . . and can not be deduced from any part of it without an inadmissible latitude of construction and a reliance on insufficient precedents."

The promoters of the bill in Congress had argued that building roads and improving rivers at federal expense would "render more easy and less expensive the means and provisions for the common defense." Madison retorted: "To refer the power in question to the clause 'to provide for the common defense and general welfare would be contrary to the established and consistent rules of interpretation." He added: "Such a view of the Constitution would have the effect of giving to Congress a general power of legislation instead of the defined and limited one hitherto understood to belong to them, the terms 'common defense and general welfare' embracing every object and act within the purview of a legislative trust."

Madison concluded that twisting the General Welfare clause in this way "would have the effect of subjecting both the Constitution and the laws of the several States in all cases not specifically exempted to be superseded by laws of Congress."

These words from Madison carry exceptional weight because he was a chief architect of the U.S. Constitution. At the convention in Philadelphia in 1787, Madison sat in front of the presiding officer. He never missed an important speech, and he took copious notes on the proceedings. When he says that the General Welfare clause cannot be used to give Congress "a general power of legislation instead of the defined and limited one," he is echoing the original intent of the Founders.

Even so, Madison's veto may have surprised Congress because earlier he had conceded that "establishing throughout our country the roads and canals . . . can best be executed under the national authority. No objects within the circle of political economy so richly repay the expense bestowed upon them." Madison believed, however, that the country was better off following the Constitution rather than twisting its meaning to secure more rapid economic growth. If we want federal road-building, then pass a constitutional amendment to permit it.

Madison's principled veto of the Bonus Bill of 1817 set a precedent that lasted for generations. The Erie Canal, for example, never received federal funds. In 1830, however, Congress tested the resolve of President Andrew Jackson with the Maysville Road Bill, which would have used federal funds to build a turnpike in Kentucky.

Jackson scrupulously followed Madison's lead and vetoed the bill. Sure, the proposed turnpike might be economically sound, Jackson conceded, but if the country used federal funds to build a turnpike in Kentucky, "there can be no local interest that may not with equal propriety be denominated national." He echoed Madison by adding, "A disregard of this distinction would of necessity lead to the subversion of the federal system."

Madison and Jackson were also following George Washington's advice in his Farewell Address. "[Avoid] the accumulation of debt," Washington admonished, "not only by shunning occasions of expense, but by vigorous exertions in time of peace to discharge the debts which unavoidable wars have occasioned, not ungenerously throwing upon posterity the burthen which we ourselves ought to bear."

Debt Retired

During Jackson's presidency the United States fulfilled Washington's request and retired all its national debt. In large part, Jackson argued, the new annual surpluses reflected the frugality exemplified by refusing to use federal funds for internal improvements. The government had raised a small amount of revenue each year through tariffs, the sale of land, and excise taxes, especially on whiskey. But the nation had followed the Constitution and limited spending mainly to national defense—two wars with Britain and occasional Indian removal.

In Jackson's veto of the Maysville Road, he observed that on "the national debt we may look with confidence to its entire extinguishment in the short period of four years." We were a nation "free from debt and with all her immense resources unfettered! What a salutary influence would not such an exhibition [of restraint] exercise upon the cause of liberal principles and free government throughout the world!"

James Madison, who lived to see the national debt removed, could point to his veto of the Bonus Bill as crucial in this achievement.

—*BWF, January 2008*

4

Chapter **Four**

Principled Parties

Imagine a political movement that says it's committed to "equal rights"—and means it. Not just equality in a few cherry-picked rights but all human rights, including the most maligned, property rights. Imagine a movement whose *raison d'être* is to oppose any and all special privileges from government for anybody.

When it comes to political parties, most of them in recent American history like to at least say they're for equal rights. If we've learned anything from politics, though, surely the first lesson is this: What the major parties say and do are two different things.

In American history no such group has ever been as colorful and as thorough in its understanding of equal rights as one that flashed briefly across the political skies in the 1830s and '40s. They were called "Locofocos." If I had been around back then, I would have proudly joined their illustrious ranks.

The Locofocos were a faction of the Democratic Party of President Andrew Jackson, concentrated mostly in the Northeast and New York in particular, but with notoriety and influence well beyond the region.

Formally called the "Equal Rights Party," they derived their better known sobriquet from a peculiar event on October 29, 1835.

Turn On The Lights, The Party's Starting

Democrats in New York City were scrapping over how far to extend Jackson's war against the federally chartered national bank at a convention controlled by the city's dominant political machine, Tammany Hall. (He had killed the bank in 1832 by vetoing its renewal.) When the more conservative officialdom of the convention expelled the radical William Leggett, editor of the *Evening Post*, they faced a full-scale revolt by a sizable and boisterous rump. The conservatives walked out, plunging the meeting room into darkness as they left by turning off the gas lights. The radicals continued to meet by the light of candles they lit with matches called "loco focos" (Spanish for "crazy lights").

With the Tammany conservatives gone and the room once again illuminated, the Locofocos passed a plethora of resolutions. They condemned the national bank as an unconstitutional tool of special interests and an engine of paper-money inflation. They assailed all monopolies, by which they meant firms that received some sort of privilege or immunity granted by state or federal governments. They endorsed a "strict construction" of the Constitution and demanded an end to all laws "which directly or indirectly infringe the free exercise of equal rights." They saw themselves as the true heirs of Jefferson, unabashed advocates of laissez faire and of minimal government confined to securing equal rights for all and dispensing special privileges for none.

Three months later, in January 1836, the Locofocos held a convention to devise a platform and endorse candidates to run against the Tammany machine for city office in April. They still considered themselves Democrats, hoping to steer the party of Jefferson and Jackson to a radical reaffirmation of its principled roots rather than bolt and form a distinct opposition party. "We utterly disclaim any intention or design of instituting any new party, but declare ourselves the original Democratic party," they announced.

The "Declaration of Principles" the Locofocos passed at that January gathering is a stirring appeal to the bedrock concept of rights, as evidenced by these excerpts:

> The true foundation of Republican Government is the equal rights of every citizen, in his person and property, and in their management.

The rightful power of all legislation is to declare and enforce only our natural rights and duties, and to take none of them from us. No man has a natural right to commit aggression on the equal rights of another; and this is all the law should enforce on him.

The idea is quite unfounded that on entering into society, we give up any natural right.

The convention pronounced "Hostility to any and all monopolies by legislation," "unqualified and uncompromising hostility to paper money as a circulating medium, because gold and silver are the only safe and constitutional currency," and "Hostility to the dangerous and unconstitutional creation of vested rights by legislation."

These days Congress and the legislatures of our 50 states routinely bestow advantages on this or that group at the expense of those whom the same laws *disadvantage*—from affirmative action to business subsidies. The Locofoco condemnation of such special privilege couldn't be clearer: "We ask that our legislators will legislate for the whole people and not for favored portions of our fellow-citizens, thereby creating distinct aristocratic little communities within the great community. It is by such partial and unjust legislation that the productive classes of society are . . . not equally protected and respected as the other classes of mankind."

William Leggett, the man whose expulsion from the October gathering by the regular Democrats of Tammany Hall sparked the Locofocos into being, was the intellectual linchpin of the whole movement. After a short stint editing a literary magazine called *The Critic*, he was hired as assistant to famed poet and editor William Cullen Bryant at the *New York Evening Post* in 1829. Declaring "no taste" for politics at first, he quickly became enamored of Bryant's philosophy of liberty. He emerged as an eloquent agitator in the pages of the *Post*, especially in 1834 when he took full charge of its editorial pages while Bryant vacationed in Europe. He struck a chord with the politically unconnected and with many working men and women hit hard by the inflation of the national bank.

In the state of New York at the time, profit-making corporations could not come into being except by special dispensation from the legislature. This meant, as historian Richard Hofstadter explained in a 1943 article, that "men whose capital or influence was too small to win charters from the lawmakers were barred from such profitable lines of corporate enterprise as bridges, railroads, turnpikes and ferries, as well as banks."

Leggett railed against such privilege: "The bargaining and trucking away of chartered privileges is the whole business of our lawmakers." His remedy was "a fair field and no favor," free market competition unfettered by favor-granting politicians. He and his Locofoco followers were not antiwealth or antibank, but they were vociferously opposed to any unequal application of the law. To Leggett and the Locofocos, the goddess of justice really was blindfolded!

The Locofocos won some local elections in the late 1830s and exerted enough influence to see many of their ideas embraced by no less than Martin Van Buren when he ran successfully for president in 1836. By the middle of Van Buren's single term, the Locofoco notions of equal rights and an evenhanded policy of a small federal government were reestablished as core Democratic Party principles. There they would persist through the last great Democratic president, Grover Cleveland, in the 1880s and 1890s. Sadly, those essentially libertarian roots have long since been abandoned by the party of Jefferson and Jackson.

If you're unhappy that today's political parties give lip service to equal rights as they busy themselves carving yours up and passing out the pieces, don't blame me. I'm a Locofoco.

—LWR, January 2010

5

Chapter **Five**

Andrew Johnson and the Constitution

Before 1998 "Andrew Johnson" used to be the answer to the question "Who was the only U.S. president to be impeached?" But Andrew Johnson, the self-educated tailor, deserves to be remembered more for his ideas, especially his defense of the Constitution in a troubled time.

Johnson was born in poverty in North Carolina in 1808 and moved to Greenville, Tennessee, as a teenager when he heard the town needed a tailor. He established a strong business there and at age 26 won election to the state legislature, where he spent several terms. He strongly supported fellow Tennessean Andrew Jackson (president 1829–1837), and eventually won election to the U.S. House and Senate. In Congress, Johnson became a constitutional watchdog on federal spending and special subsidies to favored groups. The protective tariff he called "a system of humbug," and he wanted entrepreneurs, not the federal government, to build the nation's canals and railroads. He often tried to get a law passed for across-the-board pay cuts for federal employees, whom he resented because they lived comfortably in Washington from the tax dollars of hard-working artisans, farmers, and laborers.

Charity, Johnson argued, begins with people, not government. This issue came up when he ran for governor of Tennessee in 1853. Gustavus Henry, the Whig candidate, attacked Johnson vigorously in a public debate for voting against a bill to give federal aid to Ireland. The severe potato famine, Henry insisted, called for American help. Johnson responded that people, not government, had the responsibility of helping their fellow men in need. Any politician could be generous with other people's money, which was forcibly collected in taxes. He then took from his pocket a receipt for the $50 he had sent to the hungry Irish. "How much did you give, sir?" he challenged Henry, who had given nothing. The audience, according to the *Memphis Appeal*, gave Johnson "prolonged and deafening applause." Such adherence to the Constitution, Johnson believed, helped him narrowly win the governor's chair that year.

When the Civil War began, Governor Johnson left Tennessee rather than break with the union. That loyalty endeared him to President Lincoln, who asked the Democrat Johnson to be his vice-presidential candidate in the 1864 election. The Lincoln-Johnson campaign won, and when Lincoln was assassinated Johnson became president for four turbulent years.

As president, Johnson was not a consistent devotee of liberty. He believed that blacks were not as capable as whites, and he was reluctant to give blacks full voting rights. But when the Thirteenth Amendment (abolishing slavery) became law, Johnson, as a strict constitutionalist, "fully recognized the obligation to protect and defend that class of our people whenever and wherever it shall become necessary, and to the full extent compatible with the Constitution of the United States."

Vetoes Bill

Johnson found himself caught in the middle. On one hand were southern racists, who passed Black Codes that denied basic civil liberties to former slaves. On the other were Radical Republicans who not only wanted full voting rights for blacks, but sometimes special privileges as well. For example, Republicans had set up the Freedmen's Bureau during the war to help freed blacks get food, clothing, and other necessities of life. After the war, the Freedmen's Bureau expanded its efforts to help blacks get land and education as well. In 1866 Congress voted to extend the life of the Freedmen's Bureau and expand its scope.

Johnson, however, vetoed the bill. In a nutshell, his view was this: Civil liberties for blacks, yes; special legislation, no. "In time of war,"

Johnson said, "it was eminently proper that we should provide for those who were passing suddenly from a condition of bondage to a state of freedom. But this bill proposes to make the Freedmen's Bureau . . . a permanent branch of the public administration, with its powers greatly enlarged." These powers "in my opinion are not warranted by the Constitution."

Johnson built his case around the provisions in the bill that put the government in the business of establishing schools for blacks and of taking land from plantation owners to give to former slaves without due process of law. On the first point, Johnson noted that Congress "has never founded schools for any class of our own people, not even for the orphans of those who have fallen in the defense of the Union, but has left the care of education to the much more competent and efficient control of the States, of communities, of private associations, and of individuals."

The president hoped that blacks would be protected in their civil liberties and would thereby use their freedom to gain skills and work their way up in society. "The idea on which the slaves were assisted to freedom was that on becoming free they would be a self-sustaining population." He added that "any legislation that shall imply that they are not expected to attain a self-sustaining condition must have a tendency injurious alike to their character and their prospects."

Granted, Johnson was overly optimistic that his southern brethren would allow blacks sufficient civil liberties to compete for jobs and establish fair contracts. But, as in the earlier case of charity to the Irish, he believed that compassionate people, not a government program, were the solution to the problem. They would build the schools and train the newly freed slaves. He was ever faithful to the Constitution when he said that establishing schools was a state, not a federal, function and that the federal government should not favor "one class or color of our people more than another."

Interestingly, Johnson's vision of self-help for blacks somewhat paralleled that of black leader Booker T. Washington, who agreed that caring people, not bureaucrats at the Freedmen's Bureau, needed to take the lead in promoting black education. In the spirit of Johnson's veto of the Freedmen's Bureau, Washington set up Tuskegee Institute, with help from whites, as a black-operated college. Blacks and whites also worked together to set up Fisk College and Meharry Medical

College in Nashville. In fact, dozens of private black colleges were established in the years immediately after emancipation. Black literacy skyrocketed from 20 percent in 1870 to 83 percent in 1930, a period marred by forced segregation. That increased literacy was the tool that blacks used to win their struggle to have their rights recognized in the coming decades.

Andrew Johnson's arguments are still cogent today. The Constitution does not guarantee special privileges for any class of citizens.

—BWF, September 2003

6

Chapter **Six**

A Supreme Court to Be Proud Of

In the closing months of the current U.S. Supreme Court session, pundits of every stripe will be assessing the impact of recent changes in the Court's composition. If the justices themselves are interested in how they measure up, there may be no better standard than the Court's record under Chief Justice Melville W. Fuller.

It's a sad commentary that in the mainstream media, courts are tagged with such confusing and superficial labels as "conservative" or "liberal"—terms loaded with political baggage and often manipulated by those with an ax to grind. I prefer more clarifying questions: Does a court interpret law or manufacture it? Does it apply the Constitution according to what its text says or is it willing to abandon it to accommodate current whims, trendy ideologies, or alleged "needs" of the moment? Were our liberties more or less secure after it did its work?

The Fuller Court, encompassing a parade of justices who came and went during Fuller's 22 years as chief, was not consistent on all counts. But unlike any subsequent Court, it stretched neither the law nor the Constitution beyond what the words say. When it found law to be in conflict with the Constitution, it usually sided with the latter because liberty under the rule of law was its highest priority. It upheld the importance of a limited federal role, strengthened the role of the states in our federal system, and defended contract and property rights against a rising tide of egalitarian agitation.

Melville Weston Fuller was born in Augusta, Maine, in 1833. Both sides of his family were staunch Jacksonian Democrats—hard money and a small federal government being foremost among the principles they embraced. After graduation from Bowdoin College in 1853, Fuller was admitted to the bar in 1855. A year later he started a successful law practice in Illinois, where he would reside until his elevation to the Supreme Court by President Grover Cleveland in 1888.

As a one-term Democratic legislator in Illinois's lower house in 1862, Fuller condemned the Lincoln administration's arbitrary arrests, suspension of habeas corpus, and other wartime indiscretions as assaults on liberties guaranteed by the Constitution. He opposed both secession and slavery, but didn't believe in quashing dissent and due process to vanquish them. As a Democratic activist and adviser to candidates for national office, he opposed protectionism as special-interest legislation that hurt consumers. He decried irredeemable paper money as a form of theft and fraud, even voting to forbid the Illinois treasury from receiving greenbacks as payment for state taxes. He scrutinized public spending for waste and favoritism, once earning the wrath of his colleagues by publicly opposing (unsuccessfully) a bill to give gold pens to each member of the Illinois House.

In what biographer Willard L. King terms "the greatest public speech of his career," Fuller seconded the 1876 nomination of Indiana's Thomas Hendricks for president in unmistakably Jeffersonian terms: "[T]he country demands a return to the principles and practices of the fathers of the Republic in this the hundredth year of its existence, and the restoration of a wise and frugal government, that shall leave to every man the freest pursuit of his avocation or his pleasures, consistent with the rights of his neighbors, and shall not take from the mouth of labor the bread it has earned."

The 1876 Democratic Convention nominated Samuel Tilden instead of Hendricks, but many Democrats around the country remembered Melville Fuller. One of them was Grover Cleveland. The last Jacksonian Democrat to hold the highest office, Cleveland wanted a chief justice with an unblemished record of integrity who not only shared his limited-government philosophy but was also a good business manager who could fix the three-year backlog of cases at the high court.

Fuller, 55, who had argued many cases before the Supreme Court over a 16-year period, was precisely what Cleveland was looking for. The President admired the fact that in his visits and meetings with Fuller, the Illinois lawyer had never asked him for anything, even turning down three high posts within the administration. And he had taken considerable public heat in defending the President's hard money stance and his numerous vetoes of spending bills. To thwart a possible decline by Fuller, Cleveland announced his nomination before Fuller even gave his consent. He was literally dragged into an office for which he didn't lust but in which he quickly distinguished himself as one of its most able and important holders.

Fuller charmed his colleagues on the Court with his good humor, thoughtful scholarship, and remarkable capacity for friendly persuasion and mediation. He began a custom still in use today of requiring each justice at the start of a working day to shake the hand of every other justice. He resolved the Court's crowded docket.

The Fuller Court should be most admired, however, for its jurisprudence. Certainly Americans who share the Founders' vision can find much about it to applaud. Fuller himself was at the center of it, often arguing for the majority. When freedom of commerce was at issue, the Fuller Court did not carelessly allow governmental interference. For example: Prohibitionists in Iowa secured passage of a law forbidding the sale of an interstate shipment of liquor, but the Court, with Fuller himself writing the majority opinion, declared it an unconstitutional violation of the Commerce Clause.

Restricted Sherman Act

In other commerce-related rulings, the Fuller Court restricted the application of the almost incoherently broad language of the Sherman Anti-Trust Act. Regulating the terms of interstate commerce and transportation, as the Constitution provided for, was one thing, but federal meddling in manufacturing and production was quite anathema to Fuller and most of his colleagues. It was left to later Courts to distort the Commerce Clause and justify federal regulation of virtually every corner of the economy.

The Fuller Court staunchly defended the sanctity of contract by treating it, in the words of James W. Ely, Jr., a Vanderbilt University law professor and biographer of the Court, "as the controlling constitutional norm." It resisted attempts at congressional price- and rate-fixing. It once unanimously threw out a Louisiana law that prohibited a person from obtaining insurance from a company that was not qualified to do business in that state. Its feelings in this regard were summed up in another ruling in which the majority declared that "The legislature may not, under the guise of protecting the public interest, arbitrarily interfere with private business, or impose unusual and unnecessary restrictions upon lawful occupations." Likewise, the Court was far friendlier to property rights in eminent-domain cases than the recent Supreme Courts.

One of the finest moments of the Fuller Court was its rejection in 1895 of a federal income tax passed the previous year. Pleas that Congress needed the money, class warfare, and egalitarian claims against other people's wealth carried little weight with this Court. The Constitution forbade direct taxation of that kind, and that was enough to ditch it. Melville Weston Fuller never succumbed to the temptations of power and ego or discovered vast new constitutional duties for the Washington establishment to inflict on the people. He and most of his colleagues actually took seriously their oath to defend the supreme law of the land, a notion that seems sadly quaint in an age where sweeping judicial activism is a mainstream law-school principle.

—LWR, March 2006

7

Chapter **Seven**

Two Presidents, Two Philosophies, and Two Different
Outcomes

Richard Weaver's observation that "ideas have consequences" is especially valid when we study the growth of government in America. If we compare the attitudes of Woodrow Wilson and Calvin Coolidge on the Constitution and the Declaration of Independence we can see how their views on government intervention were a logical outcome of their conceptions of these documents.

The Declaration of Independence reflected a generation of thinking on the subject of natural rights—"that all men are created equal, that they are endowed by their Creator with certain unalienable rights, that among these are life, liberty, and the pursuit of happiness." The Constitution later separated the powers of government to protect life, liberty, and property from future encroachments by potential tyrants.

Woodrow Wilson had only limited use for the Founders and the Declaration. "If you want to understand the real Declaration of Independence," Wilson urged, "do not read the preface." Government did not exist merely to protect rights. Instead, Wilson argued that the Declaration "expressly leaves to each generation of men the determination of what they will do with their lives. . . . In brief, political liberty is the right of those who are governed to adjust the government to their own needs and interests." "We are not," Wilson insisted, "bound to adhere to the doctrines held by the signers of the Declaration of Independence."

The limited government enshrined in both the Declaration and the Constitution may have been an advance for the Founders, Wilson conceded, but society had evolved since then. The modern state of the early 1900s was "beneficent" and "indispensable." Separation of powers hindered modern governments from promoting progress. "[T]he only fruit of dividing power," Wilson asserted, "was to make it irresponsible."

A better "constitutional government," Wilson urged, was one "whose powers have been adapted to the interests of its people." A strong executive was needed, he believed, to translate the interests of the people into public policy. The president was the opinion leader, the "spokesman for the real sentiment and purpose of the country." And what the country needed was "a man who will be and who will seem to the country in some sort of an embodiment of the character and purpose it wishes its government to have—a man who understood his own day and the needs of his country."

In the White House, Wilson intended to be a strong president working with a "living Constitution." He promoted the expanding of "beneficent" government into new areas. In his second year as president he concluded that shipping rates were too high, and he blessed his secretary of treasury's plan to regulate overseas shipping rates and the companies doing the shipping. Later he promoted a plan to make loans to farmers at federally subsidized rates. Then he pushed through Congress a bill fixing an eight-hour day for railroad workers.

Article 1, Section 8, of the Constitution gives no power to the federal government to regulate the prices of trade, the hours of work, or to make special loans to farmers or any other group. But Wilson said he was operating with a "living Constitution" and that increased government in these cases reflected appropriately the greater will of the people. Likewise, when Wilson helped centralize banking with the Federal Reserve system and when he further restricted trade by promoting the Clayton Antitrust Act, he believed that this work for the general good outweighed any loyalties to the rigid construction set up by the Founders in the original Constitution.

Not all Americans agreed with Wilson 's evolving Constitution. The Adamson Act, which required the eight-hour day for railroad workers, was challenged and went to the Supreme Court. It was sustained by a 5–

4 majority, but Justice William Day was appalled at the constitutional violations in the bill. "Such legislation, it seems to me," Day said, "amounts to the taking of the property of one and giving it to another in violation of the spirit of fair play and equal right which the Constitution intended to secure in the due process clause to all coming within its protection."

Such growth of government came with a cost, but Wilson was ready with the progressive income tax to pay for his new programs. World War I clearly influenced Wilson's use of the tax and his centralization of power—he promoted an increase in the top tax rate from 7 to 15 percent in 1916; then, during the war, Wilson secured an increase to a 77 percent marginal rate on the country's largest incomes.

Where Wilson supported an evolving Constitution that gave him authority to increase the power of government and centralize power, President Calvin Coolidge, who was on the ticket that succeeded Wilson, believed that the Declaration and the Constitution should be accepted as the Founders wrote them.

In July 1926, on the sesquicentennial of the signing of the Declaration, Coolidge gave a speech reaffirming the need for limited government. "It is not so much then for the purpose of undertaking to proclaim new theories and principles that this annual celebration is maintained, but rather to reaffirm and reestablish those old theories and principles which time and the unerring logic of events have demonstrated to be sound."

Coolidge added that "there is a finality" about the Declaration. "If all men are created equal, that is final. If they are endowed with inalienable rights, that is final. If governments derive their just powers from the consent of the governed, that is final. No advance, no progress can be made beyond these propositions. If anyone wishes to deny their truth or their soundness, the only direction in which he can proceed historically is not forward, but backward toward the time when there was no equality, no rights of the individual, no rule of the people. Those who wish to proceed in that direction can not lay claim to progress. They are reactionary."

Coolidge's attitude as president reflected his belief in the ideas of the Declaration. He was not always consistent—for example, he signed the Fordney-McCumber Tariff in 1922, which slapped high and uneven taxes on some needed imports. But his efforts were largely in the direction of reducing the size of government to increase liberty. For example, Coolidge cut the size of government and was the last president to have budget surpluses every year of his presidency. Also, when the Harding-Coolidge administration came into office in 1921, the tax rate on top incomes was 73 percent; when Coolidge left the presidency eight years later it was 25 percent. The rates on the lowest incomes were also slashed.

Attacked Special Interests

Furthermore, Coolidge often attacked special interests. He vetoed a bill to give a special cash bonus to veterans; and, through President Harding, he was part of the administration that shut down a government-operated steel plant set up by Wilson, which had lost money each year of its operation.

Not once but twice Coolidge courageously vetoed the McNary-Haugen farm bill, which was popular with farmers because it promised federal price supports for them. "I do not believe," Coolidge wrote, "that upon serious consideration the farmers of America would tolerate the precedent of a body of men chosen solely by one industry who, acting in the name of the government, shall arrange for contracts which determine prices, secure the buying and selling of commodities, the levying of taxes on that industry, and pay losses on foreign dumping of any surplus."

When presidents are faithful to America 's founding documents, limited government has a chance to flourish. But when presidents emote over a "living" Declaration and Constitution, then the growth of government is upon us.

—BWF, June 2007

8

Chapter **Eight**

Andrew Mellon: The Entrepreneur as Politician

Rarely do spectacular entrepreneurs leave their realm of business for the political arena. One exception is Andrew Mellon, the third-wealthiest American of his era, who left a dazzling career in American industry to become secretary of treasury under Presidents Warren Harding, Calvin Coolidge, and Herbert Hoover.

Mellon established his career in Pittsburgh as a successful banker—always on the lookout for profitable innovations to back. His investments in Gulf Oil challenged the legendary John D. Rockefeller, and Mellon's establishment of Alcoa introduced lightweight aluminum as a significant industrial metal.

Should Mellon have given up running these and other profitable ventures in 1921 to work under President Harding, a career politician who had little understanding of economics? Mellon hesitated. But when Harding persisted, Mellon joined the president's cabinet. At age 65, Mellon had experienced a full career in business; his country, which was in economic chaos after World War I, had 11.7 percent unemployment and needed his financial guidance.

31

Confronting Crises

As treasury secretary Mellon confronted three major crises: a spiraling national debt, near confiscatory tax rates, and the repayment of large loans owed the United States by most European nations.

The soaring national debt required immediate attention. During the 140 years from the American Revolution to 1916, the United States had accumulated a national debt just over $1.2 billion. But during World War I the debt had skyrocketed to more than $24 billion. The annual interest payments alone exceeded the entire national debt before the war.

The U.S. tax system, which generated the revenue to pay the debt, was in disarray. Under President Woodrow Wilson, Harding's predecessor, the income tax had become part of American life. Wilson started with a top marginal rate of 7 percent, but he argued that the war required a drastic rise in taxes. Congress agreed, and by 1920, Wilson's last full year in office, the top rate reached 73 percent. Tax avoidance was rampant, and the annual revenue did not offset expenses.

Finally, the debts that the European allies owed the United States for food and materials during the war were over $10 billion. Britain and France, which owed the most, were balking at repayment.

Few secretaries of the treasury have ever encountered such formidable problems, and Harding (who died in 1923) and Coolidge relied on Mellon for financial advice. Mellon's attack on the debt was twofold. First, he renegotiated almost one-third of the debt at lower interest rates; second, he helped chop federal spending from $6.5 billion in 1921 to $3.5 billion in 1926. Coolidge, in particular, obliged by vetoing special-interest legislation—a bill to give a bonus to veterans and another to subsidize wheat and cotton farmers.

Mellon was not always consistent in his free-market arguments. He supported high tariffs for many products, but he recognized that a "subsidy can be paid only by taking money out of the pockets of all the people in order that it shall find its way back into the pockets of some of the people."

Mellon, meanwhile, did his part to promote thrift. He cut staff at the Treasury Department, and he reduced the size of America's paper money; the smaller bills were more durable and saved ink and paper.

The slashing of the tax rates, however, was where Mellon did his most good. He carefully studied the effects of confiscatory rates and concluded that most wealthy Americans were avoiding payment of taxes by exploiting tax loopholes—foreign investments, the buying and selling of art and coins, and the purchase of tax-exempt bonds.

Why not, Mellon argued, cut the top rate from 73 to 25 percent? In fact, why not chop all rates by the same proportion? That idea—which would be called the Mellon Plan—would not only encourage the rich to invest in the American economy, it might actually generate more revenue. "It seems difficult for some to understand," he wrote, "that high rates of taxation do not necessarily mean large revenue to the Government, and that more revenue may often be obtained by lower rates."

Coolidge fully backed the Mellon Plan, and Congress passed it in stages during the 1920s. Cutting both federal spending and tax rates across the board worked wonders for the American economy. American businessmen plowed capital into radios, cars, refrigerators, vacuum cleaners, telephones, and a variety of new inventions from the air conditioner to the zipper. Entrepreneurs knew they would be able to keep most of what they invested, and the American economy grew rapidly during the 1920s.

Measuring Misery

One measure of prosperity is the misery index, which combines unemployment and inflation. During Coolidge's six years as president, his misery index was 4.3 percent—the lowest of any president during the twentieth century. Unemployment, which had stood at 11.7 percent in 1921, was slashed to 3.3 percent from 1923 to 1929. What's more, Mellon was correct on the effects of the tax-rate cuts—revenue from income taxes steadily increased from $719 million in 1921 to over $1 billion by 1929. Finally, the United States had budget surpluses every year of Coolidge's presidency, which cut about one-fourth of the national debt.

On the issue of the Allied loans, Mellon was less successful. When the Europeans refused to begin payments on their debts, Mellon substantially lowered the interest rates on the loans and gave the Europeans 62 years to repay. At first, they agreed, and even began making small payments, but only Finland paid off its entire debt. The other countries eventually asked for a moratorium on payments, and then abandoned their debts entirely.

Oddly, the Allies had one good argument for reneging on their debts. In 1930, when the United States passed the Smoot-Hawley Tariff, the highest in American history, Europeans asked how they could repay their loans when the United States was refusing to accept their imports? Hoover ultimately appointed Mellon as ambassador to England—in part to nudge the British into honoring their debt commitment—but with the Great Depression under way, even Mellon's powers of persuasion failed to move the British.

By 1933, with the arrival of Franklin Roosevelt and the New Dealers, the times had changed for Mellon. Hoover had raised the top marginal income tax rate to 63 percent, and Roosevelt hiked it to 79 percent in 1935. Moreover, Roosevelt played politics and pressured the IRS to assess Mellon a $3 million fine for tax evasion. Mellon gladly went to court and was vindicated of all charges of wrongdoing. David Blair, the former commissioner of internal revenue, called the tax investigation "unwarranted abuse by high officials of the government."

Mellon, despite the trumped-up charges, always focused optimistically on the art of the possible. Before his death in 1937 he donated his superb art collection to the United States. In doing so, he wanted to avoid all federal expense, so he built the National Gallery of Art in Washington, D. C., to house the paintings and then donated all of it to his country. When Mellon went to Washington, he changed it more than it changed him.

—BWF, December 2008

Part II

The Trials of Unlimited Government

9

Chapter **Nine**

Where Are the Omelets?

"On ne saurait faire une omelette sans casser des oeufs."

["One can't expect to make an omelet without breaking eggs."]

With those words in 1790, Maximilian Robespierre welcomed the horrific French Revolution that had begun the year before. A consummate statist who worked tirelessly to plan the lives of others, he would become the architect of the Revolution's bloodiest phase—the Reign of Terror of 1793–94. Robespierre and his guillotine broke eggs by the thousands in a vain effort to impose a utopian society based on the seductive slogan "liberté, égalité, fraternité."

But, alas, Robespierre never made a single omelet. Nor did any of the other thugs who held power in the decade after 1789. They left France in moral, political, and economic ruin, and ripe for the dictatorship of Napoleon Bonaparte.

As with Robespierre, no omelets came from the egg-breaking efforts of Lenin, Mao, Pol Pot, Adolf Hitler, and Benito Mussolini either.

The French experience is one example in a disturbingly familiar pattern. Call them what you will—leftists, utopian socialists, radical interventionists, collectivists, or statists—history is littered with their presumptuous plans for rearranging society to fit their vision of "the common good," plans that always fail as they kill or impoverish other people in the process. If socialism ever earns a final epitaph, it will be this: "Here lies a contrivance engineered by know-it-alls and busybodies who broke eggs with abandon but never, ever created an omelet."

Every collectivist experiment of the twentieth century was heralded as the Promised Land by statist philosophers. "I have seen the future and it works," the intellectual Lincoln Steffens said after a visit to Uncle Joe Stalin's Soviet Union. In *The New Yorker* in 1984, John Kenneth Galbraith argued that the Soviet Union was making great economic progress in part because the socialist system made "full use" of its manpower, in contrast to the less efficient capitalist West. But an authoritative 846-page study published in 1997, *The Black Book of Communism*, estimated that the communist ideology claimed 20 million lives in the "workers' paradise." Similarly, *The Black Book* documented the death tolls in other communist lands: 45 to 72 million in China, between 1.3 million and 2.3 million in Cambodia, 2 million in North Korea, 1.7 million in Africa, 1.5 million in Afghanistan, 1 million in Vietnam, 1 million in Eastern Europe, and 150,000 in Latin America.

Additionally, all of those murderous regimes were economic basket cases; they squandered resources on the police and military, built vast and incompetent bureaucracies, and produced almost nothing for which there was a market beyond their borders. They didn't make "full use" of anything except police power. In every single communist country the world over, the story has been the same: lots of broken eggs, no omelets. No exceptions.

F. A. Hayek explained this inevitable outcome in his seminal work, *The Road to Serfdom*, in 1944. All efforts to displace individual plans with central planning, he warned us, must end in disaster and dictatorship. No lofty vision can vindicate the use of the brute force necessary to attain it. "The principle that the end justifies the means," wrote Hayek, "is in individualist ethics regarded as the denial of all morals. In collectivist ethics it becomes necessarily the supreme rule."

The worst crimes of the worst statists are often minimized or dismissed by their less radical intellectual brethren as the "excesses" of men and women who otherwise had good intentions. These apologists reject the iron fist and claim that the State can achieve their egalitarian and collectivist goals with a velvet glove.

But whether it is the Swedish "middle way," Yugoslavian "worker socialism," or British Fabianism, the result has been the same: broken eggs, but no omelets.

Have you ever noticed how statists are constantly "reforming" their own handiwork? Education reform. Health-care reform. Welfare reform. Tax reform. The very fact that they're always busy "reforming" is an implicit admission that they didn't get it right the first 50 times.

The list is endless: Canadian health care, European welfarism, Argentine Peronism, African postcolonial socialism, Cuban communism, on and on ad infinitum. Nowhere in the world has the statist impulse produced an omelet. Everywhere—it yields the same: eggs beaten, fried, and scrambled. People worse off than before, impoverished and looking elsewhere for answers and escape. Economies ruined. Freedoms extinguished.

It is a telling conclusion that statists have no successful model to point to, no omelet they can hold up as the pièce de résistance of their cuisine. Not so for those of us who believe in freedom. Indeed, economists James Gwartney, Robert Lawson, and Walter Block in their survey, *Economic Freedom of the World: 1975–1995*, conclude that "No country with a persistently high economic freedom rating during the two decades failed to achieve a high level of income. In contrast, no country with a persistently low rating was able to achieve even middle income status. . . . The countries with the largest increases in economic freedom during the period achieved impressive growth rates."

Perhaps no one explained the lesson of all this better than the French economist and statesman Frédéric Bastiat more than 150 years ago:

> And now that the legislators and do-gooders have so futilely inflicted so many systems upon society, may they finally end where they should have begun: May they reject all systems, and try liberty; for liberty is an acknowledgment of faith in God and His works.

—*LWR, October 1999*

10

Chapter **Ten**

The Times that Tried Men's Economic Souls

More than 230 years ago in Valley Forge, Pennsylvania, the brutal and storied winter of 1777–78 came to a long-awaited close. Nearly a quarter of George Washington's Continental Army troops encamped there had died—victims of hunger, exposure, and disease. Almost every American knows that much, but few can tell you why Congress was as much to blame as the weather.

For six years—from 1775 until 1781—representatives from the 13 colonies (states after July 4, 1776) met and legislated as the Second Continental Congress. They were America's de facto central government during most of the Revolutionary War and included some of the greatest minds and admirable patriots of the day. Among their number were Thomas Jefferson, Benjamin Franklin, John and Sam Adams, Alexander Hamilton, Patrick Henry, John Jay, James Madison, and Benjamin Rush. The Second Continental Congress produced and ratified the Declaration of Independence and the country's first written constitution, the Articles of Confederation. It also ruined a currency and very nearly the fledgling nation in the process, proving that even the best of men with the noblest of intentions sometimes must learn economics the hard way.

Governments derive their revenues primarily from one, two, or all three of these sources: taxation, borrowing, and inflating the currency.

41

Americans were deemed to be in no mood to replace London's taxes with local ones so the Second Continental Congress, which before March 1781 faced no legal prohibition to tax, opted not to. It borrowed considerable sums by issuing bills of credit, but with few moneyed interests willing to risk their capital to take on the British Empire, the expenses of war and government could hardly be covered that way. What the Congress chose as its principal fundraising method is revealed by this statement of a delegate during the financing debate: "Do you think, gentlemen, that I will consent to load my constituents with taxes when we can send to our printer and get a wagon-load of money, one quire of which will pay for the whole?"

Reports of the deliberations that led to the printing of paper money are sketchy but indications are that support for it was probably not universal. John Adams, for instance, was a known opponent. He once referred to the idea as "theft" and "ruinous." Nonetheless, he and Ben Franklin were among five committee members appointed to engrave the plates, procure the paper, and arrange for the first printing of Continental dollars in July 1775. Many delegates were convinced that issuing unbacked paper would somehow bind the colonies together in the common cause against Britain.

In any event, not even the skeptics foresaw the bottom of the slippery slope that began with the first $2 million printed on July 21. Just four days later, $1 million more was authorized. Franklin actually wanted to stop the presses with the initial issue and opposed the second batch, but the temptation to print proved too alluring. By the end of 1775 another $3 million in notes were printed. After war erupted, the states demanded more paper Continentals from Congress. A fourth issue—this time for $4 million—was ordered in February 1776, followed by $5 million more just five months later and another $10 million before the year was out.

In the marketplace the paper notes fell in value even before independence was declared. The consequences of paper inflation at the hands of American patriots were no different from what they ever were (or still are) when rampant expansion of the money supply is conducted by rogues or dictators: prices rise, savings evaporate, and governments resort to draconian measures to stymie the effects of their own folly. As author Ayn Rand would advise in another context nearly two centuries later, "We can evade reality, but we cannot evade the consequences of evading reality."

Americans increasingly refused to accept payment in the Continental dollar. To keep the depreciating notes in circulation, Congress and the states enacted legal-tender laws, measures that are hardly necessary if people have confidence in the soundness of the money. Though he used the power sparingly, George Washington was vested by Congress with authority to seize whatever provisions the army needed and imprison merchants and farmers who wouldn't sell goods for Continentals. At harvest time in 1777, with winter approaching and the army in desperate need of supplies, even farmers who supported independence preferred to sell food to the redcoats because they paid in real money—gold and silver. Washington ordered guards placed along the Schuylkill River to stop supplies from reaching the British.

Another 13 Million Paper Dollars

Congress cranked out another 13 million paper dollars in 1777. With prices soaring the Pennsylvania legislature compounded the effects of bad policy: it imposed price controls on precisely those commodities required by the army. Washington's 11,000 men at Valley Forge froze and starved while not far away the British army spent the winter in relative comfort, subsisting on the year's ample local crops. It wasn't the world's first, nor would it be its last, experiment with price controls.

Congress recognized the mistake on June 4, 1778, when it adopted a resolution urging the states to repeal all price controls. But the printing presses rolled on, belching out 63 million more paper Continentals in 1778 and 90 million in 1779. By 1780 the stuff was virtually worthless, giving rise to a phrase familiar to Americans for generations: "not worth a Continental."

A currency reform in 1780 asked everyone to turn in the old money for a new one at the ratio of 20 to 1. Congress offered to redeem the paper in gold in 1786, but this didn't wash with a citizenry already burned by paper promises. The new currency plummeted in value until Congress was forced to get honest. By 1781 it abandoned its legal-tender laws and started paying for supplies in whatever gold and silver it could muster from the states or convince a friend (like France) to lend it. Not by coincidence, supplies and morale improved, which helped to bring the war to a successful end just two years later.

The early years of our War for Independence were truly, as Tom Paine wrote, "times that tr[ied] men's souls" and not just because of Mother Nature and British troops. Pelatiah Webster, America's first economist, summed up our own errors rather well when he wrote, "The people of the states had been . . . put out of humor by so many tender acts, limitations of prices, and other compulsory methods to force value into paper money . . . and by so many vain funding schemes, declarations and promises, all of which issued from Congress but died under the most zealous efforts to put them into operation and effect."

History texts often bestow great credit on the men of the Second Continental Congress for winning American independence. A case can also be made, however, that we won it in spite of them.

—LWR, March 2008

11

Chapter **Eleven**

The Forgotten Robber Barons

Conventional wisdom, which often is mostly convention and very little wisdom, confidently instructs us that rapacious capitalists dominated and victimized American society in the latter half of the nineteenth century. The white knight of government then rode to the rescue of hapless workers and consumers. The message: business bad, government good.

Honest, objective historians of the so called"robber baron" era, such as Gabriel Kolko and Burton Folsom, know that the capitalist bogeyman perspective is simplistic and overwrought. Even a bad apple or two does not a rotten barrel make. But while recently reading a forgotten little gem of a book, I came to appreciate a fact that is vastly understated in the literature, even by defenders of the market: government of the day was hardly a model of virtue. The critics zero in on a few abuses to indict private enterprise in general. But if they were consistent, they'd draw up a similar, sweeping indictment of the public sector too.

The book to which I refer is *Plunkitt of Tammany Hall*. The first of many editions appeared in 1905 with a rather lengthy subtitle:"A Series of Very Plain Talks On Very Practical Politics, Delivered by Ex-Senator George Washington Plunkitt, The Tammany Philosopher, From His Rostrum—The New York County Court House Bootblack Stand," dutifully recorded and compiled by William L. Riordan of the *New York Evening Post.*

Plunkitt's motto, repeated several times in this slim volume, would undoubtedly be well-known to generations of American high-schoolers if a captain of industry had ever said it: "I seen my opportunities and I took 'em!" Plunkitt was no captain of industry. Indeed, he never did much of anything in the private sector except work briefly at a butcher shop after he quit school at the age of 11. He decided as a teenager to make politics his life's work, and he never looked back. His vehicle was Tammany Hall, a vast political machine that maintained a formidable hold on power through a patronage-fed bureaucracy in the nation's largest city, New York. Plunkitt was a district leader within the organization, and used its considerable connections to crawl his way up the political ladder—as did thousands of others over three-quarters of a century, including Richard Croker, John Kelly, and perhaps the best-known of all the Democratic Party bigwigs of Tammany Hall, the infamous William Marcy "Boss" Tweed.

If anything of the day deserved to be labeled a Frankenstein monster, it was Tammany— frightening in its reach and corrupt to the core. It was a patronage juggernaut, at one time filling 12,000 municipal positions with its hand-picked, often incompetent, but always politically correct loyalists. It milked the taxpayers like cows, took care of its own, and turned out the votes of its followers, living and dead, on election day. For decades, it thwarted reform efforts by buying the reformers. It did more than just rig the system; it was the system.

Plunkitt himself became a millionaire at the game, and was proud of it. When he delivered his series of talks recorded by Riordan, he crowed about how he made his money through "honest graft"—by which he meant being in the right place at the right time with the right inside information. Knowing, for example, that the city planned to announce a site for a new park, Plunkitt would buy up the land in the area. Then he would later sell it to the city at inflated prices. Or he would bid on city property and arrange to get it at dirt-cheap prices because he'd offer jobs or money to the other bidders to drop out. Outright stealing from the city treasury, which Plunkitt regarded as "dishonest graft," wasn't necessary because political pull could earn you all the cash you could imagine.

Politics doesn't require a person to be book-smart, well-spoken, or even possess good business sense, according to Plunkitt. It just requires that you know how to pick and reward your friends. Here's his advice for getting started in the trade:

> Get a followin', if it's only one man, and then go to the district leader and say: 'I want to join the organization. I've got one man who'll follow me through thick and thin.' The leader won't laugh at your one-man followin'. He'll shake your hand warmly, offer to propose you for membership in his club, take you down to the corner for a drink and ask you to call again. But go to him and say: 'I took first prize at college in Aristotle; I can recite all Shakespeare forwards and backwards; there ain't nothin' in science that ain't as familiar to me as blockades on the elevated roads and I'm the real thing in the way of silver-tongued orators.' What will he answer? He'll probably say: 'I guess you are not to be blamed for your misfortunes, but we have no use for you here.'

Padding the city payroll with your friends? Tammany made an art form of it. When civil-service reform later cut into the number of jobs the Democratic machine could fill, Plunkitt decried the result with a straight face: "Just think! Fifty-five Republicans and mugwumps holdin' $3,000 and $4,000 and $5,000 jobs in the tax department when 1,555 good Tammany men are ready and willin' to take their places! It's an outrage!" To Plunkitt, taking from some and giving to others was a key ingredient in the recipe for re-election. He saw nothing at all wrong with it, morally or otherwise. Using the political machine to bestow benefits and buy votes came quite naturally to him. "It's philanthropy, but it's politics too—mighty good politics," he said. Referring to the assistance he passed out to victims of a fire in the city, he declared, "Who can tell how many votes one of these fires bring me? The poor are the most grateful people in the world, and, let me tell you, they have more friends in their neighborhoods than the rich have in theirs." Plunkitt and his associates had quite a nice little welfare state going—the usual kind, in which the politicians get well and everybody else pays the fare.

Tammany Hall was not the only big-city political machine in the country in those days, but it was undoubtedly the biggest. It bilked citizens of millions of dollars and used its political power to secure its place and put everybody else in theirs. Strange, isn't it?, that in almost all the literature critical of this era of American life, the sachems of Tammany Hall are never listed among the so-called "robber barons" of the day.

—LWR, January 2003

12

Chapter **Twelve**

Teddy Roosevelt and the Progressive Vision of History

Over a hundred years ago, on August 31, 1910, Teddy Roosevelt gave his famous "New Nationalism" speech in Osawatomie, Kansas. In that speech the former president projected his vision for how the federal government could regulate the American economy. He defended the government's expansion during his presidency and suggested new ways that it could promote "the triumph of a real democracy."

Roosevelt's quest for "a real democracy" and for centralizing power was a clear break with the American founders. James Madison, for example, distrusted both democracy and human nature; he believed that separating power was essential to good government. He urged in Federalist No. 51 that "those who administer each department" of government be given "the necessary constitutional means and personal motives to resist the encroachments of others. . . . Ambition must be made to check ambition." If power was dispersed, Madison concluded, liberty might prevail and the republic might endure.

Roosevelt argued in this speech that the recent rise of corporations gave businessmen too much economic control. Madison's constitutional restraints, therefore, allowed too much wealth to be concentrated in too few hands. Redistribution of wealth by government, Roosevelt thought, would achieve "a more substantial equality of opportunity."

The economic power of railroads triggered Roosevelt's ire during his presidency. He was frustrated that railroads gave rebates to large customers. In effect, the railroads charged varying rates for carrying the same products the same distance. Roosevelt thought rates should be roughly similar for large shippers and small shippers, especially if the small shippers were far from major cities.

He posed the problem this way: "Combinations in industry are the result of an imperative economic law which cannot be repealed by political legislation. The effort at prohibiting all combination has substantially failed. The way out lies, not in attempting to prevent such combinations, but in completely controlling them in the interest of the public welfare."

In practical terms, "completely controlling" railroads in the public interest meant that the Interstate Commerce Commission (ICC) would have power to set rates so that larger shippers would not get such big discounts on their high volume of business. James J. Hill, president of the Great Northern Railroad, argued that large shippers received higher rebates because their massive business created "economies of scale" for the railroads—that is, railroads could reduce their costs best when shipping large amounts of goods over the rails. The bigger shippers contributed more to the reduced costs of shipping, so they got larger rebates.

To Roosevelt and to the smaller shippers, rebates for the bigger shippers were "unfair money-getting" and have "tended to create a small class of enormously wealthy and economically powerful men, whose chief object is to hold and increase their power." The founders may have provided a "right to life, liberty, and the pursuit of happiness," but Roosevelt believed that the pursuit of happiness and private property were not absolute. "We grudge no man a fortune which represents his own power and sagacity," Roosevelt said—but then added, "when exercised with entire regard to the welfare of his fellows." If railroads were enriching themselves and larger shippers disproportionately to the smaller shippers, then Roosevelt believed such power to set rates needed to be limited: "The Hepburn Act, and the amendment [Mann-Elkins Act] to the act in the shape in which it finally passed Congress at the last session [1910], represent a long step in advance, and we must go further."

The Hepburn Act gave the ICC the power to reduce railroad rates and placed the burden on railroads to show their rates were reasonable. One intervention led to another. The railroads now had to prove that the rates they set were fair, so Congress created a Bureau of Valuation, which was empowered with a huge staff to value railroad property. According to historian Ari Hoogenboom, the bureau's "final report, issued after a twenty-year study costing the public and the railroads hundreds of millions of dollars, disproved assumptions by Progressives that railroads were . . . making fabulous returns on their true investment."

The lesson that Roosevelt learned from passing the Hepburn Act was that federal power was needed to break up those businesses that engaged in price discrimination. "The citizens of the United States," Roosevelt said, "must effectively control the mighty commercial forces which they have called into being."

Once Roosevelt established that the federal government should regulate the prices railroads charged for shipping, the next step was to intervene in other industries as well. "In particular," Roosevelt argued in his speech, "there are strong reasons why . . . the United States Department of Agriculture and the agricultural colleges and experiment stations should extend their work to cover all phases of farm life. . . ." He added, "The man who wrongly holds that every human right is secondary to his profit must now give way to the advocate of human welfare, who rightly maintains that every man holds his property subject to the general right of the community to regulate its use to whatever degree the public welfare may require it."

The shift from the individual rights of the founders to the community rights of the Progressives was a watershed transition in American thought in the early 1900s. But Roosevelt needed a federal income tax to help him redistribute wealth in the national interest. The title "New Nationalism" reflected his view that he and other leaders could determine the national interest and redistribute wealth and power accordingly.

Of the income tax Roosevelt said, "The really big fortune, the swollen fortune, by the mere fact of its size, acquires qualities which differentiate it in kind as well as in degree from what is possessed by men of relatively small means, Therefore, I believe in a graduated income tax on big fortunes, and in another tax which is far more easily collected and far more effective—a graduated inheritance tax on big fortunes, properly safeguarded against evasion, and increasing rapidly in amount with the size of the estate."

Three years after Roosevelt's speech, the Sixteenth Amendment, authorizing a federal income tax without regard to source, became law. Roosevelt had his wish—the 1913 tax was progressive: Most people paid no income tax, and the top rate was 7 percent. Roosevelt probably envisioned rates not much higher than that, but once Congress established the principle that some people could be taxed more than others, there was no way to calculate or determine what the national interest was.

Within one-third of a century after Roosevelt's speech, the United States had a top marginal income tax rate of more than 90 percent.

When the individual liberty of the founders was transformed into the national interest of Teddy Roosevelt and the Progressives, we were only one generation away from a major threat to all our personal liberties. That threat still exists today.

—BWF, October 2010

13

Chapter **Thirteen**

Of Meat and Myth

One hundred years ago, a great and enduring myth was born. Muckraking novelist Upton Sinclair wrote a novel entitled *The Jungle*—a tale of greed and abuse that still reverberates as a case against a free economy. Sinclair's "jungle" was unregulated enterprise; his example was the meat-packing industry; his purpose was government regulation. The culmination of his work was the passage in 1906 of the Meat Inspection Act, enshrined in history, or at least in history books, as a sacred cow (excuse the pun) of the interventionist state.

A century later, American schoolchildren are still being taught a simplistic and romanticized version of this history. For many young people, *The Jungle* is required reading in high-school classes, where they are led to believe that unscrupulous capitalists were routinely tainting our meat, and that moral crusader Upton Sinclair rallied the public and forced government to shift from pusillanimous bystander to heroic do-gooder, bravely disciplining the marketplace to protect its millions of victims.

But this is a triumph of myth over reality, of ulterior motives over good intentions. Reading *The Jungle* and assuming it's a credible news source is like watching *The Blair Witch Project* because you think it's a documentary.

Given the book's favorable publicity, it's not surprising that it has duped a lot of people. Ironically, Sinclair himself, as a founder of the Intercollegiate Socialist Society in 1905, was personally suckered by more than a few intellectual charlatans of his day. One of them was fellow "investigative journalist" Lincoln Steffens, best known for returning from the Soviet Union in 1921 and saying, "I have seen the future, and it works." [1]

In any event, there is much about *The Jungle* that Americans just don't learn from conventional history texts.

The Jungle was, first and foremost, a novel. As is indicated by the fact that the book originally appeared as a serialization in the socialist journal "Appeal to Reason," it was intended to be a polemic—a diatribe, if you will—not a well-researched and dispassionate documentary. Sinclair relied heavily both on his own imagination and on the hearsay of others. He did not even pretend that he had actually witnessed the horrendous conditions he ascribed to Chicago packinghouses, nor to have verified them, nor to have derived them from any official records.

Sinclair hoped the book would ignite a powerful socialist movement on behalf of America's workers. The public's attention focused instead on his fewer than a dozen pages of supposed descriptions of unsanitary conditions in the meat-packing plants. "I aimed at the public's heart," he later wrote, "and by accident I hit it in the stomach."[2]

Though his novelized and sensational accusations prompted congressional investigations of the industry, the investigators themselves expressed skepticism about Sinclair's integrity and credibility as a source of information. In July 1906, President Theodore Roosevelt stated his opinion of Sinclair in a letter to journalist William Allen White: "I have an utter contempt for him. He is hysterical, unbalanced, and untruthful. Three-fourths of the things he said were

---

[1] www.spartacus.schoolnet.co.uk/Jsteffens.htm
[2] Gabriel Kolko, *The Triumph of Conservatism: A Reinterpretation of American History, 1900–1916* (Quadrangle Books, 1967), p. 103.

absolute falsehoods. For some of the remainder there was only a basis of truth."[3]

Sinclair's fellow writer and philosophical intimate, Jack London, wrote this announcement of *The Jungle*, a promo that was approved by Sinclair himself:

> Dear Comrades: . . . The book we have been waiting for these many years! It will open countless ears that have been deaf to Socialism. It will make thousands of converts to our cause. It depicts what our country really is, the home of oppression and injustice, a nightmare of misery, an inferno of suffering, a human hell, a jungle of wild beasts.
>
> And take notice and remember, comrades, this book is straight proletarian. It is written by an intellectual proletarian, for the proletarian. It is to be published by a proletarian publishing house. It is to be read by the proletariat. What *Uncle Tom's Cabin* did for the black slaves *The Jungle* has a large chance to do for the white slaves of today.[4]

The fictitious characters of Sinclair's novel tell of men falling into tanks in meat-packing plants and being ground up with animal parts, then made into "Durham's Pure Leaf Lard." Historian Stewart H. Holbrook writes, "The grunts, the groans, the agonized squeals of animals being butchered, the rivers of blood, the steaming masses of intestines, the various stenches . . . were displayed along with the corruption of government inspectors"[5] and, of course, the callous greed of the ruthless packers.

Most Americans would be surprised to know that government meat inspection did not begin in 1906. The inspectors Holbrook cites as being mentioned in Sinclair's book were among *hundreds* employed by federal, state, and local governments for more than a decade. Indeed, Congressman E.D. Crumpacker of Indiana noted in testimony before the House Agriculture Committee in June 1906 that not even one of those

---

[3] Roosevelt to William Allen White, July 31, 1906, Elting E. Morison and John M. Blum, eds., *The Letters of Theodore Roosevelt*, (Harvard University Press, 1951–54), vol. 5, p. 340.

[4] Mark Sullivan, *Our Times: The United States, 1900–1925*; vol. 2: *America Finding Herself* (Charles Scribner's Sons, 1927), p. 473.

[5] Stewart H. Holbrook, *The Age of the Moguls* (Doubleday & Company, 1953), pp. 110–111.

officials "ever registered any complaint or [gave] any public information with respect to the manner of the slaughtering or preparation of meat or food products." [6]

To Crumpacker and other contemporary skeptics, "Either the Government officials in Chicago (were) woefully derelict in their duty, or the situation over there (had been) outrageously overstated to the country."[7] If the packing plants were as bad as alleged in *The Jungle* surely the government inspectors who never said so must be judged as guilty of neglect as the packers were of abuse.

Some two million visitors came to tour the stockyards and packing-houses of Chicago every year. Thousands of people worked in both. Why is it that it took a novel written by an anticapitalist ideologue who spent but a few weeks in the city to unveil the real conditions to the American public?

All the big Chicago packers combined accounted for less than 50% of the meat products produced in the United States, but few if any charges were ever made against the sanitary conditions of the packinghouses of other cities. If the Chicago packers were guilty of anything like the terribly unsanitary conditions suggested by Sinclair, wouldn't they be foolishly exposing themselves to devastating losses of market share?

In this connection, historians with an ideological axe to grind against the market usually ignore an authoritative 1906 report of the Depart-ment of Agriculture's Bureau of Animal Husbandry. Its investigators provided a point-by-point refutation of the worst of Sinclair's allegations, some of which they labeled as "willful and deliberate misrepresentations of fact," "atrocious exaggeration," and "not at all characteristic."[8]

Instead, some of these same historians dwell on the Neill-Reynolds Report of the same year because it at least tentatively supported Sinclair. It turns out that neither Neill nor Reynolds had any experience in the meat-packing business and spent a grand total of two and a half weeks in the spring of 1906 investigating and preparing what turned out to be a carelessly written report with predetermined conclusions.

---

[6] U.S. House Committee on Agriculture, "Hearings on the So-called 'Beveridge Amendment' to the Agriculture Appropriation Bill," 59th Congress, 1st Session, 1906, p. 194.

[7] Ibid., p. 194

[8] Ibid., pp. 346–350.

Gabriel Kolko, a socialist but nonetheless a historian with a respect for facts, dismisses Sinclair as a propagandist and assails Neill and Reynolds as "two inexperienced Washington bureaucrats who freely admitted they knew nothing"[9] of the meat-packing process. Their own subsequent testimony revealed that they had gone to Chicago with the intention of finding fault with industry practices so as to get a new inspection law passed.[10]

According to the popular myth, there were no government inspectors before Congress acted in response to *The Jungle* and the greedy meat packers fought federal inspection all the way. The truth is that not only did government inspection exist, but meat packers themselves supported it and were in the forefront of the effort to extend it so as to ensnare their smaller, unregulated competitors.[11]

When the sensational accusations of *The Jungle* became worldwide news, foreign purchases of American meat were cut in half and the meat packers looked for new regulations to give their markets a calming sense of security. The only congressional hearings on what ultimately became the Meat Inspection Act of 1906 were held by Congressman James Wadsworth's Agriculture Committee between June 6 and 11. A careful reading of the deliberations of the Wadsworth committee and the subsequent floor debate leads inexorably to one conclusion: knowing that a new law would allay public fears fanned by *The Jungle*, bring smaller rivals under control, and put a newly laundered government seal of approval on their products, the major meat packers strongly endorsed the proposed act and only quibbled over who should pay for it.

In the end, Americans got a new federal meat inspection law, the big packers got the taxpayers to pick up the entire $3 million price tag for its implementation, as well as new regulations on the competition, and another myth entered the annals of anti-market dogma.

To his credit, Sinclair actually opposed the law because he saw it for what it really was—a boon for the big meat packers. He had been a fool and a sucker who ended up being used by the very industry he hated. But then, there may not have been an industry that he didn't hate.

---

[9] Kolko, op. cit., p. 105.

[10] "Hearings," p. 102.

[11] Upton Sinclair, "The Condemned-Meat Industry: A Reply to Mr. J. Ogden Armour," *Everybody's Magazine*, XIV, 1906, pp. 612–613.

Sinclair published more than 90 books before he died (at the age of 90) in 1968—*King Coal, Oil!, The Profits of Religion, The Flivver King, Money Writes!, The Moneychangers, The Goose-Step: A Study of American Education, The Goslings: A Study of the American Schools*, et cetera—but none came anywhere close to the fame of *The Jungle*. One (*Dragon's Teeth*), about the Nazi rise to power, earned him a Pulitzer in 1942, but almost all the others were little-noticed and even poorly-written class warfare screeds and shabby "exposés" of one industry or another. Many were commercial flops. Friend and fellow writer Sinclair Lewis took Sinclair to task for his numerous errors in a letter written to him in January 1928:

> I did not want to say these unpleasant things, but you have written to me, asking my opinion, and I give it to you, flat. If you would get over two ideas—first that anyone who criticizes you is an evil and capitalist-controlled spy, and second that you have only to spend a few weeks on any subject to become a master of it—you might yet regain your now totally lost position as the leader of American socialistic journalism.[12]

On three occasions, Sinclair's radical socialism led him into electoral politics. Running on the Socialist Party ticket for a congressional seat in New Jersey in 1906, he captured a measly 3% of the vote. He didn't fare much better as the Socialist candidate for governor of California in 1926. In 1934, however, he secured the nomination of the Democratic Party for the California governorship and shook up the political establishment with a program he called EPIC ("End Poverty in California"). With unemployment in excess of 20% and the state seething in discontent, most Californians still couldn't stomach Sinclair's penchant for goofy boondoggles and snake oil promises. Nonetheless, he garnered a very respectable 38% against the incumbent Republican Frank Merriman.

The EPIC platform is worth a mention, if only to underscore Sinclair's lifelong, unshakeable fascination with crackpot central-planning contrivances. It called for a massive tax increase on corporations and utilities, huge public employment programs (he wanted to put the unemployed to work on farms seized by the state for failure to pay taxes), and the issuance of money-like "scrip" based on goods produced by state-employed workers. He thought the Depression was probably a

---

[12] www.spartacus.schoolnet.co.uk/Jupton.htm

permanent affliction of capitalism and seemed utterly unaware of the endless state interventions that had brought it on in the first place (see my "Great Myths of the Great Depression" at FEE.org).

Was Upton Sinclair a nincompoop? You decide. This much is clear: early in the 20th century, he cooked up a work of fiction as a device to help in his agitation for an economic system (socialism) that doesn't work and that was already known not to work. For the next six decades he learned little if anything about economics, but he never relented in his support for discredited schemes to put big government in charge of other people's lives.

Myths survive their makers. What you've just read about Sinclair and his myth is not at all "politically correct." But defending the market from historical attack begins with explaining what really happened in our history. Those who persist in the shallow claim that *The Jungle* stands as a compelling indictment of the market should take a look at the history surrounding this honored novel. Upon inspection, there seems to be an unpleasant odor hovering over it.

—LWR, February 2002

14

Chapter **Fourteen**

Our Presidents and the National Debt

During the last 75 years the United States has failed to balance its annual budget over 90 percent of the time. What's worse, the government has spent money so recklessly that we now owe over $8.2 trillion, and Congress recently raised the debt ceiling to $9 trillion.

Such a trend is ominous because a country's national debt is a mirror of its economic future and its national character as well. With our piles of IOUs, we borrow from the future to indulge the present. If we study our national debt, we can discover some generalizations that help us understand how our presidents and our national character have changed over time.

1. Our first presidents took the national debt seriously and handled it with courage and integrity.

Our nation began with dangerous financial liabilities. When we fought the Revolutionary War we borrowed over $75 million in cash and supplies from individual patriots, from all 13 colonies, and from France and Holland. Our Founders, led by President George Washington and his treasury secretary, Alexander Hamilton, were determined to establish the U.S. credit by passing a tariff and a whiskey tax that would generate the revenue to help retire our war debt.

Washington, in his Farewell Address, described public credit as "a very important source of strength and security." He recommended that we "use it as sparingly as possible, avoiding occasions of expense by cultivating peace. . . ." Avoid "the accumulation of debt. . . ," Washington urged, "by vigorous exertions in time of peace to discharge the debts which unavoidable wars have occasioned, not ungenerously throwing upon posterity the burthen which we ourselves ought to bear." Not only did Washington wage the war, serve as president, and help establish our institutions of liberty, but he urged his generation to pay off the national debt as well.

Our first seven presidents were committed to Washington's goal. They chipped away so steadily at the national debt that James Madison, one of those presidents and the "Father of the Constitution," lived to see the entire debt eradicated. In fact, by his death in 1836, the United States had actually begun running a surplus.

How to handle the national surplus became a political issue that President Andrew Jackson had to address. "It appears to me," Jackson said, "that the most safe, just, and federal disposition which could be made of the surplus revenue, would be its apportionment among the several states according to their ratio of representation."

When Jackson's suggestion became law, the effect was immediate and nationwide. The residents of the Michigan Territory, for example, frantically clamored for statehood so that they would be eligible to scoop up some of the overflow from the federal treasury. Washington's dream of a creditworthy nation had become a reality.

2. Wars have spiked the national debt.

The national debt has not increased slowly; instead, it has increased sharply during major wars, starting with the Civil War. The earlier wars—the Revolutionary War, the War of 1812, and the Mexican War—all created small jumps in the national debt, but the presidents who followed them all whittled down those debts quickly. In the Civil War, however, the national debt skyrocketed from $60 million to $2.7 billion—more than a 45-fold increase, which is the greatest proportional leap of any war in U.S. history.

Interestingly, in the 50 years after the Civil War, from 1866 to 1916, the presidents were committed to restoring American credit, and the national debt was slashed from $2.7 billion to $1.2 billion. But World War I sent the debt spiraling again, this time to $24 billion by 1920. World War II added another digit to the nation's debt, which leaped from $43 billion to $259 billion from 1940 to 1945.

Those war debts have had a strong impact on U.S. tax policy. The income tax was introduced in America during the Civil War, but it was removed shortly after the war in 1872. After the Sixteenth Amendment was passed in 1913, the new income tax had a top marginal rate of 7 percent. But five years later, in the midst of World War I, the top rate was hiked to 77 percent. It was lowered in the 1920s, but during World War II the marginal tax rate jumped to 90 percent. President Franklin Roosevelt also introduced the idea of withholding income (proposed by a Treasury staff that included a young Milton Friedman) and forcing the employers to do the paperwork.

3. Most presidents have run surpluses, not deficits.

In fact, from 1791 to 1931, we had annual surpluses over 70 percent of the years. After the Civil War, for example, we ran surpluses for 28 straight years. Oddly, those presidents who obtained the most dramatic surpluses have often been those most condemned in the leading presidential polls. In Arthur Schlesinger's 1962 poll, four of the bottom five presidents—Coolidge, Pierce, Grant, and Harding—secured budget surpluses in each of their 20 total years as presidents. Under Franklin Pierce, for example, the entire national debt was cut almost in half. Under Harding and Coolidge, the national debt was almost slashed by one-third.

On the other hand, Lincoln, Wilson, and Franklin Roosevelt, whom Schlesinger's historians ranked among the top four presidents, broke all records for budget deficits. It is astonishing but true that these three presidents incurred more debt in their administrations than the entire national debt of $259 billion in 1945. In other words, of the first 32 presidents, under 29 of them we had a budget surplus of $4 billion; under Lincoln, Wilson, and Roosevelt we had a budget deficit of $263 billion.

Granted, they were war presidents, but that is a key point. Yet Washington had fought a major war, and as president he wanted to pay off the debt from that war in his generation. Lincoln, Wilson, and Roosevelt did not do that and do not seem to have had any ambition to do so.

Modern presidents, those who have served since the 1962 poll, are eager to secure their place in history. They may realize that fame and adulation are no longer given to those who "use [public credit] as sparingly as possible." Perhaps the slogan of the modern presidents could be, "It is better to have spent and lost than never to have spent at all."

4. Regardless of war or political party, modern presidents have tended to double the national debt about every nine years.

Even as late as post-World War II (1945–1960) the national debt increased at less than 1 percent per year. But since the Kennedy era and the Schlesinger poll, we have had four Democratic and five Republican presidents. Under these nine men, the national debt has doubled almost five times, from $289 billion in 1961 to a newly proposed ceiling of $9 trillion. Whether the issue has been hurricanes, farm subsidies, or medical care (none of which is a subject for federal aid, according to the Constitution), all these presidents have spent first and asked questions later.

Should that pattern of doubling the national debt every nine years continue—and there are very few politicians who wish to stop it—our debt by the end of the 21st century will increase to about $9 quadrillion, or (even if the U. S. population triples) about $10 million per person.

In discussing public debt, Washington said that congressmen needed to bear responsibility for retiring the debt, and "that public opinion should cooperate" as well. Will we heed the advice of this thrifty president and demand accountability from our elected officials?

—BWF, August 2006

15

The Progressive Income Tax in U.S. History

America's founders rejected the income tax entirely, but when they spoke of taxes they recognized the need for uniformity and equal protection to all citizens. "[A]ll duties, imposts and excises shall be uniform throughout the United States," reads the U.S. Constitution. And 80 years later, in the same spirit, the Fourteenth Amendment promised "equal protection of the laws" to all citizens.

In other words, the principle behind the progressive income tax—the more you earn, the larger the percentage of tax you must pay—would have been appalling to the founders. They recognized that, in James Madison's words, "the spirit of party and faction" would prevail if Congress could tax one group of citizens and confer the benefits on another group.

In Federalist No. 10, Madison asked, "[W]hat are the different classes of legislators but advocates and parties to the causes which they determine?" He went on to say, "The apportionment of taxes on the various descriptions of property is an act which seems to require the most exact impartiality; yet there is, perhaps, no legislative act in which greater opportunity and temptation are given to a predominant party to trample on the rules of justice."

During the 1800s economic thinking in the United States usually conformed to the founders' guiding principles of uniformity and equal protection. One exception was during the Civil War, when a progressive income tax was first enacted. Interestingly, the tax had a maximum rate of 10 percent, and it was repealed in 1872. As Representative Justin Morrill of Vermont observed, "in this country we neither create nor tolerate any distinction of rank, race, or color, and should not tolerate anything else than entire equality in our taxes."

When Congress passed another income tax in 1894—one that only hit the top 2 percent of wealth holders—the Supreme Court declared it unconstitutional. Stephen Field, a veteran of 30 years on the Court, was outraged that Congress would pass a bill to tax a small voting bloc and exempt the larger group of voters. At age 77, Field not only repudiated Congress's actions, he also penned a prophecy. A small progressive tax, he predicted, "will be but the stepping stone to others, larger and more sweeping, till our political contests will become a war of the poor against the rich."

In 1913, almost 20 years later, the ideas of uniform taxation and equal protection of the law for all citizens were overturned when a constitutional amendment permitting a progressive income tax was ratified. Congress first set the top rate at a mere 7 percent—and married couples were only taxed on income over $4,000 (equivalent to $80,000 today). During the tax debate, William Shelton, a Georgian, supported the income tax "because none of us here have $4,000 incomes, and somebody else will have to pay the tax." As Madison and Field had feared, the seeds of class warfare were sown in the strategy of different rates for different incomes.

It took the politicians less than one generation to hike the tax rates and fulfill Field's prophecy. Herbert Hoover and Franklin Roosevelt, using the excuses of depression and war, permanently enlarged the income tax. Under Hoover, the top rate was hiked from 24 to 63 percent. Under Roosevelt, the top rate was again raised—first to 79 percent and later to 90 percent. In 1941, in fact, Roosevelt proposed a 99.5 percent marginal rate on all incomes over $100,000. "Why not?" he said when an adviser questioned him.

After that proposal failed, Roosevelt issued an executive order to tax all income over $25,000 at the astonishing rate of 100 percent. Congress later repealed the order, but still allowed top incomes to be taxed at a marginal rate of 90 percent.

Subsidies for Friends, Audits for Enemies

Roosevelt thus became the first president to practice on a large scale what Madison had called "the spirit of party and faction" and what Field had called the "war of the poor against the rich." With a steeply progressive income tax in place, Roosevelt used the federal treasury to reward, among others, farmers (who were paid not to plant crops), silver miners (who had the price of their product artificially inflated), and southerners in the vote-rich Tennessee Valley (with dams and cheap electricity).

In the 1936 presidential election, Senator Hiram Johnson of California, a Roosevelt supporter, watched in amazement as the President mobilized "the different agencies of government" to dole out subsidies for votes. "He starts with probably 8 million votes bought," Johnson calculated. "The other side has to buy them one by one, and they cannot hope to match his money." In that campaign, Roosevelt defeated the Republican Alf Landon by an electoral vote of 523–8.

The flip side of rewards for supporters was investigations of opponents. Senator James Couzens of Michigan, who supported Roosevelt even more vigorously than Johnson did, had said before Roosevelt took office, "Give me control of the Bureau of Internal Revenue and I will run the politics of the country."

Couzens lived to see the bureau begin to investigate Roosevelt's opponents. It started with an investigation of Senator Huey Long of Louisiana, who had threatened to run for president against Roosevelt. Next came an audit of William Randolph Hearst, whose newspaper empire strongly opposed Roosevelt for president in 1936. Moses Annenberg, publisher of the *Philadelphia Inquirer*, vehemently opposed Roosevelt's re-election campaign in 1936; the next year he had a full-scale audit, which was followed by a prison term.

Elliott Roosevelt, the president's son, conceded in 1975 that "my father may have been the originator of the concept of employing the IRS as a weapon of political retribution." But he was quick to add that "each of his successors followed his lead." That is a key point: once the machinery of retribution is in place, it is hard for politicians to resist using it. When Richard Nixon, a Republican, became president, he sounded like his Democrat counterparts when he described whom he wanted as commissioner of internal revenue. Nixon said, "I want to be sure that he is . . . ruthless . . . that he will do what he is told, that every income-tax return I want to see, I see. That he will go after our enemies and not go after our friends. It is as simple as that."

If we want to lessen "the spirit of party and faction," as Madison recommended, and if we want to avoid a "war of the poor against the rich," as Field anticipated, we would do well to scrap the progressive income tax.

—BWF, May 2003

16

Chapter **Sixteen**

Cigarette Taxes Are Hazardous to Our Health

"In the great chess-board of human society," wrote Adam Smith in *The Theory of Moral Sentiments*, "every single piece has a principle of motion of its own, altogether different from that which the legislature might chuse to impress upon it."

With monotonous regularity legislatures are busy fine-tuning the lives and habits of millions of citizens—utterly oblivious, in most cases, to Smith's time-honored wisdom. As if keeping the peace, dispensing justice, and protecting the nation from foreign aggressors were petty, part-time assignments, nanny-state lawmakers are forever prodding us to moderate or abandon certain pastimes they say aren't good for us (even if many legislators engage in those very pastimes themselves). And if in the process of altruistically prodding us they make a few bucks for their favorite government program, well, that's just what the nanny state is really all about anyway.

If Adam Smith were with us today he could point to cigarette taxes as proof of what he wrote more than 200 years ago. Armed with the rhetoric of moral righteousness, the Carry Nations of the cigarette wars are jacking up taxes on smokes higher than smoke itself. It'll discourage a bad habit, they tell us, as they spend the revenues at least as fast as they roll in.

This past summer New York City raised its municipal cigarette tax from eight cents a pack to $1.50. New York State imposes the nation's highest per-pack tax, also $1.50, which means that $3 of every $7 pack of cigarettes in the Big Apple goes just for the government's take at the retail level. Never mind the baked-in hidden taxes from the tobacco farm to the local 7-Eleven that go into the retail price.

When Mayor Michael Bloomberg signed the latest tax hike into law at a news conference on June 30, a citizen tossed him a very cogent inquiry. According to the *New York Times*, Audrey Silk of Citizens Lobbying Against Smoker Harassment asked His Honor, "I know that you love to eat chunky peanut butter with bacon and bananas. How about I come out and start a campaign to tax that bacon that's going to cause heart disease, and tax that super-chunky peanut butter that's going to kill you?" After conferring with an expert at his side, the Mayor essentially said that smoking was different because it's addictive. Besides, the city's deficit-ridden budget needed the expected $111 million a year the $1.50 per pack would yield.

Who's really the addict here? I know of many people who have given up smoking. I don't know of any politicians who have given up on making money from it.

Indeed, federal, state, and local governments are the overwhelming reason why the average price of a pack of cigarettes has doubled in the past five years. In the mid-'90s my own state of Michigan tripled its tax from 25 to 75 cents. In August of this year it added another 50 cents. I hasten to add that my concern is not for my own pocketbook; I've never smoked anything but a paycheck. My first concern is personal liberty, which, if it means anything, surely means the right to enjoy risky pursuits like hang-gliding or even smoking as long as your actions don't aggress against others.

But more to the point, the ever-higher taxes on cigarettes are counterproductive in certain crucially important ways. As Adam Smith suggested, people are going to find ways to do what they want to do even if their friendly congressman would prefer that they didn't. Cigarette taxes are producing some of the same effects that alcohol prohibition brought in the 1920s and early '30s and that drug prohibition brings today.

In his 1963 book, *How Dry We Were: Prohibition Revisited*, Henry Lee explained what happened between 1919 and 1933 when alcohol was banned: The law drove the production and consumption of booze underground, and people who wanted to either make or drink the stuff turned to crime (and amazing creativity) to satisfy their desires. Profits in the trade soared, thanks to the ban itself. Smuggling became an art form. Likewise, today's endless and costly drug war has produced side effects that even a diehard drug warrior can't deny: an entire subculture that guarantees both violence and drugs to whoever wants them.

Legal Loophole

And so it is with cigarettes. It will be ever more so if taxes reach prohibitive levels. At least one legal loophole for avoiding the taxes is helping to keep the cigarette trade relatively peaceful for the moment: Indian reservations can sell cigarettes tax-free and sales at their stores and websites are soaring.

Meantime, low-tax, tobacco-growing states like Kentucky and North Carolina are magnets for smugglers who buy smokes there and truck them to high-tax, high-price states like Michigan. Authorities concede that smuggling is on the rise. An untold and growing volume of tax dollars is being spent to fight it.

In a recent commentary for the Mackinac Center for Public Policy, researcher James Damask revealed an especially seamy and disturbing side of cigarette-tax evasion. On July 21, 2000, 13 months before the World Trade Center attack, FBI agents raided a house in Charlotte, North Carolina, used as a smuggling base. Inside they found cash, weapons (including shotguns, rifles, and an AK-47), documents written in Arabic-and cigarettes. Lots of cigarettes. Why? Because, Damask says, "the operation exploited the tax differential between North Carolina, which has low cigarette taxes at 5 cents a pack, and Michigan, with high taxes at 75 cents a pack" (now $1.25).

Apparently, the smugglers would drive the 680 miles from Charlotte to Detroit in a rented van with 800 to 1,500 cartons of cigarettes purchased with cash in North Carolina. The cigarettes would then be sold to convenience stores in Detroit, which sold them to customers. Authorities say that each trip—which required absolutely no special skills for the 13-hour drive—would net $3,000 to $10,000. The profits would then be shuttled back to Charlotte. The homeowner and recipient of the profits was a man believed to have ties to foreign terrorist organizations.

The lesson? Like Prohibition, high taxes lead to big profit opportunities for people who break the law, which leads to smuggling, which in turn invites some pretty nasty people into the business. Politicians who say they're helping our health by taxing cigarettes so heavily are not counting all the costs of their effort with as much care as they count their tax revenue. And Adam Smith was right as rain.

—*LWR, November 2002*

17

Chapter **Seventeen**

A Man Who Knew the Value of Liberty

A television audience in the millions feasts on the glitz and glamor of Hollywood whenever the Academy Awards are bestowed. My thoughts are elsewhere that Sunday night—on a friend who won an Oscar nearly 30 years ago. February 25, usually a few days after the ceremony, marks the anniversary of the day he was killed.

On the night of the 57th Oscars in 1985, *Amadeus* claimed Best Picture, F. Murray Abraham won for best actor, and Sally Field for best actress. Then came the announcement of the winner of the award for best supporting actor. To the stage bearing the widest grin of his life bounced a man few Americans had ever heard of. He had acted in only one motion picture. He had been trained as a physician in his native Cambodia, where he had witnessed unspeakable cruelty and endured torture before escaping and finding his way to America barely five years earlier. He was Dr. Haing S. Ngor.

Ngor's Oscar-winning performance in *The Killing Fields* gave him a platform to tell the world about the mass murder that occurred between 1975 and 1979 in Cambodia at the hands of the Khmer Rouge communists. When I met Ngor at a conference in Dallas a few months after Oscar night, I was struck by the intensity of his passion. Perhaps no one loves liberty more than one who has been denied it at the point of a gun. We became instant friends and stayed in frequent contact. When he decided to visit Cambodia in August 1989 for the first time since his escape ten years before, he asked me to go with him. Dith Pran, the photographer Ngor portrayed in the movie, was among the small number in our entourage. Experiencing Cambodia with Ngor and Pran so soon after the genocide left me with vivid impressions and lasting memories.

But Cambodia in 1989 was still a universe away from the Cambodia of 1979. In spite of the country's continued suffering on a grand scale, I knew it was a playground compared to the three and a half years that Ngor and Pran lived through and miraculously survived.

During that time, crazed but battle-hardened and jungle-toughened revolutionaries who had seized power in 1975 set about to remake Cambodian society. Their leader, Pol Pot, embraced the most radical versions of class warfare, egalitarianism, and state control. Mao and Stalin were his heroes. In the warped minds of Pol Pot and his Khmer Rouge hierarchy, the "evils" they aspired to destroy included all vestiges of the former governments of Cambodia: city life, private enterprise, the family unit, religion, money, modern medicine and industry, private property, and anything that smacked of foreign influence. They savaged an essentially defenseless population already weary of war. The Khmer Rouge manufactured the killing fields for which the film was later named.

One day after taking power, the Khmer Rouge forcibly evacuated the populations of all urban areas, including the capital, Phnom Penh, a city swollen by refugees to at least two million inhabitants. Many thousands of men and women—including the sick, elderly, and handicapped—died on the way to their "political rehabilitation" in the countryside. Survivors found themselves slaving away at the most grueling toil in the rice fields, often separated from their families, routinely beaten and tortured for trifling offenses or for no reason at all, kept hungry by meager rations, and facing certain death for the slightest challenge to authority.

Thon Hin, a top official in the Cambodian foreign ministry at the time of our 1989 visit, told me of the propaganda blasted daily from speakers as citizens labored in the fields: "They said that everything belonged to the state, that we had no duty to anything but the state, that the state would always make the right decisions for the good of everyone. I remember so many times they would say, 'It is always better to kill by mistake than to not kill at all.' "

Churches and pagodas were demolished and thousands of Buddhist monks and worshippers were murdered. Schools were closed down, and modern medicine was forbidden in favor of quack remedies and sinister experimentation. By 1979 only 45 doctors remained alive in the whole country; more than 4,000 had perished or fled. Eating in private and scavenging for food were considered crimes against the state. So was wearing eyeglasses, which was seen as evidence that one had read too much.

Early estimates of the death toll from starvation, disease, and execution during Pol Pot's tyranny ranged as high as three million—in a nation of only eight million inhabitants when he took power. Most now put the figure in the neighborhood of two million deaths.

Haing Ngor didn't just see these things; he endured them. He had to get rid of his eyeglasses and disappear as a doctor. He reappeared as a cab driver, hoping he and his wife would not draw the attention of the Khmer Rouge. Nonetheless, on more than one occasion, he fell prey to their brutality. In one torturous episode, one of his fingers was sliced off. In another, his wife died in his arms from complications during childbirth. Ngor's skills as a physician might have saved her, but he knew if he revealed he was a doctor they both would have been executed on the spot. He eventually escaped Cambodia through Thailand, landing in America in 1980, a year and a half after a Vietnamese invasion eradicated the Khmer Rouge regime.

Haing Ngor believed the world must know these things, fully and graphically. When fate led to a chance to act in a movie about the period, he grabbed it and performed brilliantly. He deserved the Oscar it earned him, even though he often said that he really didn't have to "act." He had personally suffered through calamities much worse than those depicted in the film. He was driven to do well so that the rest of us would remember what happened and those to whom it happened.

One cold morning in February 1996 I learned that Dr. Haing S. Ngor had been shot and killed the day before—not somewhere in Southeast Asia, but in downtown Los Angeles. The perpetrators, it turned out, were ordinary gang thugs trying to rob him as he got out of his car. They took a locket that held the only picture he still had of his deceased wife.

For Haing Ngor, rediscovering his freedom after experiencing hell on earth wasn't enough. He couldn't relax, breathe sighs of relief, or resume living a quiet or anonymous life. He felt compelled to tell his story so others would know what awful things total government can do. He forced us to ponder and appreciate life more fundamentally than ever before.

Enjoy the Oscars if you watch them. We should be thankful for people like Haing Ngor, who did more to educate for liberty in a few short years than most people who take their liberty for granted will ever do in their lifetimes.

—LWR, January 2009

Part III

Our Cousins Stand for Liberty

18

Chapter **Eighteen**

Scotland: Seven Centuries since William Wallace

I am an American of Scottish extraction, and few things stir my blood more than the colorful history of my ancestral homeland. Through the centuries, rugged Scots stand tall among those heroes who gave every ounce of their lives for such noble ideals as liberty, independence, and self-reliance.

Mel Gibson's epic film *Braveheart*, released in 1995, introduced many non-Scots to one of our greatest heroes, William Wallace. A fierce and uncompromising Scottish patriot, Wallace gave English invaders fits for years until his capture on August 5, 1305. He was hauled to London to face charges of insurrection, found guilty, and brutally executed by Edward I seven centuries ago, on August 23, 1305.

Edward was deservedly known as the "Hammer of the Scots." His designs on Scotland were apparent shortly after he ascended to the English throne in 1272, when Wallace was but two years old. While the Scottish people themselves may have been staunch in their desire to retain their own national identity, many of their nobility were unprincipled opportunists who connived with Edward to allow English encroachment in exchange for political favors. More than a dozen of them claimed the Scottish throne in 1290 and then invited Edward's arbitration to settle the question.

The English king chose John Balliol to be his royal puppet in exchange for the Scottish king's oath of loyalty to England. But in 1296 Balliol found the spine to differ with Edward over an important issue, and the two nations went to war.

Young Wallace emerged early as a Scottish patriot of special mettle, leading his countrymen to a smashing victory at the Battle of Stirling Bridge on September 11, 1297. "All powerful as a swordsman and un-rivalled as an archer," John D. Carrick wrote in his classic *Life of Sir William Wallace of Elderslie*, "his blows were fatal and his shafts un-erring: as an equestrian, he was a model of dexterity and grace; while the hardships he experienced in his youth made him view with indifference the severest privations incident to a military life."

Wallace's courage united Scotland, but 11 months after Stirling, the Scots were outnumbered at Falkirk and dealt a crushing blow. His forces scattered, Wallace took his campaign for independence to the courts of Europe in search of foreign alliances. When he returned to Scotland in 1303, he was the most-wanted fugitive in the country, and he was betrayed to Edward in the summer of 1305. The evidence is strong that it wasn't commoners who broke faith with him, but highly placed Scottish officials who sold out to Edward. In London he was hanged and then drawn and quartered while still alive. Before his torture and execution, he responded to the charges against him with these words:

> I cannot be a traitor, for I owe him no allegiance. He is not my Sovereign; he never received my homage; and whilst life is in this persecuted body, he never shall receive it. To the other points whereof I am accused, I freely confess them all. As Governor of my country I have been an enemy to its enemies; I have slain the English; I have mortally opposed the English King; I have stormed and taken the towns and castles which he unjustly claimed as his own. If I or my soldiers have plundered or done injury to the houses or ministers of religion, I repent me of my sin; but it is not of Edward of England I shall ask pardon.

Avenging Wallace's death became a rallying cry in the years thereafter. Edward died in 1307 with Scotland still simmering in revolt. Under Robert the Bruce, the forces of Edward II were decisively defeated at Bannockburn in 1314. Six years later, a group of Scottish leaders issued the famous Declaration of Arbroath in hopes that the Pope would convince the English to leave Scotland alone. This declaration, written a full four and a half centuries before the American Declaration of Independence, enunciated the principle that a king must rule by the consent of the governed, who in turn have a duty to get rid of him if he doesn't. It includes these stirring words: "It is not for honors or glory or wealth that we fight, but for freedom alone, which no good man gives up except with his life."

The crowns of England and Scotland were united in the early seventeenth century and the parliaments were merged a hundred years later but Scotland retains a strong national identity within the United Kingdom. Wallaceite rugged individualism was apparent in the ideas of the Scottish Enlightenment, which produced Adam Smith, David Hume, and other eighteenth-century thinkers committed to limited government, self-reliance, freer markets, and personal freedom. William Ewart Gladstone, one of Britain's greatest prime ministers and an ardent opponent of excessive government, had deep roots in Scotland.

Though my Scottish blood and love of liberty make me proud of this heritage, I worry that Scots in more recent decades have forsaken their history. The spirit of Wallace and the contributions of Hume, Smith, and Gladstone are perfunctorily recognized, but in practice Scottish policymakers seem wedded to the coercive nanny state. The great Scots of the past would probably be shocked to know how extensively their descendents now depend on the largess of government. As Alexander Hamilton, an American of Scottish ancestry, once wisely warned, "Control of a man's subsistence is control of his will."

Modern Reality

"Scotland is the most socialist part of Britain," says John Blundell, former director of the Institute of Economic Affairs in London. "It even has strong credentials as the most socialist part of the European Union. Its public sector, including municipal agencies, consumes more of the [gross domestic product] than in any other OECD nation." The romantic, noble image of proud and independent Scots has given way to a very different reality: a heavily subsidized population that overwhelmingly supports political candidates who demand even more subsidies.

Still, 705 years after the death of William Wallace, Scots know who Wallace was and admire him. Many seem to know instinctively something very fundamental to the greatness of their past and their distinction as a people: Their proudest heritage is one of keeping government at bay, not granting it broad power over their lives and livelihoods. As a Scot in America, that's what I celebrate every chance I get. I hope someday the Scots of Scotland will do so once again as well.

—LWR, December 2010

19

Chapter **Nineteen**

Happy Birthday, Adam Smith!

The birthday of a great man just passed virtually unnoticed—even in his homeland—though he shaped the modern world perhaps as much as anybody. That man was Adam Smith, the world's first economist.

Smith was baptized on June 5, 1723, in Kirkcaldy, Scotland. It's not known for certain, but presumed that he was either born on that very day, or a day or two before. Whichever date it was, he entered a world that his reason and eloquence would later transform.

For 300 years before Smith, Western Europe was dominated by an economic system known as "mercantilism." Though it provided for modest improvements in life and liberty over the feudalism that came before, it was a system rooted in error that stifled enterprise and treated individuals as pawns of the state.

Mercantilist thinkers believed that the world's wealth was a fixed pie, giving rise to endless conflict between nations. After all, if you think there's only so much and you want more of it, you've got to take it from someone else.

Mercantilists were economic nationalists. Foreign goods, they thought, were sufficiently harmful to the domestic economy that govern-ment policy should be marshaled to promote exports and restrict imports. Instead of imported goods, they wanted exports to be paid for by foreigners in gold and silver. To the mercantilist, the precious metals were the very definition of wealth, especially to the extent that they piled up in the coffers of the monarch.

Because they had little sympathy for self-interest, the profit motive and the operation of prices, mercantilists wanted governments to bestow monopoly privileges upon a favored few. In Britain, the king even granted a protected monopoly over the production of playing cards to a particular, highly-placed noble.

Economics in the late 18th century was not yet a focused subject of its own, but rather a poorly organized compartment of what was known as "moral philosophy." Smith's first of two books, *The Theory of Moral Sentiments*, was published in 1759 when he held the chair of moral philosophy at Glasgow University. He was the first moral philosopher to recognize that the business of enterprise—and all the motives and actions in the marketplace that give rise to it—was deserving of careful, full-time study as a modern discipline of social science. The culmination of his thoughts in this regard came in 1776. As American colonists were declaring their independence from Britain, Smith was publishing his own shot heard round the world, *An Inquiry into the Nature and Causes of the Wealth of Nations*, better known ever since as simply *The Wealth of Nations.*

Smith's choice of the longer title is revealing in itself. Note that he didn't set out to explore the nature and causes of the poverty of nations. Poverty, in his mind, was what happened when nothing happens, when people are idle by choice or force, or when production is prevented or destroyed. He wanted to know what brings the things we call material wealth into being, and why. It was a searching examination that would make him a withering critic of the mercantilist order.

Wealth was not gold and silver in Smith's view. Precious metals, though reliable as media of exchange and for their own industrial uses, were no more than claims against the real thing. All of the gold and silver in the world would leave one starving and freezing if they couldn't be exchanged for food and clothing. Wealth to the world's first economist was plainly this: goods and services. Whatever increased the supply and quality of goods and services, lowered their price or enhanced their value made for greater wealth and higher standards of living. The "pie" of national wealth isn't fixed; you can bake a bigger one by producing more.

Baking that bigger pie, Smith showed, results from investments in capital and the division of labor. His famous example of the specialized tasks in a pin factory demonstrated how the division of labor works to produce far more than if each of us acted in isolation to produce everything himself. It was a principle that Smith showed works for nations precisely because it works for the individuals who make them up. He was consequently an economic internationalist, one who believes in the widest possible cooperation between peoples irrespective of political boundaries. He was, in short, a consummate free trader at a time when trade was hampered by an endless roster of counterproductive tariffs, quotas and prohibitions.

Smith wasn't hung up on the old mercantilist fallacy that more goods should be exported than imported. He exploded this "balance of trade" fallacy by arguing that since goods and services constituted a nation's wealth, it made no sense for government to make sure that more left the country than came in.

Self-interest, frowned upon for ages as acquisitive, anti-social behavior, was celebrated by Smith as an indispensable spur to economic progress. "It is not from the benevolence of the butcher, the brewer, or the baker, that we can expect our dinner," he wrote, "but from their regard to their own interest." Moreover, self-interest was an unsurpassed incentive: "The natural effort of every individual to better his own condition ... is so powerful, that it is alone, and without any assistance, not only capable of carrying on the society to wealth and prosperity, but of surmounting a hundred impertinent obstructions with which the folly of human laws too often encumbers its operations."

In a free economy, he reasoned, no one can put a crown on his head and command that others provide him with goods. To satisfy his own desires, he must produce what others want at a price they can afford. Prices send signals to producers so that they will know what to make more of and what to provide less of. It wasn't necessary for the king to assign tasks and bestow monopolies to see that things get done. Prices and profit would act as an "invisible hand" with far more efficiency than any monarch or parliament. And competition would see to it that quality is improved and prices are kept low.

Smith's view of competition was undoubtedly shaped by the way he saw the universities of his day, loaded with coddled, tenured professors whose pay had little to do with their service to their pupils or the public at large. While a student at Oxford in the 1740s, he observed the lassitude of his professors who "had given up altogether even the pretense of teaching."

If it seems that Smith put much more faith in people and markets than in kings and edicts, it's because that's precisely right. With characteristic eloquence, he declared that ". . .[I]n the great chess-board of human society, every single piece has a principle of motion of its own, altogether different from that which the legislature might chuse to impress upon it."

Smith displayed an understanding of government that eclipses that of many citizens today when he wrote, "It is the highest impertinence and presumption, therefore, in kings and ministers, to pretend to watch over the economy of private people, and to restrain their expense . . . . They are themselves always, and without any exception, the greatest spendthrifts in the society. Let them look well after their own expense, and they may safely trust private people with theirs. If their own extravagance does not ruin the state, that of their subjects never will."

The ideas of Adam Smith exerted enormous influence before he died in 1790 and especially in the 19th century. America's Founders were greatly affected by his insights. *The Wealth of Nations* became required reading among men and women of ideas the world over. A tribute to him more than any other individual, the world in 1900 was much freer and more prosperous than anyone imagined in 1776. The march of free trade and globalization in our own time is further testimony to the enduring legacy of Adam Smith. A think tank in Britain bears his name and seeks to make that legacy better known.

Ideas really do matter. They can change the world. Adam Smith proved that in spades, and we are all immeasurably better off because of the ideas he shattered and the ones he set in motion.

—LWR, June 2006

20

Chapter **Twenty**

The Man Who Didn't "Grow" In Office

Seven miles north of Escanaba in Michigan's Upper Peninsula sits a little town with a very big name. More than a hundred years after the death of the town's namesake it's unlikely that many of today's 5,000 residents of Gladstone could tell you much about him. But in the nineteenth century and for a long time thereafter, he was widely considered to be one of the world's greatest statesmen.

Gladstone, Michigan, wasn't always so named. It was originally christened "Minnewasca," the Sioux Indian word for "White Water," in 1887. Shortly thereafter, a local businessman pushed to rename the town after British Prime Minister William Ewart Gladstone. A nearby railroad was partially funded by British capital and area residents appreciated the resulting economic development.

Just who was this son of Scottish parents who read 20,000 books in his lifetime and could speak Greek, Latin, Italian, and French, in addition to English? Biographer Philip Magnus wrote that "at the time of his death [1898] he was . . . the most venerated and influential statesman in the world." Another biographer (who currently sits in Britain's House of

Lords), Roy Jenkins, declares that Gladstone "stamped the Victorian age even more than did [Queen] Victoria herself, and represented it almost as much."

No individual in history had a longer or more distinguished career in the British government: 62 years in the House of Commons; in charge of the nation's finances as Chancellor of the Exchequer for 14 budgets in four administrations; leader of a major political party (the Liberals) for almost 40 years; four times prime minister, for a total of 12 years. Gladstone was 84 years old when he retired as P.M. in 1894, the oldest prime minister in British history. He was hailed as the "Grand Old Man" for his leadership and stature and as "England's Great Commoner" because he was not of royal blood and refused to accept any titles of nobility. When he died, a quarter million citizens attended his funeral, one of the largest the country ever saw.

What made Gladstone both great and memorable was what he accomplished while he served in government. Biographer Magnus says that Gladstone "achieved unparalleled success in his policy of setting the individual free from a multitude of obsolete restrictions."

Today, when a citizen gets elected to make government smaller but ends up doing the opposite, the conventional wisdom credits him with having "grown in office." Gladstone's philosophy evolved, but in precisely the opposite direction—from a hodgepodge of statist notions to principled liberty. He entered Parliament at age 22 in 1832 as a protectionist, a defender of the tax-subsidized Church of England, and an opponent of reform. The eminent British historian Thomas Babington Macaulay described him as "the rising hope of the stern and unbending Tories."

Ardent Free Trader

By 1850 he had become an ardent free trader and by 1890 he was largely responsible for reducing Britain's tariffs from 1,200 to just 12. He slashed government spending, taxes, and regulations. He ended tax subsidies for the Church of England in Ireland. He pushed through reforms that allowed Jews and Catholics to serve in Parliament and that extended the vote to millions of taxpaying workers. He extolled the virtues of self-help and private charity.

Gladstone's administrations were not paragons of unqualified libertarianism. In domestic policy he sometimes supported interventionist measures. But it is undeniable that Britons were considerably freer when he died in 1898 than their fathers and grandfathers had been at the start of the century.

It wasn't the instruction he received while a student at Oxford that converted Gladstone to the liberation of the individual. Indeed, he offered this observation in later years: "I trace in the education of Oxford of my own time one great defect. Perhaps it was my own fault; but I must admit that I did not learn when at Oxford that which I have learned since—namely, to set a due value on the imperishable and inestimable principles of human liberty. The temper which, I think, too much prevailed in academic circles was to regard liberty with jealousy." Anyone familiar with the prevailing orthodoxy of today's academia would have to conclude that in this respect, the more things have changed the more they've stayed the same.

It was as president of the Board of Trade in the ministry of Sir Robert Peel in the 1840s that a young Gladstone came to champion free trade. The disastrous Irish potato famine was a powerful argument against laws forbidding the importation of grain for a starving populace.

Gladstone befriended the Anti-Corn Law League's John Bright, became convinced of the logic of free trade, and secured the repeal of the protectionist Corn Laws over the objections of many in his own Conservative, or Tory, Party. The measure split the Conservatives, which paved the way for Gladstone and others a decade later to give birth to the Liberal Party.

Gladstone's conversion to free trade made him a big name in liberal circles in Britain and a rising star abroad as well. His international reputation soared in 1851 when, after a visit to Naples, he revealed to the world the appalling conditions in Neapolitan prisons. Reformers there were being locked up for speaking out on behalf of freedom. Gladstone's vigorous denunciation reverberated around the globe and later prompted the Italian patriot Garibaldi to credit the British parliamentarian with having "sounded the first trumpet call of Italian liberty."

In foreign policy, with a painful exception or two that he mostly later regretted, Gladstone practiced retrenchment. He opposed the imperialist policies of his arch-rival Benjamin Disraeli. He said he preferred the Golden Rule over intervention. He fought hard but failed to secure Home Rule for Ireland; if Parliament had been as wise as he on that issue, Ireland today might still be a part of the United Kingdom.

In February 1893, in his 83rd year, he delivered what one biographer terms "a lucid and brilliant speech" upholding the sanctity of sound money and the gold standard.

Gladstone often urged the British people to look to the ideas of America's Founding Fathers for inspiration. "I was brought up to distrust and dislike liberty; I learned to believe in it," he told a friend in 1891. "I view with the greatest alarm the progress of socialism at the present day," he said. "Whatever influence I possess will be used in the direction of stopping it."

Today, in little Gladstone, Michigan, a portrait of the Grand Old Man hangs in City Hall. The residents there can and should be very proud that their town's name didn't stay "Minnewasca" for long.

—LWR, April 2002

21

Chapter **Twenty-One**

Prophets of Property

In 1800, fewer than 1 million people lived in London; a century later, it was home to well over 6 million. As the 20th century dawned, London had already been the most populous city on the planet for seven decades. Britain's population as a whole soared from 8 million in 1800 to 40 million in 1900. In the previous 2,000 years, even a fraction of such population growth anywhere in Europe was usually nipped in the bud by famine, disease, falling incomes and population retrenchment.

But Britain in the 19th century was a special place, the legendary "workshop of the world." London had become the capital of capital, with private investment in agriculture and manufacturing burgeoning at a record-breaking pace in the latter half of the century. The year Victoria ascended to the throne, 1837, saw fewer than 300 patent applications for new inventions, but by the end of the century the number exceeded 25,000 annually. Per capita income on the eve of World War I was three times what it was a century before and life expectancy had risen by 25 percent. There were many more mouths to feed and bodies to clothe, but British entrepreneurship was feeding and clothing them better than the world had ever experienced. It was the greatest flowering of problem-solving creativity, ingenuity, and innovation in history.

Colin Pullinger, a carpenter's son from Selsea, typified the 19th century British entrepreneur. He designed a "perpetual mousetrap" that could humanely catch a couple dozen mice per trap in a single night, and then sold 2 million of them. Perhaps Emerson had Pullinger in mind when he famously wrote, "If a man write a better book, preach a better sermon, or make a better mousetrap than his neighbour, tho' he build his house in the woods, the world will make a beaten path to his door."

As the 1800s drew to a close, the framework that made possible these extraordinary achievements—capitalism—fell under assault. As poverty declined massively for the first time, the very presence of the poverty that remained prompted impatient calls for forcible redistribution of wealth. Around the world, Marxists painted capitalists as exploiters and monopolists. In Britain, Charles Kingsley argued that Christianity demanded a socialist order, and the Fabian Society was formed to help bring it about. Many unscrupulous businessmen turned to the state for favors and protections unavailable to them in competitive markets. Would anyone come to the defense of the capitalism with as much vigor and passion as those who opposed it?

At least one group did: the Liberty and Property Defence League. Though its work has been largely forgotten, what the world learned about socialism in the following century surely vindicates its message. Its name derived from the members' belief that liberty and property were inseparable and that unless successfully defended, both could be swept away by the beguiling temptations of a coercive state.

The founder of the League in 1882 was a pugnacious Scot by the name of Lord Elcho, later the 10th earl of Wemyss as a member of the House of Lords and thereafter known simply as "Wemyss." Originally elected to parliament in 1841 as a protectionist Tory, he eventually embraced free trade and repeal of the Corn Laws by 1846. He later evolved into a full-throated advocate for what we today would call "classical liberal" ideas. At the organization's third annual meeting in 1885, he expressed his hope that its efforts to educate the public would "cause such a flood as will sweep away, in the course of time, all attempts at state interference in the business transactions of life in the case of every Briton of every class . . . . No nation can prosper with undue state interference, and unless its people are allowed to manage their own affairs in their own way. . . ."

Wemyss and his friends rounded up spokespersons and financial support. They enlisted writers and public speakers. They published and circulated essays and leaflets. The organization operated as an activist think tank with a lobbying arm. The League attempted to mobilize public opinion against specific bills, functioning as a "day-to-day legislative watchdog" in the view of historian Edward Bristow. It even arranged testimony before parliamentary hearings. One League pamphlet attacked the introduction of "grandmotherly legislation" as a transgression against the freedom of contract. Armed with arguments provided by League members and sympathizers, Wemyss' allies in Parliament killed hundreds of interventionist bills in the 1880s and 1890s.

Opponents often accused the League of being motivated by its members' bottom line drive for profits, but in actuality its philosophical ideals were paramount. Among its members were some of the brightest intellects of the era, Herbert Spencer being perhaps the most notable. Author of the libertarian classic, "The Man Versus the State," Spencer was the best-selling philosopher of his day and was nominated for a Nobel in literature. Spencer saw liberty as the absence of coercion and as the most indispensable prerequisite for human progress. The ownership of property was an individual right that could not be morally infringed unless an individual first threatened the property of another. Spencer has been demonized as an apostle of a heartless "survival of the fittest" Darwinism by those who choose to ignore or distort his central message, namely that individual self-improvement can accomplish more progress than political action. One creates wealth, the other merely takes and reapportions it.

Auberon Herbert was a Spencer acolyte whose championship of voluntarism found fertile soil among fellow League members. His now century-old warning about the danger of state intervention is positively prophetic: "No amount of state education will make a really intelligent nation; no amount of Poor Laws will place a nation above want; no amount of Factory Acts will make us better parents . . . . To have our wants supplied from without by a huge state machinery, to be regulated and inspected by great armies of officials, who are themselves slaves to the system which they administer, will in the long run teach us nothing, (and) will profit us nothing."

In a 1975 essay in *The Historical Journal* from Cambridge University Press, historian Bristow contended that the Liberty and Property

Defence League changed the language in one important, lasting way. Prior to the 1880s, "individualism" was a term of opprobrium in most quarters, referring to "the atomism and selfishness of liberal society." The League appropriated the word and elevated its general meaning to one of respect for the rights and uniqueness of each person.

But was the League successful in its mission to thwart the socialist impulse? In the short run, lamentably, no. By 1914, socialists had convinced large numbers of Britons that they could (and should) vote themselves a share of other people's property. Two world wars and a depression in between seemed to cement the socialists' claim that their vision for society was inevitable.

Good ideas, however, have a way of resisting attempts to quash them. Bad ideas sooner or later fail and teach a valuable lesson or two in the process. Britain and most of the world gave socialism in all its varieties one hell of a run in the 20th century. The disastrous results now widely acknowledged underscore the warnings of those who said that we could depart from liberty and property only at our peril.

The warriors of the Liberty and Property Defence League may have lost the battle in their lifetimes, but a hundred years later they offer prophetic wisdom to those who will listen.

—LWR, July 2007

22

Chapter **Twenty-Two**

Wilfrid Laurier: A Canadian Statesman

Owing to where most Americans trace their ancestry from, we tend to know more European history than the history of our immediate neighbors to the north and south, Canada and Mexico. We can name famous entrepreneurs and political leaders from across the sea but rarely one from right next door.

Not too long ago in a casual dinner conversation with Canadian liber-tarians in Vancouver, I named the better presidents and prime ministers, respectively, of the United States and Great Britain. It suddenly occurred to me that I couldn't name a single Canadian counterpart.

So I asked my dinner friends, "Among Canada's political leaders, did you ever have a Grover Cleveland or a William Ewert Gladstone, a prime minister who believed in liberty and defended it?"

One name emerged, almost in unison: Sir Wilfrid Laurier. Embarrassed by my ignorance, I had to admit I had never heard of him. Never mind that he's the guy with the bushy hair on the Canadian five-dollar bill; I just never noticed. Now that I've done a little research, I'm a fan.

Laurier's political resume is impressive: fourth-longest-serving prime minister in Canada's history (1896–1911, the longest unbroken term of office of all 22 PMs). Forty-five years in the House of Commons, an all-time record. Longest-serving leader of any Canadian political party (almost 32 years). Across Canada to this day, he is widely regarded as one of the country's greatest statesmen.

It's not his tenure in government that makes Laurier an admirable figure. It's what he stood for while he was there. He really meant it when he declared, "Canada is free and freedom is its nationality" and "Nothing will prevent me from continuing my task of preserving at all cost our civil liberty."

A think tank in Ottawa now honors Laurier and another Canadian PM, John MacDonald, in its name: the MacDonald-Laurier Institute. Founders Brian Crowley, Jason Clemens, and Niels Veldhuis authored a book, *The Canadian Century: Moving Out of America's Shadow*, in which they explain the political principles and institutions the great Laurier stood for: limited government, light taxes, fiscal discipline, free trade, private property, and the rule of law.

At a time when others in the British Commonwealth had begun to emulate the welfare-state policies of Bismarckian Germany, Laurier had a better idea. Crowley, Clemens, and Veldhuis write:

Laurier's objection to such schemes, like that of his Liberal colleagues, was one of principle: when people were expected to take responsibility for themselves and their famil[ies], they made better provision for their needs and directed their productive efforts where they would do the country and themselves the greatest good. When this natural necessity to strive was diluted by an easy access to the public purse, the ever-present danger was of the enervation of the individual and the stagnation of the progress of society. "If you remove the incentives of ambition and emulation from public enterprises"—by which he meant the economic undertakings of individuals and businesses, not state enterprises—Laurier said on the subject in 1907, "you suppress progress, you condemn the community to stagnation and immobility."

Born in Quebec in 1841, Laurier rose in popularity in spite of his expressed belief in the separation of church and state. The province's Roman Catholic bishops urged voters to steer clear of him but he built a firm base of local support. The people appreciated his solid character and his desire for goodwill and conciliation among the disparate cultures of Canada. As prime minister he worked to keep the country together by keeping the central government small. Toleration and decentralized federalism became hallmarks of his long legacy in politics.

Relying on Markets

To help Canadians compete with the colossus to the south, Laurier hoped the country would rely on private enterprise and open markets. A key ingredient, he believed, would have to be a lower cost of government and a lower tax burden in Canada than in the United States. He made it clear, in the words of Crowley, Clemens, and Veldhuis, "that people who came to Canada from south of the border or beyond the seas would find in the Dominion a society of free men and women where everyone was expected to work hard, and where, if they did so, they would keep more of the fruits of their labours than anywhere else, including the United States of America."

Laurier never achieved the degree of free trade his conscience supported, but against powerful opposition he pushed Canada away from high protectionist tariffs. He wanted lower duties aimed more to raise revenue than to favor certain industries or regions at the expense of others. He made progress on some other fronts as well. He proposed balanced budgets as a way to keep Canada's debt low and manageable. His policies opened the door for an explosion of immigration. Half a million hard-working immigrants rushed to Canada during his tenure, building a strong economy and a melting pot of countless cultures in the process.

Laurier's record was not perfect from a libertarian perspective. For example, he supported subsidies to transcontinental railroads, a major departure from his otherwise pro-enterprise, limited-government philosophy. But as twentieth-century Canadian prime ministers go, he clearly stands apart and above. My friends in Vancouver don't believe any PM since Laurier did as much for liberty as he did.

I now keep a Canadian five-dollar bill in my wallet just for those occasions when I meet a Canadian and the conversation turns to politics. We will lament the caliber of more recent politicians on both sides of the border but at least I can now point to Laurier's picture and say, "We can do better, and indeed, you have."

—*LWR, November 2010*

23

Chapter **Twenty-Three**

From Crystal Palace to White Elephant in 150 Years

Mention the ill-fated Millennium Dome to almost any citizen of Great Britain and you'll get an earful about one of the greatest government sponsored, scandal-ridden fiascoes of all time. Costing more than a billion dollars, it was a white elephant that bled red ink from its public opening on New Year's Day 2000 until it closed a year later. It was intended in part to rival a famous project of a century and a half earlier but, by any important measure, it never came close.

The Millennium Dome's colossal flop prompted Prime Minister Tony Blair to remark, "If I had my time again, I would have listened to those who said governments shouldn't try to run big visitor attractions." Two years before, Blair and his whiz kids in the London bureaucracy thought there was nothing about the Great Exhibition of 1851 that couldn't be improved with a generous dose of modern central planning and loot from the taxpayer. How wrong they were. If the Dome sparks renewed interest in that earlier show, it will serve perhaps its most useful purpose. What happened in 1851 was a spectacular tribute to the enterprising spirit of that day.

By the middle of the nineteenth century, Britain was the industrial "workshop of the world," producing more than half of all coal, iron, and cotton cloth. Powered by a relatively free economy that was becoming freer by the decade, Britain's railroads, factories, and machine technology were well ahead of any other nation's. It was time to celebrate not only Britain's remarkable achievements, but also those of free trade and free enterprise the world over. Around the mid-1840s, these thoughts came to animate Queen Victoria's husband, Albert, the Prince Consort.

Albert and his advisers felt that Britain should host a fair to showcase the industrial might of all nations. Like so many people of the time, they were ecstatic about the potential of capitalist invention and the peaceful, international trade it fostered. In January 1850, Victoria named Albert to head a 24-man Royal Commission to make the "Great Exhibition of the Industries of All Nations" a reality.

Prince Albert declared at the start of the commission's deliberations that the Exhibition should not and would not be funded by government. This was to be a celebration of private enterprise, and it seemed only logical for private, enterprising citizens to foot the bill. Everything from the building that would house it to the exhibits themselves would be paid for by voluntary contributions, fundraising campaigns, and admission fees. The Millennium Dome of 2000, by contrast, was a giant public works scheme from its inception—filled with uninspiring, politically correct, and just plain boring displays and financed by taxes and the government's national lottery.

As soon as London's Hyde Park was chosen for the 1851 site, the Royal Commission solicited proposals for a building to house the Exhibition during the expected six months it would be open to the public. The project was in danger of foundering amid designs deemed too costly, when entrepreneur Joseph Paxton came forth with plans for a monster edifice made entirely of glass panes (nearly a quarter million of them) and the supporting iron framework. Thanks to the repeal in 1845 of Britain's longstanding and onerous "window tax," the price of glass had fallen by 80 percent, making Paxton's design affordable.

When the "Crystal Palace" opened its doors on May 1, 1851, the sheer immensity of it made for a grand show all by itself: 1,851 feet long (a dimension intended to fit the year), 408 feet wide, and 108 feet high at the entrance. It was built to accommodate as many as 60,000 people at one time, in addition to nearly 14,000 exhibits. There was nothing like it in all the world. Michael Leapman, author of *The World for a Shilling: How the Great Exhibition of 1851 Shaped a Nation*, calls it "the first mass spectacle that appealed to almost every social class."

For a visitor to give every exhibit the attention it deserved would have required 200 hours in the building, according to London's most famous newspaper of the day, *The Times*. There were the huge and fabulous Koh-i-Noor diamond from India; a 40-foot scale model of the Liverpool docks, complete with 1,600 meticulously accurate miniature ships; sophisticated threshing machines and other labor-saving farm equipment; a knife with 1,851 blades; exotic fabrics and furnishings, looms, sewing machines, and even a prototype submarine; gas cookery, electric clocks, and one of the earliest versions of a washing machine.

The Latest from America

The wide array of displays representing the very latest of industry from America included a set of unpickable locks, a model of Niagara Falls, a 16,400-pound lump of zinc, a McCormick reaper, a Colt revolver, and, in Leapman's words, "a piano that could be played by four people at once and a violin and piano joined in such a way that a single musician could play them both at the same time on a single keyboard."

The Exhibition itself gave birth to new inventions. One of many examples was provided by George Jennings, a sanitary engineer. His ingenious flush toilets and decorative, space-saving urinals prevented a potential health hazard. They sparked so much public interest and fascination that his designs were subsequently copied in cities around the world.

Some of Britain's best known businesses can trace their origins to the Great Exhibition. Thomas Cook, the firm that today boasts more than 4,000 affiliated travel agencies around the world, got its start when its namesake began offering low-price excursion packages to get people from all corners of Britain to the Palace in Hyde Park. The big profits Charles Harrod earned serving visitors in his modest grocery store proved to be the capital he needed to create one of the most famous department stores in the world.

When the Exhibition closed its doors on October 18 after five and a half months, more than six million people had come through it—almost the same number who visited the Millennium Dome over a 12-month period 150 years later. Factor in the time-consuming difficulties of transportation in 1851 compared to the ease and speed of the space age and the contrast is all the more stunning. And unlike the Dome of 2000, the unsubsidized Crystal Palace of 1851 produced a financial surplus.

Tony Blair was right. He should have listened to those who warned that government has enough trouble doing what it's supposed to do, that it doesn't need to do what it shouldn't.

—LWR, March 2003

Part IV

The Positive Power of the Entrepreneur

Chapter **Twenty-Four**

From Kleenex to Zippers: The Unpredictable Results of Entrepreneurs

The 1920s taught us many lessons in economics—perhaps foremost among them is that cutting tax rates encouraged entrepreneurs to invest in a variety of revolutionary products, from radios to refrigerators.

A corollary lesson, however, is also important: When entrepreneurs are turned loose and their property rights are protected, what they eventually produce can't be predicted—even by them. I want to describe four products that became part of American life in the 1920s—Kleenex tissues, the zipper, air conditioning, and Scotch tape.

Kimberly-Clark developed the material in Kleenex tissues from wood pulp in World War I as a substitute for cotton, which was in short supply. Originally called cellucotton, it was first used in wadded form as a surgical dressing. Later in the war, in its modern tissue form, it was used as a filter in gas masks.

After the war Kimberly-Clark had large supplies of cellucotton on hand and the company searched for years for new uses for their product. Finally, in 1924 the cellucotton became Kleenex tissues. The marketing staff at Kimberly-Clark believed the tissues had a niche market for removing cold cream and other cosmetics. Endorsements from Hollywood stars such as Helen Hayes and Gertrude Lawrence promoted Kleenex as soft and efficient for cleaning their faces.

Fortunately for Kimberly-Clark, their marketers were wise enough to read their mail, and expand their market. Many letters from customers asked,"Why don't you ever say it's good for blowing your nose?" That led the company to do test-marketing—and yes, indeed, more customers preferred Kleenex tissues to handkerchiefs. In fact, the company now boasted that tissues were healthier because they were disposable. "Don't put a cold in your pocket" was the theme of the next wave of advertising. In 1929 Kimberly-Clark introduced the pop-up box. Sales grew further and were even strong during the Great Depression of the 1930s.

The zipper, like Kleenex tissues, had a variety of uses in its early years. Perhaps what is most surprising about the zipper, however, is that someone ever thought it up at all. The U.S. patent office was stunned by the product and hardly knew how to classify it.

Originally known as a "slide fastener," the zipper was first used on shoes. In 1914 one of its promoters, Gideon Sundback, finally produced a zipper that would consistently work. He called it "hookless no. 2" and during World War I sold several thousand for use on money belts for sailors. Sundback also sold some to the Navy for a "flying suit" it was developing. Garment manufacturers and tailors, however, preferred buttons and shunned the zipper.

Finally, in 1923 B. F. Goodrich took a chance and bought 150,000 hookless slide fasteners for its rubber galoshes. The company called their galoshes "Zipper Boots," and the name stuck. Only after that success did the textile industry explore the larger market for zippers on clothing.

The market for air conditioning seems obvious now, but it was not so at the beginning of the 1920s. Willis Carrier, its inventor, worked on air conditioning as a sideline at his job with the Buffalo Forge Co. in New York. Carrier was assigned to help a publisher in Brooklyn figure out how to stabilize the humidity in the printing room. Pages of newsprint expanded and contracted when the humidity rose and fell, and ink dried at different rates when the humidity changed.

When Carrier developed a system of air flows to dehumidify the print room, he ended up cooling the room as well. He had solved the newspaper issue, but was fascinated with the broader implications of producing "air conditioning" to cool and clean the air in stuffy buildings. His employers did not share his vision, and Carrier left to start his own company in 1914. His air-conditioning units were huge, cumbersome, and expensive, but he sold enough to acquire the capital to keep improving the product.

Carrier's big breakthrough came in the expanding movie industry. Most theaters closed down in the summer because the heat and stuffiness made patrons focus more on waving fans than watching the screen. In 1925 the Rivoli Theatre owners in Manhattan decided to install air conditioning to attract moviegoers in the summer. The patrons were enthusiastic; many were more excited over what was happening in the air than in the movie. By 1930 Carrier was supplying air conditioning to over 300 theaters in America. Factories soon followed, and finally, after World War II, Carrier was able to make home air conditioning units affordable and popular.

Scotch tape was developed in connection with painting of cars. By the 1920s Henry Ford's all-black Model-Ts were out of fashion. Improved lacquers and automatic spray guns allowed automakers to give customers more appealing two-tone cars. Scotch tape, two inches wide, was invented by Minnesota Mining and Manufacturing (3M) to give the clear sharp edge where the two paint tones met. Before long, 3M was selling dozens of different types of Scotch tape for a variety of sealing purposes.

No Obvious Mass Market

These inventions had no obvious mass use or market when they were developed. Entrepreneurs had to invest energy and talent to figure out how best to sell their products, and ultimately consumers decided that Kleenex tissues were best marketed as disposable handkerchiefs, zippers as clothes fasteners, Scotch tape for household sealing, and air conditioning for home cooling. The common uses for these products seem obvious now, but that was not so in 1920. Trial and error, unexpected consumer interest, and sometimes desperation were part of developing these now popular, and seemingly indispensable, products. No planning board could ever have invented these products, much less figured out how to market them. Even their inventors were often mystified by the direction of consumer interest in them.

Perhaps we should not be surprised that so many new products of the 1920s were created for one purpose and ultimately marketed for another. Two inventions of the previous generation also fit this pattern. Josephine G. Cochrane, the daughter of a civil engineer, invented the dishwasher in the 1880s to protect her valuable china from being broken during washing by careless servants. Even when the sanitary value of a dishwasher was realized, its next market was large-scale cleaning for hotels. Popular home use didn't come until the 1950s, almost 70 years after it was invented.

Melville Bissell invented the carpet sweeper in the 1870s, not to market commercially, but simply to help his wife clean the floor of sawdust from packaging in her crockery shop. He and his wife only thought of marketing their sweepers when customers were more fascinated by the cleaning of the shop than by the cups and dishes being sold there.

Entrepreneurship is a strange and unpredictable process. We need it, and our lives have been improved by it. We must have strong property rights to sustain it. But what entrepreneurs will produce, and the marketing route they will take, will probably remain as strange and circuitous as it was in the 1920s.

—BWF, December 2005

25

Chapter **Twenty-Five**

A Camera Reaches 100

This month marks a centennial anniversary that deserves to be noted. It was 100 years ago, in February 1900, that George Eastman first intro-duced the Kodak Brownie box camera. The price tag was one dollar; film sold for 15 cents a roll. Eastman was about to do for cameras what Steven Jobs would do for computers almost eight decades later. For the first time, taking pictures was within the reach of almost every American family.

Whether you're a camera buff or not, you probably have seen and perhaps have even used a Brownie. Nowadays, they show up at rummage sales and antique shows, but I can remember when they were still widely used in my childhood days during the 1950s. They were simple to operate and took great pictures.

The Brownie not only ushered in the era of modern photography; it was also a genuine cultural phenomenon in America. Millions were sold. Thousands of American youngsters signed up as members of The Brownie Camera Club and entered Kodak photo contests. Men and women who went on to become famous photographers got their start with Eastman's little invention.

Student of Photography

The man who gave us the Brownie camera was no stranger to photography in 1900. In the 1870s, when Eastman was in his twenties and picture-taking wasn't much older, what would become the passion of his life started out as a hobby. In 1871 at the age of 17, he bought almost a hundred dollars' worth of photographic equipment and hired a photographer to instruct him in the art. He read everything he could find on the subject and with a backpack and a wheelbarrow, he hauled his equipment everywhere he wanted to capture an image.

Cameras in the 1870s were as big as microwave ovens. The tools of the professional photographer's trade—including a bulky, unreliable camera, a tripod, and various liquid chemicals—were more than a single man could carry, "a pack-horse load," as Eastman described it. He resolved to downsize, simplify, and reduce the cost of the "burden" of taking pictures.

Though he lived his entire life in the area where he was born—upstate New York—Eastman traveled widely. He once visited Michigan's Mackinac Island, where he set up his camera equipment to take photos of the natural bridge, a stone landmark. A crowd of gawking tourists gathered, assuming Eastman would take their pictures and offer the photos for sale. When he informed them he was making pictures for his own purposes and not for sale, a disappointed tourist chewed him out: "Then why did you let us stand in the hot sun for a full half-hour while you fooled around with your contraptions! You ought to wear a sign saying that you are an amateur!"

Eastman experimented endlessly and discovered new techniques and processes for producing better film and lighter, less expensive cameras. A self-taught chemist, he ended the era of sloppy, wet-plate photography by inventing a process that used dry chemicals, though not without many disappointments. His Eastman Dry Plate Company almost went bankrupt in the 1880s, in spite of his hard work and sleepless nights. But in America's golden age of invention, when taxes were low and rewards for persistence were often great, this genius who had dropped out of school at the age of 13 went on to build an extraordinarily successful business.

Praise from the Pros

Professional photographers praised the pioneering work of Eastman. They called his prints and negatives "the best dry plate work on the market." Journals and newspapers began publishing articles about his inventions. In 1929, when Eastman met Thomas Edison for the first time, each of the elderly men revealed they had purchased a product made by the other as early as the 1880s. "Pretty good film," Edison told Eastman.

By 1888, Eastman had simplified the camera into a small, easily held box measuring three and three-quarter inches high, three and a quarter inches wide, and six and a half inches long. He needed a name for it, a catchy trademark that could be easily pronounced and spelled. "K" was his favorite letter because, he said, it was "a strong, incisive sort of letter." After toying with various combinations of letters, he hit on one that rang some sort of internal bell in his mind, "Kodak." But the first Kodak camera, priced at $25 when it debuted in 1888, was still unaffordable for most Americans.

Eastman and his team of expert craftsmen worked feverishly to cut costs and improve quality. The result was a camera that would reach people, in Eastman's words, "the same way the bicycle has reached them"—the Kodak Brownie. It took the world by storm. The first run of 5,000 cameras flew off the shelves and orders piled up at an amazing pace that exceeded the most optimistic projections. Even corner drugstores were selling them.

A new term was coined during a 1905 trial to describe the millions of people caught up in the craze: "Kodak freaks." In her biography of George Eastman, Elizabeth Bayer quotes the court transcript, which read, "Wherever they go, and whomever they see, and whatever place they have come to, they have got to have a Kodak along for the purpose of getting pictures." In 1904, reports Bayer, when the Dalai Lama fled from his Tibetan palace, he took his Brownie with him.

Eastman inspired great loyalty among his employees, in large measure because of what biographer Bayer notes were "his countless acts of kindness, his enlightened personnel policies, and his tireless working habits." He was an American original—a self-made man whose dreams and commitment have made the everyday lives of generations of people happier by allowing moments of those lives to be captured on film.

The estimated 70 billion pictures Americans alone will take this year are the direct descendants of the Kodak Brownie, the first mass-produced camera in history. Its creator was a superb businessman as well as a talented inventor, and became one of America's wealthiest citizens. He gave away more than $100 million to universities and charities before his death in 1932.

If, as the saying goes, one picture is worth a thousand words, then the story of George Eastman and the Kodak Brownie is worth 70 trillion words.

—LWR, February 2000

26

Chapter **Twenty-Six**

Charles Schwab and the Steel Industry

When asked for the secret of his success in the steel industry, Charles Schwab (1862–1939) always talked about making the most with what you have, using praise, not criticism, giving liberal bonuses for work well done, and "appeal[ing] to the American spirit of conquest in my men, the spirit of doing things better than anyone has ever done them before." He liked to tell this story about how he handled an unproductive steel mill:

> I had a mill manager who was finely educated, thoroughly capable and master of every detail of the business. But he seemed unable to inspire his men to do their best.
>
> "How is it that a man as able as you," I asked him one day, "cannot make this mill turn out what it should?"
>
> "I don't know," he replied. "I have coaxed the men; I have pushed them, I have sworn at them. I have done everything in my power. Yet they will not produce."
>
> It was near the end of the day; in a few minutes the night force would come on duty. I turned to a workman who was standing

beside one of the red-mouthed furnaces and asked him for a piece of chalk.

"How many heats has your shift made today?" I queried.

"Six," he replied.

I chalked a big "6" on the floor, and then passed along without another word. When the night shift came in they saw the "6" and asked about it.

"The big boss was in here today," said the day men. "He asked us how many heats we had made, and we told him six. He chalked it down."

The next morning I passed through the same mill. I saw that the "6" had been rubbed out and a big "7" written instead. The night shift had announced itself. That night I went back. The "7" had been erased, and a "10" swaggered in its place. The day force recognized no superiors. Thus a fine competition was started, and it went on until this mill, formerly the poorest producer, was turning out more than any other mill in the plant. (Charles M. Schwab, *Succeeding with What You Have* [New York: Century Co., 1917], pp. 39–41)

Schwab showed the ability to find solutions to problems even as a lad growing up in Loretto, Pennsylvania. According to one of his teachers, "Charlie was a boy who never said, 'I don't know.' He went on the principle of pretend that you know and if you don't, find out mighty quick." Schwab knew early that he would have to live by his wits; his parents and immigrant grandparents weaved and traded wool products, jobs which put food on the table but not much money in the bank. Young Charlie, therefore, started work early in life. In one job he was a "singing cabby": he drove passengers from nearby Cresson to Loretto and entertained them with ballads along the way. One of his passengers, impressed with the gregarious youth, gave him a travel book. Schwab later said, "It opened my eyes to the glories of the outside world, and stimulated my imagination tremendously." Soon, Loretto, Pennsylvania, population 300, would be too small to contain the ambitious Schwab. With his parents' blessing, he left home at age 17 to clerk in a general store in Braddock, a suburb of Pittsburgh.

Braddock was a steel town, varied in its cultural and urban life. Working in the store, young Charlie often pleased customers with his good looks, wit, and charm; one man whom he impressed was William "Captain Bill" Jones, the mill superintendent at Braddock for Carnegie

Steel. Jones offered Schwab a job as a stake driver for the engineering corps who designed plans for building furnaces. Schwab accepted, proved himself capable, and soon became a draftsman. Here, he worked overtime to master his craft; within six months he became Jones' right-hand man at the mill. As Jones' messenger boy, Schwab came into contact with the mill owner, the Scottish immigrant Andrew Carnegie. Carnegie took a special liking to Schwab, who wisely spent some of his off hours playing Scottish ballads on Carnegie's piano.

Schwab worked hard to please Jones and Carnegie. Doing so allowed him to advance in the Carnegie organization. Fortunately for Schwab, Carnegie did not recruit his leaders on the basis of wealth or family standing. He used a merit system; he wanted people who could make the best steel possible at the lowest price. To succeed under Carnegie's system, Schwab would have to master the methods of steel production.

The Carnegie System

Carnegie stressed cutting costs: in fact his motto was "Watch the costs and the profits will take care of themselves." This meant hard work in innovating, accounting, and managing. Purchases, for example, were made in bulk to achieve economies of scale. Also, Carnegie strived for vertical integration, the control of his steel business from the buying of raw materials to the marketing of finished steel.

At the heart of Carnegie's system were bonuses and partnerships for those who excelled. Strong incentives were given employees who could figure out how to save on iron ore, coke, and limestone; or how to produce a harder, cheaper steel; or how to capture new markets for steel. Carnegie explained that success "flows from having interested exceptional men in our service; thus only can we *develop ability* and hold it in our service." In fact, Carnegie said, "Every year should be marked by the promotion of one or more of our young men."

Captain Jones had risen to mill superintendent this way. Among other things he had invented the Jones mixer, a device that cut costs in the transferring of steel from the blast furnace to the Bessemer converter. For his inventions and know-how, Carnegie paid him the highest salary in the business, $25,000—the same salary as that of the President of the United States.

Schwab rose through the ranks just as Jones did. He completed small tasks and was given larger ones. At age 23, he designed and built a bridge over the Baltimore and Ohio Railroad tracks; he saved time and money doing the job and received as a bonus ten $20 gold pieces from Carnegie himself. Other assignments followed: he installed meters in the factories and reduced waste of natural gas; he redesigned a rail-finishing department and saved 10 cents per ton of steel; he helped in calming down workers during a violent strike in the Homestead plant. When Captain Jones died in a blast furnace explosion in 1889, Schwab was the logical choice for superintendent at Braddock.

Gregarious and competent, Schwab became Carnegie's problem solver. For example, the workers at Braddock were turning out "seconds," or substandard rails. Schwab's solution: give $20 cash bonuses to those steel-makers producing the fewest seconds. The quality of the rails shot up and the resulting increase in profits more than paid the bonuses given. No wonder that Carnegie soon gave Schwab a small partnership in Carnegie Steel, with the promise of more to come if he could keep producing. Carnegie even wrote one of his senior partners, Henry Clay Frick, that Schwab "gives every promise of being the man we have long desired" eventually to run the business.

Schwab idolized Carnegie and found him amazing to watch. Carnegie's efficiency and his thorough knowledge of the industry made him a terror among fellow steel producers. He spied on them, used their annual reports against them, and even wrote them to secure information on costs of production. Meanwhile, Carnegie Steel was a closed corporation; he told outsiders nothing of his costs or his future plans. Carnegie disdained "pools," secret agreements among competitors to divide up the market and keep prices high. Pools were for the weak; Carnegie wanted to "scoop the market [and] run the mills full."

Not that Carnegie didn't use friendships and other means to help him. In bidding on a large Union Pacific contract for rails, he may have outmaneuvered the veteran Scranton family. Joseph Scranton was a director of the Union Pacific as well as president of the Lackawanna Iron and Coal Company. But Carnegie had done a favor for Sidney Dillon, the president of the Union Pacific, and Dillon agreed to give Carnegie the contract if he would match the lowest bid.

Carnegie vs. the Scrantons

In the case of the Scrantons, Carnegie showed no mercy. When Carnegie went into the steel business in 1872, he was told that he could never compete against the Lackawanna Company; Joseph Scranton was a founding father of American rail-making; he had a generation of experience making rails. But that year Joseph Scranton died, and his sons William and Walter would be the ones to challenge Carnegie: first with the Lackawanna Company, then with their Scranton Steel Company. Carnegie and the Scrantons joined the Bessemer Steel Association in 1875, but their approaches were different: the Scrantons wanted a pool, but Carnegie told them and others that unless he got the largest share he would "withdraw from it and undersell you all in the market—and make good money doing it."

The Scrantons and the others were bluffed by Carnegie and gave him his way. Carnegie then studied the Scrantons and learned their strengths and weaknesses. He discovered that they (and others) were discarding the thin steel shavings, called "scale," that fell on the floor when the steel passed through the rollers. When he learned this, he regularly sent a man to Scranton to cart away tons of the Scrantons' scale, almost free of charge, and brought it to Pittsburgh to use in making rails for Carnegie Steel.

As Carnegie moved to the top of the American steel business, Schwab watched, learned, and proved himself time and again. In 1897, the 35-year-old Schwab became president of Carnegie Steel and the two men ran the company together. Business was never better. Schwab put in 16 new furnaces at the Homestead plant, and costs per ton of finished steel fell 34 per cent in one year. To promote espirit de corps, Schwab held Saturday meetings with all of his superintendents to work out problems. Meanwhile, the results of large-scale production took hold: the cost of making rails fell from $28 to $11.50 per ton between 1880 and 1900, but the profits from the larger volume of business went from $2 million in 1888 to $4 million in 1894, to $40 million in 1900. Some people wondered if Carnegie Steel might soon capture the steel trade of the entire world.

Such speculation was premature. The next year, at age 65, Carnegie retired and, with Schwab as his emissary, sold Carnegie Steel to J. P. Morgan for $480 million. Morgan then combined Carnegie Steel with other companies to create U.S. Steel, the first billion-dollar company in American history. The choice for president of the company: Charles Schwab.

Reporters and critics condemned "The Steel Trust," as they called U.S. Steel, for its size and its potential to monopolize. Who would be able to compete, they asked, with such a large vertically integrated company? At his disposal, Schwab would have 213 steel mills and transportation companies, 41 iron ore mines, and 57,000 acres of coal land—enough, critics charged, to dwarf competitors and keep prices high.

Schwab discovered, however, that he would not be able to use the Carnegie system at U.S. Steel. In fact, he would not have authority to run the company at all. Morgan and his friend Elbert Gary had organized U.S. Steel so that an executive committee, headed by Gary, and the board of directors would set the policies of the company; Schwab, as president, would carry them out. Morgan and Gary were interested in business stability, not in innovating or in cutting the price of steel. For example, when Schwab wanted to secure more ore land, Gary said no. He also opposed price-cutting, aggressive marketing, giving bonuses, and adopt-ing new technology. Schwab later said, "Gary, who had no real knowl-edge of the steel business, forever opposed me on some of the methods and principles that I had seen worked out with Carnegie— methods that had made the Carnegie Company the most successful in the world."

Personal Problems

Schwab's personal life, more than disputes over policy, seems to have led to his downfall at U.S. Steel. He showed he had the values of a dissipater as well as those of an entrepreneur. When Carnegie was in control, Schwab consciously restrained his extravagant tastes; Carnegie deplored living beyond one's income, gambling, and adultery. But out from under Carnegie's grip, Schwab engaged in all three and almost mined his marriage and his career. In New York City, Schwab built "Riverside," a gargantuan mansion, which consumed one whole block of the city and $7 million of his cash. He also gambled at Monte Carlo, which made bad newspaper copy and cost him credibility. Finally, he had an affair with a nurse, which resulted in a child. Though Schwab hid this from the press, he could not do so from his wife, Rana. The strain of his adulterous behavior, combined with the pressure of Monte Carlo, the expense of Riverside, and the barbs from Elbert Gary wrecked Schwab's health. He went to Europe to recover and, in 1904, resigned as president of U.S. Steel.

Schwab, the man who said, "I cannot fail," seemed to have failed. He was depressed for months. Even Carnegie repudiated Schwab and this added to the pain. During his troubles he had insomnia, he lost weight, his arms and legs were regularly numb, and sometimes he fainted. His wife forgave him for his adultery and this no doubt eased the strain; but she was still not happy because she wanted a child of her own and never had one. She didn't covet the extravagant life, so dear to her husband, and she spent many lonely days at Riverside.

Schwab was out at U.S. Steel, but he already had the makings for a comeback. When he was president of U.S. Steel, Schwab had bought Bethlehem Steel as a private investment. He was criticized for this, espe-cially when he merged Bethlehem Steel with some unsound companies into an unprofitable shipbuilding trust. This merger eventually col-lapsed; but when Schwab stepped down at U.S. Steel, he still had Bethlehem Steel as his own property. The demotion from being pres-ident of a company worth over one billion dollars, to being president of one worth less than nine million dollars would have embarrassed some men, but not Schwab. He would have full control in running the company and would succeed or fail on his own abilities.

Before Schwab took over Bethlehem Steel, its future had not looked promising. It had been founded in 1857 and soon produced rails for the Lehigh Valley Railroad. This was more than coincidence because entrepreneur Asa Packer, who had built the Lehigh Valley Railroad, held a large interest in what was then Bethlehem Iron. Packer, a Connecticut Yankee, had the vision and ability to promote both of these investments and make them profitable. His rise from carpenter to railroad tycoon had made him a legend in Pennsylvania; he was worth $17 million by the late 1870s. When he died in 1879, his sons, sons-in-law, and nephews took over his investments, but did not have the success that Packer did. The Lehigh Valley Railroad floundered and went into receivership in the Panic of 1893. Bethlehem Iron almost shared the same fate.

Led by Philadelphians and the Packer group, Bethlehem Iron became very conservative after Packer's death. The younger leaders singlemind-edly produced rails, even though Carnegie was doing it cheaper, and they had the expense of importing most of their iron ore from Cuba. They es-caped a price squeeze in 1885 when, reluctantly, they shifted from making rafts to producing military ordnance, which commanded a higher price than rails. Such an imaginative strategy, as one might expect, did not originate within the Packer group; in fact, they resisted it until declining profits on rails presented them with no alternative.

From Rails to Armor Plate

The wise, if belated, switch from rails to gun-forgings and armor plate led to profits because Bethlehem Iron was the only bidder on its first government contract for ordnance in 1887. Other contracts were forthcoming and Bethlehem Iron "established a reputation for quality and reliability," if not for aggressiveness and efficiency. Regarding the last, its operations were so inefficient that the company in 1898 hired Frederick W. Taylor, master of scientific management, to suggest ways of improving worker productivity. Yet the Packer group soon became hostile to Taylor's cost-cutting ideas. Of one suggestion to reduce the number of workers handling raw materials, Taylor observed that the owners "did not wish me, as they said, to depopulate South Bethlehem." He further commented, "They owned all the houses in South Bethlehem and the company stores and when they saw we [Taylor and his assistants] were cutting the labor force down to about one-fourth, they did not want it." They also rejected Taylor's suggestions to standardize job functions and give raises to key personnel.

Surviving, then, on government contracts, Bethlehem Iron stumbled into the twentieth century—a profitable operation in spite of itself. In the midst of this conservatism, Schwab came to Bethlehem in 1904 and boldly announced that he would "make the Bethlehem plant the greatest armor plate and gun factory in the world." Taking the helm, Schwab "backed Bethlehem with every dollar I could borrow." This backing included buying new branch plants and closing unprofitable ones, getting new contracts by selling aggressively, and reorganizing the company as Bethlehem Steel. Planning for the future, Schwab bought large tracts of land for the company east of South Bethlehem. He also bought or leased more ore land and mechanized the company's Cuban iron fields to spur production there.

Schwab's entrepreneurship clashed with the Packer group's cautiousness right from the start. As one historian said, "Many of the veteran Bethlehem executives preferred the old, pre-Taylor and pre-Schwab way." Soon after arriving in South Bethlehem, Schwab ousted the inbred Packer group from authority. In the new president's remarkable words, "I selected 15 young men right out of the mill and made them my partners." Two of these "partners" were Eugene Grace, the son of a sea captain, and Archibald Johnston, a local Moravian. They later became presidents of Bethlehem Steel.

After reorganization, Schwab wanted to diversify his company and challenge U.S. Steel. To do this, he began making rails and moving Bethlehem Steel away from its dependence on government contracts. Schwab adopted open-hearth technology because it produced better rails than the Bessemer system did. As historian Robert Hessen notes:

> U.S. Steel, the nation's largest rail producer, did not follow Schwab's lead; it would have had to replace its Bessemer facilities with open hearth equipment. Being a late starter, Bethlehem enjoyed a clear advantage: with no heavy investment in obsolete equipment to protect, it could adopt the newest and most efficient technological processes. (*Steel Titan: The Life of Charles M. Schwab*, Oxford University Press, 1975], p. 169).

Schwab's reorganization of the Cuban ore mines also improved Bethlehem's competitive position at the expense of U.S. Steel.

> Cuban ore was richer in iron and lower in phosphorus than was the Mesabi range ore used by U.S. Steel. It also had another advantage: it contained large amounts of nickel, so that Bethlehem could produce nickel steel at no extra cost. For a ton of iron Bethlehem's cost was $4.31; U.S. Steel's was $7.10. (*Steel Titan: The Life of Charles M. Schwab*, p. 171)

Now that Schwab was running an efficient, diversified company he turned his attention to cutting costs. He reasoned that employees would work harder if they knew it would result directly in a raise. Therefore, he set up a bonus system for productive laborers, foremen, and managers throughout the company. As Schwab described it, "Do so much and you get so much; do more and you get more—that is the essence of the system." At U.S. Steel, by contrast, Gary tied bonuses to the overall profitability of the company, not to individual performance. Under that system, Schwab noted, a worker could toil hard and creatively, but receive no reward.

Improvements in Structural Steel

Schwab's biggest move at Bethlehem was his challenge to U.S. Steel in the making of structural steel. Here he focused on an innovation in making the steel beams that went into bridges and skyscrapers. Schwab had been listening to Edward Grey, who had the idea of making steel beams directly from an ingot, as a single section, instead of riveting smaller beams together. Grey claimed that his invention provided "the greatest possible strength with the least dead weight and at the lowest cost."

The other steelmakers rejected Grey's theory; but Schwab was eager to try it even though it would cost $5 million to design the plant, build the mill, and pay Grey's royalties. The problem was that the experts were so skeptical that Schwab had trouble raising money. In fact he almost backed out, but then jumped back in with the statement: "If we are going bust, we will go bust big." He staked his own money, and that of his company, on the Grey beam, but still he needed more. So Schwab buttonholed wealthy investors for large personal loans and then, through remarkable salesmanship, persuaded his major suppliers, the Lehigh Valley and the Reading Railroads, to give him credit on deliveries of the new steel. Schwab then aggressively recruited big contracts for the "Bethlehem beam": the Chase National Bank and the Metropolitan Life Insurance Company in New York were among them. The experiment worked. This cheaper and more durable beam quickly became Schwab's greatest innovation and he captured a large share of the structural steel market from U.S. Steel.

Schwab's actions had consequences for the American steel industry. From 1905 to 1920, Bethlehem Steel's labor force doubled every five years. By contrast, U.S. Steel often stagnated; one officer noted after Schwab left that "works standing idle have deteriorated . . . the men are disheartened and a certain amount of apathy exists." By the 1920s, the chagrined leaders at U.S. Steel secretly began making Bethlehem beams; as an official there observed, "The tonnage lost on account of competition with Bethlehem . . . is . . . ever increasing . . . we are obliged to sell at unusually low prices in order to compete." Schwab discovered their ploy, however, and forced U.S. Steel to pay him royalties.

Schwab had transformed Bethlehem Steel. Even before World War I his company had become the second largest steelmaker in America. The *New York Times* praised Bethlehem Steel as "possibly the most efficient, profitable self-contained steel plant in the country." By 1920, it employed 20,000 people in the Lehigh Valley and was among the largest enterprises in the world. In 1922, it absorbed Lackawanna Steel, the company that launched America's rail-making industry 75 years earlier.

During World War I, Schwab's abilities were needed by the U.S. government. In April 1918, one year after America entered the war, victory was uncertain. Delays in shipping cargo and troops from America to Europe threatened the Allies with defeat. More ships were needed; but in the U.S. shipyards few ships were forthcoming. Within the Wilson administration some blamed the owners of the shipyards, others blamed the workers, still others blamed radical unions. In the midst of this finger-pointing, Franklin K. Lane, the Secretary of Commerce, posed a solution: "The President ought to send for Schwab and hand him a treasury warrant for a billion dollars and set him to work building ships, with no government inspectors or supervisors or accountants or auditors or other red tape to bother him. Let the President just put it up to Schwab's patriotism and put Schwab on his honor. Nothing more is needed. Schwab will do the job."

The Schwab Formula

That month Schwab became Director-General of the Emergency Fleet Corporation for the U.S. government. In his investigation, he discovered cases of laziness, incompetence, work slowdowns, and poor coordination of the shipbuilding. As usual, though, Schwab said, "The best place to succeed is where you are with what you have." He quickly rearranged incentives: he eliminated the "cost-plus" system whereby shipyards were paid whatever it cost them to build ships plus a percentage of that as a profit. Instead, Schwab tied profits to cost-cutting by paying a set price per ship. Cost overruns would be paid by the shipbuilders who would have to be efficient to make a profit. As usual, bonuses were part of the Schwab formula. He paid them, sometimes out of his own pocket, to shipbuilders who exceeded production goals.

Schwab enjoyed being a showman, so he went to the shipyards himself: he rallied the workers, praised the owners, and even drew applause in a speech to the Industrial Workers of the World, a radical union. Never one to ignore symbols for achievement, Schwab had Rear Admiral F. F. Fletcher head a group to award flags and medals to plants and workers whose work had been outstanding. By the fall of 1918, ships were being completed on time and even ahead of schedule. President Wilson and the leaders of the Shipping Board were astonished with the change and gave Schwab the credit. Carnegie, in the last year of his life, called it "a record of accomplishment such as has never been equaled."

Not all of Schwab's dealings with the federal government were so productive. The armor plate business is an example of this. The making of military equipment—armor plate for ships, gun forgings, ordnance, and shrapnel—brought Schwab into regular contact with government purchasers. Throughout his career, Schwab had problems with these government contracts. Even at Carnegie Steel, Schwab had quarreled with government officials over allegedly defective armor plate; the issue never was amicably settled.

The problem began in the 1880s when various officials began urging the United States to build a large navy. At the time the American steel companies were mostly making rails, so President Cleveland and others began urging the companies to diversify. Making military equipment was complicated and expensive, however; only reluctantly did Bethlehem Iron and Carnegie Steel shift into ordnance. Had the government not promised them Navy contracts they would not have switched.

Four things in the military supply business made for tension between the federal government and the steel companies. First, the federal government was the largest and sometimes the only buyer of military equipment; and the government's notions of quality sometimes differed from that of the producers. Often both sides had legitimate points of view. Second, since the demand for military equipment was limited and the costs of building a factory to produce it were high, only U.S. Steel, Bethlehem Steel, and later Midvale Steel made armor plate. The potential for either a monopoly or for price-rigging bothered some government officials. Third, a ton of military equipment was more expensive to make than a ton of rails or a ton of structural steel; some purchasers thought that $450 for a ton of armor plate was price-gouging if rails sold for only $25 per ton. Finally, the ordnance producers sometimes made lower bids on foreign contracts than they did on domestic ones. To some in the American government, this was evidence they were being overcharged; to the steel companies, lower bids meant they had to cut their profit margins to almost zero to overcome tariffs in foreign countries. Also, when American needs were low, the steel men argued they had to get foreign business to keep their factories operating.

The government's solution to these four problems was to threaten to go into the military supply business and build an armor-plate factory with Federal funds. Schwab countered that the government would not be able to make armor plate cheaper than he could. After all, Bethlehem had a veteran work force, a good bonus system, and could buy materials more cheaply in bulk. Any vertically integrated company would have an advantage over companies purchasing supplies in the open market. A government factory, Schwab insisted, would waste the taxpayers' money.

Misdirected Incentives

If Schwab had been a mediator, not a participant, he might have been able to settle this dispute. Part of the problem was the same as that of the low productivity of the American shipyards during World War I: misdirected incentives. When the navy took bids for contracts from the three steel companies, it naturally accepted the lowest bid. But then Navy officials went to the two higher bidders and offered them part of the contract if they would agree to accept the lowest bid. They did this so that all three producers could survive; that way, a future monopoly of ordnance would be prevented. The problem was that this strategy gave the three companies an incentive to collude and fix prices high. Why should they bid low if all of them would get part of the contract anyway? A winner-take-all approach would have provided an incentive for lower bidding, but the Navy was unwilling to do this. Not surprisingly, then, year after year the steel companies submitted nearly identical bids for military equipment.

This problem reached a crisis during the Wilson administration. In 1913, Josephus Daniels, Wilson's Secretary of the Navy, and Ben Tillman, Senator from South Carolina, investigated the armor business. Both men urged Wilson to back a government armor plant. They held hearings in Congress on the armor business but did not like what they heard. The leaders of the three steel companies all said their bids were reasonable. In fact, Schwab submitted figures showing that he and the others charged less for armor plate than did England, France, Germany, and Japan. If others didn't believe it, then let the Federal Trade Commission look at the accounts and fix a price. Daniels and Tillman rejected this. They were convinced that the government could make armor plate cheaper: the head of the Bureau of Ordnance estimated that $10.3 million would build an armor plant and that plate could be made for less than $300 per ton, instead of $454 per ton, which was a typical bid from the steel companies.

In 1916, then, Daniels and Tillman began the campaign to convince Congress to spend $11 million for an armor factory. In the Senate, Tillman argued that the government would save money and no longer would be at the mercy of identical bids from the "greedy and hoggish" steel companies. President Wilson backed Tillman and said, "I remember very well my promise to help all I could with the bill for the construction of an armor plant and I stand ready to redeem my promise."

Schwab led the effort to defeat the bill. He spoke out against it in public and ran ads in over 3,000 newspapers challenging the need for a government plant. He stressed the fairness angle. He said that years ago the government had asked Bethlehem to make armor; they had done so only when the government agreed to buy from them. Now, with $7 million invested in equipment, the government was planning to build its own plant and make Bethlehem's useless.

Most Congressmen, however, bought the arguments of Tillman and Daniels. The bill passed the Senate and the House by about two-to-one margins, and Wilson signed it. As Senator Albert Cummins of Iowa said, "It is [one of] my profoundest convictions that the manufacture of armor-plate for battleships is a government function. I hope the private enterprises will be entirely eliminated."

Dozens of cities lobbied to be the site for the new plant. From Rome, Georgia, to Kalamazoo, Michigan, city after city was put forth as being uniquely situated to produce armor plate. The winner of this competition was South Charleston, West Virginia. Congress soon raised the appropriation to $17.5 million and authorized the South Charleston plant to make guns and projectiles, as well as armor.

Construction began in 1917 on the new factory and on hundreds of houses for the workers. The war delayed the building, but it was continued later. Higher construction costs after the war meant an overrun of several million dollars. By 1921, the new plant was making guns, projectiles, and armor—an at prices apparently much higher than that of Bethlehem Steel. Within a year the whole plant was shut down, put on "inoperative status," and never run again.

Looking Backward

Schwab turned 60 in 1921 and was beginning to look backward more than forward. There was much to see: whether he had made rails, beams, or armor plate, he had been successful. Even Carnegie, near death, had written Schwab, "I have never doubted your ability to triumph in anything you undertook. I cannot help feeling proud of you for having far outstripped any of my 'boys.'"

In the 1920s and 1930s, however, Schwab seemed to lose his entrepreneurial spirit. Producing a better product at a lower price no longer seemed to dominate his thinking. Let's "live and let live" Schwab told the steelmakers at the American Iron and Steel Institute in 1927. Next year, he urged them to fix prices and avoid cutting them. The year after this, Schwab, the father of the Bethlehem beam, urged the steel men not to expand but to use their existing plant capacity.

When the Great Depression took hold in the 1930s, Schwab's public addresses were full of anecdotes and preaching that "the good . . . lies ahead." One of Schwab's remedies for the ailing economy was a high protective tariff. He had always favored a tariff on imported steel but usually settled for low duties. The Smoot- Hawley Tariff of 1930 created the highest duties in American history on many items.

Some writers have argued that the Smoot-Hawley Tariff triggered the Great Depression; others say it merely made the depression worse. One thing is certain: many nations retaliated against high American tariffs by closing their borders to American-made goods. The demand for American goods, therefore, declined and this put more people out of work. When Cordell Hull, Roosevelt's Secretary of State, tried to lower American tariffs in 1934, Schwab opposed it. He was afraid of foreign competition.

During the 1930s, Schwab enjoyed his role as elder statesman of the steel industry. He was full of stories and ever ready to do interviews with reporters. He never became senile; his ability to memorize speeches and his knack for remembering names and faces was still amazing. He just preferred to let Eugene Grace and others run Bethlehem Steel, while he worked the crowd.

When Schwab retired as an entrepreneur, his fortune became jeopardized. He had earlier shown the traits of a dissipater and still had the potential to run through his $25 million fortune. Liberated from work, Schwab traveled, gambled, and flirted more than ever. He joined the New York Whist Club and played there for high stakes. He frequented the roulette tables in Monte Carlo with his favorite mistress. The art of speculation, an anathema to Carnegie, appealed to Schwab: he installed a ticker tape in his mansion to keep tabs on Wall Street; he also invested in a variety of companies and knew almost nothing about some of them. Gambling wasn't the only drain on Schwab's wealth: he co-signed one million dollars worth of notes—usually worthless—for "friends" and also gave monthly allowances to 27 people.

Schwab refused to cut back on expenses, even during the Great Depression. He still hired the most famous musicians of the era to give private recitals for him at Riverside. The mansion itself—complete with swimming pool, wine cellar, gymnasium, bowling alley, six elevators, and 90 bedrooms—needed 20 servants to keep it functioning. He also hired 300 men to care for his 1000-acre estate at Loretto. So Schwab desperately needed his $250,000 annual salary from Bethlehem, given for past services, just to pay his expenses.

From 1935 to 1938, a small group of rebel stockholders attended the company's annual meetings; they challenged Schwab's salary and told him he had "outlived his usefulness." He finally stopped them by privately telling one of the critics that he desperately needed the money to live on. Actually he needed more. He couldn't pay the taxes on Riverside and couldn't sell it either, even at a $6 million loss. He couldn't even give it away, when he offered it as the residence for the mayor.

Schwab's last years were also marked by poor health and the death of his wife. After her funeral, Riverside was taken by creditors; Schwab moved into a small apartment. Schwab, who had shown the world a vision of entrepreneurship, now had only a vision of death. "A man knows when he doesn't want to be alive," he said, "when the will to continue living has gone from him." Schwab died nine months after he said this, at age 77, with debts exceeding assets by over $300,000.

—*BWF, September 1988*

For full footnote citations on quoted materials and other sources, see *Entrepreneurs vs. The State.* Readers are especially directed to Robert Hessen's excellent study, *Steel Titan: The Life of Charles M. Schwab* (New York: Oxford University Press, 1975).

27

Chapter Chapter **Twenty-Seven**

Herbert Dow and Predatory Pricing

One of the sacred cows of statism is the idea that government needs to protect us from predatory price-cutting. Large corporations, according to this argument, have big advantages in the marketplace. They can cut prices, drive out their competitors, then raise prices later and gouge consumers. Antitrust laws are needed, so the argument continues, to protect small businesses and consumers from those corporations with large market shares in their industries.

The story of Herbert Dow, founder of Dow Chemical Company, is an excellent case study for those who think predatory price-cutting is a real threat to society. Dow, a small producer of bromine in the early 1900s, fought a price-cutting cartel from Germany. He not only lived to tell about it; he also prospered from it.

Born in 1866, Dow was a technical whiz and entrepreneur from childhood. His father, Joseph Dow, was a master mechanic who invented equipment for the U.S. Navy. He shared technical ideas with Herbert at the dinner table and the workbench in their home in Derby, Connecticut. He showed Herbert how to make a turbine and even how to modernize a pin factory. Whether Herbert was selling vegetables or taking an engine apart, his father was there to encourage him.

Dow's future as an inventive chemist was triggered during his senior year at the Case School of Applied Science when he watched the drilling of an oil well outside Cleveland. At the well site he noticed that brine had come to the surface. The oil men considered the oozing brine a nuisance. One of them asked Dow to taste it. "Bitter, isn't it," the driller noted. "It certainly is," Dow added. "Now why would that brine be so bitter?" the driller asked. "I don't know," Dow said, "but I'd like to find out." He took a sample to his lab, tested it, and found it contained both lithium (which helped explain the bitterness) and bromine. Bromine was used as a sedative and also to develop film. This set Dow to wondering if bromine could be extracted profitably from the abundant brine in the Cleveland area.

The key to selling bromine was finding a way to separate it cheaply from brine. The traditional method was to heat a ton of brine, remove the crystallized salt, treat the rest with chemicals, salvage only two or three pounds of bromine, and dump the rest. Dow thought this method was expensive and inefficient. Why did the salt—which was often unmarketable—have to be removed? Was the use of heat—which was very expensive to apply—really necessary to separate the bromine? And why throw the rest of the brine away? Were there economical methods of removing the chlorine and magnesium also found in brine? The answers to these questions were important to Dow: the United States was ignoring or discarding an ocean of brine right beneath the earth's surface. If he could extract the chemicals, he could change America's industrial future.

Professor Dow

After graduation in 1888, Dow took a job as a chemistry professor at the Huron Street Hospital College in Cleveland. He had his own lab, an assistant, and time to work out the bromine problem. During the next year, he developed two processes—electrolysis and "blowing out." In electrolysis he used an electric current to help free bromine from the brine; in blowing out he used a steady flow of air through the solution to separate the bromine. Once Dow showed he could use his two methods to make small amounts of bromine, he assumed he could make large amounts and sell it all over the world.

The next 15 years of bromine production were a time of testing for Dow. He started three companies. One failed, one ousted him from control, and the third, the Dow Chemical Company, struggled to survive after its founding in Midland, Michigan, in 1897.

The bromine market seemed to have potential, but Dow never had enough money because nothing ever worked as he expected it to. Electrolysis was new and untested. His brine cells were too small, and the current he passed through the brine was too weak to free all the bromine. When he strengthened the current, he freed all the bromine, but some chlorine seeped in, too. Instead of being frustrated, Dow would later go into the chlorine business as well. After all, people were making money selling chlorine as a disinfectant. So could Dow. Meanwhile, the chlorine and bromine were corroding his equipment and causing breakdowns. He needed better carbon electrodes, a larger generator, and loyal workers.

Dow found himself working 18-hour days and sleeping at the factory. He had to economize to survive, so he built his factory in Midland with cheap local pine and used nails sparingly. "Crazy Dow" is what the Midland people called him when he rode his dilapidated bike into town to fetch supplies. Laughs, not dollars, were what most townsfolk contributed to his visionary plans. To survive, Dow had to be administrator, laborer, and fundraiser, too. He looked at his resources, envisioned the possible, and moved optimistically to achieve it.

For Dow Chemical to become a major corporation, it had to meet the European challenge. The Germans in particular dominated world chemical markets in the 1800s. They had experience, topflight scientists, and monopolies in chemical markets throughout the world. For example, the Germans, with their vast potash deposits, had been the dominant supplier of bromine since it first was mass-marketed in the mid-1800s. Only the United States emerged as a competitor to Germany, and then only as a minor player. Dow and some small firms along the Ohio River sold bromine, but only within the country.

About 30 German firms had combined to form a cartel, *Die Deutsche Bromkonvention*, which fixed the world price for bromine at a lucrative 49 cents a pound. Customers either paid the 49 cents or they went without. Dow and other American companies sold bromine in the United States for 36 cents. The *Bromkonvention* made it clear that if the Americans tried to sell elsewhere, the Germans would flood the American market with cheap bromine and drive them all out of business. The *Bromkonvention* law was, "The U.S. for the U.S. and Germany for the world."

Dow entered bromine production with these unwritten rules in effect, but he refused to follow them. Instead, he easily beat the cartel's 49-cent price and courageously sold America's first bromine in England. He hoped that the Germans, if they found out what he was doing, would ignore it. Throughout 1904 he merrily bid on bromine contracts throughout the world.

A Visit from the Cartel

After a few months of this, Dow encountered in his office an angry visitor from Germany—Hermann Jacobsohn of the *Bromkonvention*. Jacobsohn announced he had "positive evidence that [Dow] had exported bromides." "What of it?" Dow replied. "Don't you know that you can't sell bromides abroad?" Jacobsohn asked. "I know nothing of the kind," Dow retorted. Jacobsohn was indignant. He said that if Dow persisted, the *Bromkonvention* members would run him out of business whatever the cost. Then Jacobsohn left in a huff.

Dow's philosophy of business differed sharply from that of the Germans. He was both a scientist and an entrepreneur: he wanted to learn how the chemical world worked, and then he wanted to make the best product at the lowest price. The Germans, by contrast, wanted to discover chemicals in order to monopolize them and extort high prices for their discoveries. Dow wanted to improve chemical products and find new combinations and new uses for chemicals. The Germans were content to invent them, divide markets among their cartel members, and sell abroad at high prices. Those like Dow who tried to compete with the cartel learned quickly what "predatory price-cutting" meant. The Bromkonvention, like other German cartels, had a "yellow-dog fund," which was money set aside to use to flood other countries with cheap chemicals to drive out competitors.

Dow, however, was determined to compete with the Bromkonvention. He needed the sales, and he believed his electrolysis produced bromine cheaper than the Germans could. Also, Dow was stubborn and hated being bluffed by a bully. When Jacobsohn stormed out of his office, Dow continued to sell bromine, from England to Japan.

Before long, in early 1905, the *Bromkonvention* went on a rampage: it poured bromides into America at 15 cents a pound, well below its fixed price of 49 cents and also below Dow's 36 cents. Jacobsohn arranged a special meeting with Dow in St. Louis and demanded that he quit exporting bromides or else the Germans would flood the American market indefinitely. The *Bromkonvention* had the money and the backing of its government, Jacobsohn reminded Dow, and could long continue to sell in the United States below the cost of production. Dow was not intimidated; he was angry and told Jacobsohn he would sell to whomever would buy from him. Dow left the meeting with Jacobsohn screaming threats behind him. As Dow boarded the train from St. Louis, he knew the future of his company—if it had a future—depended on how he handled the Germans.

On that train, Dow worked out a daring strategy. He had his agent in New York discreetly buy hundreds of thousands of pounds of German bromine at the 15-cent price. Then he repackaged and sold it in Europe—including Germany!—at 27 cents a pound. "When this 15-cent price was made over here," Dow said, "instead of meeting it, we pulled out of the American market altogether and used all our production to supply the foreign demand. This, as we afterward learned, was not what they anticipated we would do."

Dow secretly hired British and German agents to market his repackaged bromine in their countries. They had no trouble doing so because the Bromkonvention had left the world price above 30 cents a pound. The Germans were selling in the United States far below cost of production, and they hoped to offset their U.S. losses with a high world price.

Instead, the Germans were befuddled. They expected to run Dow out of business; and this they thought they were doing. But why was U.S. demand for bromine so high? And where was this flow of cheap bromine into Europe coming from? Was one of the *Bromkonvention* members cheating and selling bromine in Europe below the fixed price? The tension in the *Bromkonvention* was dramatic. According to Dow, "The German producers got into trouble among themselves as to who was to supply the goods for the American market, and the American agent [for the Germans] became embarrassed by reason of his inability to get goods that he had contracted to supply and asked us if we would take his [15-cent] contracts. This, of course, we refused to do."

More Price-Cutting

The confused Germans kept cutting U.S. prices—first to 12 cents and then to 10.5 cents a pound. Meanwhile, Dow kept buying cheap bromine and reselling it in Europe for 27 cents. These sales forced the Bromkonvention to drop its high world price to match Dow and that further depleted the *Bromkonvention*'s resources. Dow, by contrast, improved his foreign sales force, often ran his bromine plants at top capacity, and gained business at the expense of the *Bromkonvention* and all other American producers, most of whom had shut down after the price-cutting. Even when the *Bromkonvention* finally caught on to what Dow was doing, it wasn't sure how to respond. As Dow said, "We are absolute dictators of the situation." He also wrote, "One result of this fight has been to give us a standing all over the world. . . . We are . . . in a much stronger position than we ever were." He added that "the profits are not so great" because his plants had trouble matching the new 27-cent world price. He needed to buy the cheap German bromides to stay ahead, and this was harder to do once the Germans discovered and exposed his repackaging scheme.

The bromine war lasted four years (1904–08), when finally the Bromkonvention invited Dow to come to Germany and work out an agreement. Since they couldn't crush Dow, they decided to at least work out some deal so they could make money again. The terms were as follows: the Germans agreed to quit selling bromine in the United States; Dow agreed to quit selling in Germany; and the rest of the world was open to free competition. The bromine war was over, but low-priced bromine was now a fact of life.

Dow had more capital from the bromine war to expand his business and challenge the Germans in other markets. For example, Dow entered the dye industry and began producing indigo more cheaply than the dominant German dye cartel. During World War I, Dow tried to fill several gaps when Germany quit trading with the United States. Aspirin, procaine (now better known by its trademark name, Novocain), phenol (for explosives), and acetic anhydride (to strengthen airplane wings) were all products Dow began producing more cheaply than the Germans did in the World War I era. As he told the Federal Trade Commission when the war began, "We have been up against the German government in competition, and we believe that we can compete with

Germany in any product that is made in sufficient amount, provided we have the time and have learned the tricks of the trade."

Move to Magnesium

Dow's favorite new chemical from the war was magnesium. Magnesium, like bromine and chlorine, was one of the basic elements found in Michigan brine. Dow hated throwing it away and had tried since 1896 to produce it effectively and profitably. As a metal, magnesium was one-third lighter than aluminum and had strong potential for industrial use. Magnesium was a chief ingredient in products from Epsom salts to fireworks to cement.

Unfortunately for Dow, the Germans had magnesium deposits near New Stassfurt. So while he was struggling, the Germans succeeded in mining magnesium and using it as an alloy with other metals. In 1907, they had formed the *Chloromagnesium Syndikat*, or the Magnesium Trust.

Even before the war, Dow began pouring more capital into magnesium, but only during the war did he begin selling his first small amounts. After the war, Dow still could not match Germany's low cost of production, but he refused to give up. Instead, he plowed millions of dollars into developing magnesium as America's premier lightweight metal. Part of his problem was the high cost of extracting magnesium; the other problem was the fixation most businessmen had with using aluminum.

The Germans had mixed feelings as they watched Dow struggle with magnesium. On one hand, they were glad to still have their large market share. On the other hand, they were nervous that Dow would soon discover a method to make magnesium more cheaply than they could. Their solution was not to work hard on improving their own efficiency, but to invite Dow to join them in their magnesium cartel and together fix prices for the world.

In a sense, of course, the Germans were paying Dow the strongest compliment possible by asking him to join them, not fight them. What's interesting, though, is that through the battles with bromine, indigo, phenol, aspirin, and procaine, the Germans persisted in their strategy of using government-regulated cartels to fix prices and control markets. They continued to believe that monopolies were the best path to controlling markets and making profits.

Dow must have been flattered by the German offer, but he refused to join the Magnesium Trust. He had already shown the world that his company—by trying to make the best product at the lowest price—could often beat the large German cartels. Predatory price-cutting, the standard strategy of the German chemical cartels, failed again and again. By using the strategy, the Germans unintentionally helped the smaller Dow secure capital, capture markets, and deliver low prices for his products around the world.

—BWF, May 1998

28

Chapter **Twenty-Eight**

Witch-hunting For Robber Barons: The Standard Oil Story

Among the great misconceptions of the free economy is the widely-held belief that "laissez faire" embodies a natural tendency toward monopoly concentration. Under unfettered capitalism, so goes the familiar refrain, large firms would systematically devour smaller ones, corner markets, and stamp out competition until every inhabitant of the land fell victim to their power. Just as popular is the notion that John D. Rockefeller's Standard Oil Company of the late 1800s gave substance to such an evil course of events.

Regarding Standard Oil's chief executive, one noted historian writes, "He (Rockefeller) iron-handedly ruined competitors by cutting prices until his victim went bankrupt or sold out, whereupon higher prices would be likely to return."[13]

---

[13] Thomas A. Bailey, *The American Pageant: A History of the Republic*, 2 vols., 8th ed. (Boston: D. C. Heath and Company, 1966), 2:532.

Two other historians, coauthors of a popular college text, opine that "Rockefeller was a ruthless operator who did not hesitate to crush his competitors by harsh and unfair methods."[14]

In 1899, Standard refined 90 per cent of America's oil—the peak of the company's dominance of the refining business. Though that market share was steadily siphoned off by competitors after 1899, the company nonetheless has been branded ever since as "an industrial octopus."

Does the story of Standard Oil really present a case *against* the free market? In my opinion, it most emphatically does not. Furthermore, setting the record straight on this issue must become an important weapon in every free market advocate's intellectual arsenal. That's the purpose of the following remarks.

Theoretically, there are two kinds of monopoly: coercive and efficiency. A coercive monopoly results from, in the words of Adam Smith, "a government grant of exclusive privilege." Government, in effect, must take sides in the market in order to give birth to a coercive monopoly. It must make it difficult, costly, or impossible for anyone but the favored firm to do business.

The United States Postal Service is an example of this kind of monopoly. By law, no one can deliver first class mail except the USPS. Fines and imprisonment (coercion) await all those daring enough to compete.

In some other cases, the government may not ban competition outright, but simply bestow privileges, immunities, or subsidies on one firm while imposing costly requirements on all others. Regardless of the method, a firm which enjoys a coercive monopoly is in a position to harm the consumer and get away with it.

An efficiency monopoly, on the other hand, earns a high share of a market because it does the best job. It receives no special favors from the law to account for its size. Others are free to compete and, if consumers so will it, to grow as big as the "monopoly."

An efficiency monopoly has no legal power to compel people to deal with it or to protect itself from the consequences of its unethical practices. It can only attain bigness through its excellence in satisfying customers and by the economy of its operations. An efficiency

---

[14] Gilbert C. Fite and Jim E. Reese, *An Economic History of the United States*, 2nd ed. (Boston: Houghton Mifflin Company, 1965), p. 367.

monopoly which turns its back on the very performance which produced its success would be posting a sign, "COMPETITORS WANTED." The market rewards excellence and exacts a toll on mediocrity.

It is my contention that the historical record casts the Standard Oil Company in the role of efficiency monopoly—a firm to which consumers repeatedly awarded their votes of confidence.

The oil rush began with the discovery of oil by Colonel Edwin Drake at Titusville, Pennsylvania in 1859. Northwestern Pennsylvania soon "was overrun with businessmen, speculators, misfits, horse dealers, drillers, bankers, and just plain hell-raisers. Dirt-poor farmers leased land at fantastic prices, and rigs began blackening the landscape. Existing towns jammed full overnight with 'strangers,' and new towns appeared almost as quickly."[15]

In the midst of chaos emerged young John D. Rockefeller. An exceptionally hard- working and thrifty man, Rockefeller transformed his early interest in oil into a partnership in the refinery stage of the business in 1865.

Five years later, Rockefeller formed the Standard Oil Company with 4 per cent of the refining market. Less than thirty years later, he reached that all-time high of 90 percent. What accounts for such stunning success?

On December 30, 1899, Rockefeller was asked that very question before a governmental investigating body called the Industrial Commission. He replied:

> I ascribe the success of the Standard to its consistent policy to make the volume of its business large through the merits and cheapness of its products. It has spared no expense in finding, securing, and utilizing the best and cheapest methods of manufacture. It has sought for the best superintendents and workmen and paid the best wages. It has not hesitated to sacrifice old machinery and old plants for new and better ones. It has placed its manufactories at the points where they could supply markets at the least expense. It has not only sought markets for its principal products, but for all possible by-products, sparing no expense in introducing them to the public. It has not hesitated to invest millions of dollars in methods of

---

[15] D. T. Armentano, *The Myths of Antitrust: Economic Theory and Legal Cases* (New Rochelle, N.Y.: Arlington House, 1972), p. 64.

cheapening the gathering and distribution of oils by pipe lines, special cars, tank steamers, and tank wagons. It has erected tank stations at every important railroad station to cheapen the storage and delivery of its products. It has spared no expense in forcing its products into the markets of the world among people civilized and uncivilized. It has had faith in American oil, and has brought together millions of money for the purpose of making it what it is, and holding its markets against the competition of Russia and all the many countries which are producers of oil and competitors against American oil. [16]

A Master Organizer of Men and Materials

Rockefeller was a managerial genius—a master organizer of men as well as of materials. He had a gilt for bringing devoted, brilliant, and hard-working young men into his organization. Among his most outstanding associates were H. H. Rogers, John D. Archbold, Stephen V. Harkness, Samuel Andrews, and Henry M. Flagler. Together they emphasized efficient economic operation, research, and sound financial practices. The economic excellence of their performance is described by economist D. T. Armentano:

> Instead of buying oil from jobbers, they made the jobbers' profit by sending their own purchasing men into the oil region. In addition, they made their own sulfuric acid, their own barrels, their own lumber, their own wagons, and their own glue. They kept minute and accurate records of every item from rivets to barrel bungs. They built elaborate storage facilities near their refineries. Rockefeller bargained as shrewdly for crude as anyone before or since. And Sam Andrews coaxed more kerosene from a barrel of crude than could the competition. In addition, the Rockefeller firm put out the cleanest-burning kerosene, and managed to dispose of most of the residues like lubricating oil, paraffin, and vaseline at a profit.[17]

Even muckraker Ida Tarbell, one of Standard's critics, admired the company's streamlined processes of production:

---

[16] Thomas G. Manning, E. David Cronon, and Howard R. Lamar, *The Standard Oil Company: The Rise of a National Monopoly*, part 3: *Government and the American Economy: 1870 to the Present*, revised (New York: Henry Holt and Company, 1960), p. 19.

[17] Armentano, *Myths of Antitrust*, p. 67.

Not far away from the canning works, on Newton Creek, is an oil refinery. This oil runs to the canning works, and, as the newmade cans come down by a chute from the works above, where they have just been finished, they are filled, twelve at a time, with the oil made a few miles away. The filling apparatus is admirable. As the newmade cans come down the chute they are distributed, twelve in a row, along one side of a turn-table. The turn-table is revolved, and the cans come directly under twelve measures, each holding five gallons of oil—a turn of a valve, and the cans are full. The table is turned a quarter, and while twelve more cans are filled and twelve fresh ones are distributed, four men with soldering cappers put the caps on the first set. Another quarter turn, and men stand ready to take the cans from the filler and while they do this, twelve more are having caps put on, twelve are filling, and twelve are coming to their place from the chute. The cans are placed at once in wooden boxes standing ready, and, after a twenty-four-hour wait for discovering leaks, are nailed up and carted to a nearby door. This door opens on the river, and there at anchor by the side of the factory is a vessel chartered for South America or China or where not—waiting to receive the cans which a little more than twenty-four hours before were tin sheets lying on flatboxes. It is a marvellous example of economy, not only in materials, but in time and in footsteps. [18]

Market Competition Protects the Public

Socialist historian Gabriel Kolko, who argues in *The Triumph of Conservatism* that the forces of competition in the free market of the late 1800s were too potent to allow Stan dard to cheat the public, stresses that "Standard treated the consumer with deference. Crude and refined oil prices for consumers declined during the period Standard exercised greatest control of the industry . . ." [19]

Standard's service to the consumer in the form of lower prices is well-documented. To quote from Professor Armentano again:

Between 1870 and 1885 the price of refined kerosene dropped from 26 cents to 8 cents per gallon. In the same period, the Standard Oil

---

[18] Ida M. Tarbell, *The History of the Standard Oil Company*, 2 vols. in 1 (Gloucester, Mass.: Peter Smith, 1950), p. 240-241.

[19] Gabriel Kolko, *The Triumph of Conservatism: A Reinterpretation of American His tory, 1900-1916* (New York: The Macmillan Company, 1963; reprint ed., Chicago: Quad rangle Books, 1967), p. 39.

Company reduced the [refining] costs per gallon from almost 3 cents in 1870 to .452 cents in 1885. Clearly, the firm was relatively efficient, and its efficiency was being translated to the consumer in the form of lower prices for a much improved product, and to the firm in the form of additional profits. [20]

That story continued for the remainder of the century, with the price of kerosene to the consumer falling to 5.91 cents per gallon in 1897. Armentano concludes from the record that "at the very pinnacle of Standard's industry 'control,' the *costs and the prices for refined oil reached their lowest levels in the history of the petroleum industry.*" [21]

John D. Rockefeller's success, then, was a consequence of his superior performance. He derived his impressive market share not from government favors but rather from aggressive courting of the consumer. Standard Oil is one of history's classic efficiency monopolies.

But what about the many serious charges leveled against Standard? Predatory price cutting? Buying out competitors? Conspiracy? Railroad rebates? Charging any price it wanted? Greed? Each of these can be viewed as an assault not just on Standard Oil but on the free market in general. They can and must be answered.

Predatory price cutting

Predatory price cutting is "the practice of deliberately underselling rivals in certain markets to drive them out of business, and then raising prices to exploit a market devoid of competition."[22]

Professor John S. McGee, writing in the *Journal of Law and Economics* for October 1958, stripped this charge of any intellectual substance. Describing it as "logically deficient," he concluded, "I can find little or no evidence to support it.[23]

In his extraordinary article, McGee scrutinized the testimony of Rockefeller's competitors who claimed to have been victims of predatory price cutting. He found their claims to be shallow and

---

[20] Armentano, *Myths of Antitrust*, p. 70.

[21] Ibid., p. 77.

[22] Ibid., p. 73.

[23] John S. McGee, "Predatory Price Cutting: The Standard Oil (N.J.) Case," *Journal of Law and Economics*, I (October, 1958), p. 138.

misdirected. McGee pointed out that some of these very people later opened new refineries and successfully challenged Standard again.

Beyond the actual record, economic theory also argues against a winning policy of predatory price cutting in a free market for the following reasons:

1. Price is only one aspect of competition. Firms compete in a variety of ways: service, location, packaging, marketing, even courtesy. For price alone to draw customers away from the competition, the predator would have to cut substantially—enough to outweigh all the other competitive pressures the others can throw at him. That means suffering losses on every unit sold. If the predator has a war-chest of "monopoly profits" to draw upon in such a battle, then the predatory price cutting theorist must explain how he was able to achieve such ability in the absence of this practice in the first place!

2. The large firm stands to lose the most. By definition, the large firm is already selling the most units. As a predator, it must actually step up its production if it is to have any effect on competitors. As Professor McGee observed, "To lure customers away from somebody, he (the predator) must be prepared to serve them himself. The monopolizer thus finds himself in the position of selling more—and therefore losing more—than his competitors." [24]

3. Consumers will increase their purchases at the "bargain prices." This factor causes the predator to step up production even further. It also puts off the day when he can "cash in" on his hoped-for victory because consumers will be in a position to refrain from purchasing at higher prices, consuming their stockpiles instead.

4. The length of the battle is always uncertain. The predator does not know how long he must suffer losses before his competitors quit. It may take weeks, months, or even years. Meanwhile, consumers are "cleaning up" at his expense.

5. Any "beaten" firms may reopen. Competitors may scale down production or close only temporarily as they "wait out the storm." When the predator raises prices, they enter the market again. Conceivably, a "beaten" firm might be bought up by someone for a "song," and then, under fresh management and with relatively low capital costs, face the predator with an actual competitive cost advantage.

---

[24] Ibid., p. 140.

6. High prices encourage newcomers. Even if the predator drives everyone else from the market, raising prices will attract competition from people heretofore not even in the industry. The higher the prices go, the more powerful that attraction.

7. The predator would lose the favor of consumers. Predatory price cutting is simply not good public relations. Once known, it would swiftly erode the public's faith and good will. It might even provoke consumer boycotts and a backlash of sympathy for the firm's competitors.

In summary, let me quote Professor McGee once again:

> Judging from the Record, Standard Oil did not use predatory price discrimination to drive out competing refiners, nor did its pricing practice have that effect. Whereas there may be a very few cases in which retail kerosene peddlers or dealers went out of business after or during price cutting, there is no real proof that Standard's pricing policies were responsible. I am convinced that Standard did not systematically, if ever, use local price cutting in retailing, or anywhere else, to reduce competition. To do so would have been foolish; and, whatever else has been said about them, the old Standard organization was seldom criticized for making less money when it could readily have made more. [25]

Buying out competitors

The intent of this practice, the critics say, was to stifle competitors by absorbing them.

First, it must be said that Standard had no legal power to coerce a competitor into selling. For a purchase to occur, Rockefeller had to pay the *market* price for an oil refinery. And evidence abounds that he often hired the very people whose operations he purchased. "Victimized ex-rivals," wrote McGee, "might be expected to make poor employees and dissident or unwilling shareholders."[26]

Kolko writes that "Standard attained its control of the refinery business primarily by mergers, not price wars, and most refinery owners were anxious to sell out to it. Some of these refinery owners later reopened new plants after selling to Standard."[27]

---

[25] Ibid., p. 168.
[26] Ibid., p. 145.
[27] Kolko, *Triumph of Conservatism*, p. 40.

Buying out competitors can be a wise move if achieving economy of scale is the intent. Buying out competitors merely to eliminate them from the market can be a futile, expensive, and never-ending policy. It appears that Rockefeller's mergers were designed with the first motive in mind.

Even so, other people found it profitable to go into the business of build-ing refineries and selling to Standard. David P. Reighard managed to build and sell three successive refineries to Rockefeller, all on excellent terms.

A firm which adopts a policy of absorbing others solely to stifle competition embarks upon the impossible adventure of putting out the recurring and unpredictable prairie fires of competition.

Conspiracy To Fix Prices

This accusation holds that Standard secured secret agreements with competitors to carve up markets and fix prices at higher-than-market levels.

I will not contend here that Rockefeller never attempted this policy. His experiment with the South Improvement Company in 1872 provides at least some evidence that he did. I do argue, however, that all such attempts were failures from the start and no harm to the consumer occurred.

Standard's price performance, cited extensively above, supports my argument. Prices fell steadily on an improving product. Some conspiracy!

From the perspective of economic theory, collusion to raise and/or fix prices is a practice doomed to failure in a free market for these reasons:

1. Internal pressures. Conspiring firms must resolve the dilemma of production. To exact a higher price than the market currently permits, production must be curtailed. Otherwise, in the face of a fall in demand, the firms will be stuck with a quantity of unsold goods. Who will cut their production and by how much? Will the conspirators accept an equal reduction for all when it is likely that each faces a unique constellation of cost and distribution advantages and disadvantages?

Assuming a formula for restricting production is agreed upon, it then becomes highly profitable for any member of the cartel to quietly cheat on the agreement. By offering secret rebates or discounts or other "deals" to his competitors' customers, any conspirator can undercut the cartel price, earn an increasing share of the market and make a lot of money. When the others get wind of this, they must quickly break the agreement or lose their market shares to the "cheater." The very reason for the conspiracy in the first place—higher profits—proves to be its undoing!

2. External pressures. This comes from competitors who are not parties to the secret agreement. They feel under no obligation to abide by the cartel price and actually use their somewhat lower price as a selling point to customers. The higher the cartel price, the more this external competition pays. The conspiracy must either convince all outsiders to join the cartel (making it increasingly likely that somebody will cheat) or else dissolve the cartel to meet the competition.

I would once again call the reader's attention to Kolko's *The Triumph of Conservatism*, which documents the tendency for collusive agreements to break apart, sometimes even before the ink is dry.

Railroad rebates

John D. Rockefeller received substantial rebates from railroads that hauled his oil, a factor which critics claim gave him an unfair advantage over other refiners.

The fact is that most all refiners received rebates from railroads. This practice was simply evidence of stiff competition among the roads for the business of hauling refined oil products. Standard got the biggest rebates because Rockefeller was a shrewd bargainer and because he offered the railroads large volume on a regular basis.

This charge is even less credible when one considers that Rockefeller increasingly relied on his own pipelines, not railroads, to transport his oil.

The Power To Charge Any Price Wanted

According to the notion that Standard's size gave it the power to charge any price it wanted, bigness per se immunizes the firm from competition and consumer sovereignty.

As an "efficiency monopoly," Standard could not coercively prevent others from competing with it. And others did, so much so that the company's share of the market declined dramatically after 1899. As the economy shifted from kerosene to electricity, from the horse to the automobile, and from oil production in the East to production in the Gulf States, Rockefeller found himself losing ground to younger, more aggressive men.

Neither did Standard have the power to compel people to buy its products. It had to rely on its own excellence to attract and keep customers.

In a totally free market, the following factors insure that no firm, regardless of size, can charge and get "any price it wants":

1. Free entry. Potential competition is encouraged by any firm's abuse of the consumer. In describing entry into the oil business, Rockefeller once remarked that "all sorts of people . . . the butcher, the baker, and the candlestick maker began to refine oil."[28]

2. Foreign competition. As long as government doesn't hamper international trade, this is always a potent force.

3. Competition of substitutes. People are often able to substitute a product different from yet similar to the monopolist's.

4. Competition of all goods for the consumer's dollar. Every business-man is in competition with every other businessman to get consumers to spend their limited dollars on him.

5. Elasticity of demand. At higher prices, people will simply buy less.

It makes sense to view competition in a free market not as a static phenomenon, but as a dynamic, neverending, leapfrog process by which the leader today can be the follower tomorrow.

Rockefeller was greedy

The charge that John D. Rockefeller was a "greedy" man is the most meaningless of all the attacks on him but nonetheless echoes constantly in the history books.

---

[28] John A. Garraty, *The American Nation, vol. 2: A History of the United States Since 1865,* 3rd ed. (New York: Harper and Row, 1975), p. 499.

If Rockefeller wanted to make a lot of money (and there is no doubting he did), he certainly discovered the free market solution to his problem: produce and sell something that consumers will buy and buy again. One of the great attributes of the free market is that it channels greed into constructive directions. One cannot accumulate wealth without offering something in exchange!

At this point the reader might rightly wonder about the dissolution of the Standard Oil Trust in 1911. Didn't the Supreme Court find Standard guilty of successfully employing anti-competitive practices?

Interestingly, a careful reading of the decision reveals that no attempt was made by the Court to examine Standard's conduct or performance. The justices did not sift through the conflicting evidence concerning any of the government's allegations against the company. No specific finding of guilt was made with regard to those charges. Although the record clearly indicates that "prices fell, costs fell, outputs expanded, product quality improved, and hundreds of firms at one time or another produced and sold refined petroleum products in competition with Standard Oil,"[29] the Supreme Court ruled against the company. The justices argued simply that the competition between some of the divisions of Standard Oil was less than the competition that existed between them when they were separate companies before merging with Standard.

In 1915, Charles W. Eliot, president of Harvard, observed: "The organization of the great business of taking petroleum out of the earth, piping the oil over great distances, distilling and refining it, and distributing it in tank steamers, tank wagons, and cans all over the earth, was an American invention."[30] Let the facts record that the great Standard Oil Company, more than any other firm, and John D. Rockefeller, more than any other man, were responsible for this amazing development.

—*LWR, March 1980*

---

[29] D. T. Armentano, *Myths of Antitrust*, p. 83.
[30] Fite and Reese, *An Economic History*, p. 366.

29

Chapter **Twenty-Nine**

John D. Rockefeller and His Enemies

One hundred years ago John D. Rockefeller, America's first billionaire and the head of Standard Oil, faced a critical issue: what should he do about the criticisms of investigative journalist Ida Tarbell?

To Rockefeller, the solution was simple—ignore her. He was marketing 60 percent of all oil sold in the whole world. His company was popular with consumers everywhere. Therefore, let his actions speak for themselves.

Rockefeller had entered the raucous oil business during the Civil War, when oil often sold for a dollar a gallon. While most refiners dumped oil byproducts into nearby rivers, Rockefeller wisely hired research-and-development men to produce waxes, paving materials, and detergents from the seemingly unmarketable sludge that was discarded. He also developed the technology to get more kerosene out of a barrel of oil than anyone else. Rockefeller had become a billionaire by making a fraction of a cent per gallon selling millions of gallons of kerosene to illuminate every civilized part of the earth.

The result was often win-win for everyone. The U.S. became a major industrial country, and inefficient refiners in the United States sold out for Standard Oil stock, which often made them comfortable for life. As one editor in oil-rich Titusville, Pennsylvania, exclaimed, "Men until now barely able to get a poor living off poor land are made rich beyond their wildest dreaming."

However, even with cheap oil and the prospering of the United States, Ida Tarbell was unhappy. In 1904 she wrote *The History of the Standard Oil Company*, which complained loudly about Rockefeller and his company. He was a cutthroat competitor, she insisted, who relied on rebates to outsell his rivals. "The ruthlessness and persistency with which he cut and continued to cut their prices drove them to despair," she wrote. Furthermore, he low-balled those whom he sought to buy out. Innuendo became a powerful Tarbell weapon: "There came to be a popular conviction that the 'Standard would do anything.'" She concluded that Rockefeller "has done more than any other person to fasten on this country the most serious interference with free individual development."

How might we explain Tarbell's astonishing animus? The motivating force seems to be that her father, whom she adored, chose to compete with Rockefeller rather than sell to him. When Franklin Tarbell proved unable to market oil for eight cents a gallon, he brooded at home and Ida's blissful childhood was diminished. Her brother became an officer for a competing oil company, so when Ida was growing up she heard much grumbling about Standard Oil.

Tarbell serialized her book in *McClure's* magazine, which was a prominent publication of the early 1900s. The timing of her attacks meshed well with certain fears that were growing in America about large companies and their potential for monopoly and price-fixing. In 1901, for example, U.S. Steel had become the first billion-dollar corporation and it controlled more than 60 percent of the steel market. Would monopolies prevail and competition be diminished? Tarbell suggested that Standard Oil's sinister rise to power was dangerous and undesir-able. President Theodore Roosevelt agreed, and with his blessing the Justice Department began a lengthy assault on Standard Oil that resulted in its breakup into more than 30 companies.

Beware Muckraking

The Walmarts of the world need to take note: political agitation plus muckraking can defeat a competitive product enjoyed by millions of consumers. Rockefeller's decision to "let the facts speak for themselves" was naive. His "facts" were dwarfed by the negative publicity from *McClure's*, from editorial pages, and finally from the White House. In 1911 the Sherman Anti-Trust Act was used against Standard Oil.

If Rockefeller had chosen to challenge Tarbell, he could have made two useful points. First, Standard Oil rose to economic power not on rebates but on providing cheap oil to the general public. "We must ever remember," Rockefeller told one of his partners, "we are refining oil for the poor man and he must have it cheap and good." Or as he put it to another partner, "Hope we can continue to hold out with the best illuminator in the world at the lowest price."

Rockefeller did receive large rebates, but he earned them by supplying the largest shipments of oil. Without the large shipments, which came through low costs of production, he would not have had any leverage to win low shipping rates from the railroads. In any case, those low costs were mainly passed along to consumers by further reducing the price of his oil.

Second, Rockefeller avoided predatory price-cutting because it tended to hurt him more than his competitors. That point is often hard to understand, but economist John S. McGee did extensive research on Standard Oil's pricing policies and discovered that predatory price-cutting was an anathema to Rockefeller.

As McGee and others have pointed out, since Rockefeller did most of the oil business in the United States, if he cut prices he would be losing the small profits he was earning on the lion's share of the business he was already doing. Also, even if he gained a 100 percent market share, that gain would be temporary. The moment he tried to raise prices, other competitors would re-emerge, the price would fall again, and Rockefeller would (at best) be back where he started.

The charges that Rockefeller thrived on "unfair rebates" and that he was eagerly waiting to employ predatory price-cutting did him a great deal of damage and offset the favorable opinion many Americans had of him and of his oil.

Tarbell also attacked Rockefeller's character. She wrote that his "big hand reached out from nobody knew where, to steal their conquest and throttle their future. The suddenness and the blackness of the assault on their business stirred to the bottom their manhood and their sense of fair play."

Even Rockefeller's relatively modest house, Tarbell claimed, was "a monument of cheap ugliness." Yes, she conceded, his frugality was "a welcome contrast to the wanton lavishness which on every side of us corrupts taste and destroys a sense of values." However, she noted, "One would be inclined to like Mr. Rockefeller the better for his plain living if somehow one did not feel that here was something more than frugality, that here was parsimony . . . made a virtue."

If Rockefeller instead had built a magnificent mansion and had spent money lavishly, she could then have attacked him for wasting the money he greedily extracted from others. Rockefeller could not win, and that was, in part, the problem of allowing Tarbell to go unchallenged.

Sometimes Tarbell must have been perplexed. Rockefeller, she admitted, was a stable family man who was loved by his wife and children. By contrast, her boss, S. S. McClure, was a chronic adulterer. But she chided McClure in private and Rockefeller in the pages of her bestseller.

—BWF, May 2008

30

Chapter **Thirty**

It Wasn't Government that Fixed Your Clock

Remember the old Chicago song, "Does Anybody Really Know What Time It Is?" Well, if you asked that question about 120 years ago, you could have received 38 different answers in a single state and many more than that in some countries. How the invention of standard time brought order out of an astonishing degree of confusion is a sadly forgotten tale and a great tribute to ingenuity in a free society.

People in the continental United States have become so accustomed to four standardized time zones–Eastern, Central, Mountain, and Pacific–that it's hard to believe that we ever kept time any other way. But until a crucial date in 1883, what time it was depended on the nearest city or town. The time of day was a purely local matter as determined by the position of the sun. Noon was when the sun was at its highest point in the sky. Local people set their timepieces by some well-known clock in their respective communities, such as one on a prominent church steeple or in a jeweler's window.

This meant that when it was noon in Chicago, it was 12:31 p.m. in Pittsburgh, 12:24 in Cleveland, 12:13 in Cincinnati, and 12:07 in Indiana-polis. Or, when it was noon in Detroit, it was about 11:50 in Grand Rapids.

Indeed, there were at least 27 different local times within the state of Michigan alone. Indiana was slightly less confusing with just 23 local times, but Wisconsin—with 38—was a clock-watcher's nightmare.

"In every city and town," historian Stewart Holbrook wrote in his 1947 book, *The Story of American Railroads*, "the multiplicity of time standards confused and bewildered passengers, shippers, and railway employees. Too often, errors and mistakes turned out disastrously, for railroads were now running fast trains on tight schedules; a minute or two might mean the difference between smooth operation and a collision."

Traveling from north to south (or vice versa) presented no time problems but east to west (or west to east) was another story altogether. Predicting the time a train would arrive at any particular stop was no small feat in the days before standard time. In his 1990 book, *Keeping Watch: A History of American Time*, Michael O'Malley reveals that "A traveler on a westbound train, setting his watch at departure, might find after less than half an hour's travel that his watch and the local time no longer agreed. To make matters worse, individual railroad and steamship lines each ran by their own standards of time– usually the time of the city the line originated in. When two lines met, or shared a track, or terminated at a steamship landing, it threw differences in timekeeping into high relief." Something clearly had to be done.

Two men in particular are credited with "inventing" standard time and the time zones that define it. Professor C. F. Dowd, principal of Temple Grove Seminary for Young Ladies at Saratoga Springs, New York, first suggested the general concept of four or more "time belts." Later, William Frederick Allen, a railroad engineer, adapted and improved it and won acceptance for it by a crucial panel.

In 1872 railroad officials from around the country met in Missouri to arrange summer passenger schedules. To address the time problem they formed the General Time Convention. Allen was named secretary and immediately set to work on making Dowd's idea into a detailed proposal. In October 1883 the Convention approved Allen's plan. Government was not part of the picture at all; the Dowd-Allen solution to establish standardized time zones was conceived and fine-tuned to fruition entirely by the ingenuity of private citizens. The Convention chose November 18, 1883, for adoption of the new system by virtually every railroad in the country. "Railroad time" quickly became the new "local time" everywhere–or at least almost everywhere.

Detroit Holds Out

Time marched on, but Detroit didn't. The view that the sun, not man, dictates what time it is enjoyed broad support in the city. Henry Ford complained about the disparity; he designed a watch with two dials, one that kept local time for when he was in Detroit and the other that kept standard time.

Detroit stuck to local time until 1900, when the City Council ordered clocks set back 28 minutes to comply with Central Standard Time. Half the city refused to obey, and the City Council rescinded its order. It wasn't until 1905 that Detroit, by a citywide vote, adopted standard time and became part of the Central time zone.

While standardized time zones were speedily and voluntarily embraced by most of the country, the federal government actually sought to prevent it. The director of the Naval Observatory argued strenuously against any manmade challenge to the authority of the sun. The U.S. Attorney General ordered that no department of the federal government could run according to the system developed in 1883 until authorized by Congress, which took 35 years. In March 1918 Congress finally put Washington's stamp of approval on what had been accomplished through private initiative, with one major adjustment: It took Michigan and western Ohio out of the Central time zone and put them in the Eastern zone, where they remain today.

What about the rest of the world? An International Meridian Conference was held in late 1884, a year after standard time took effect in the United States. Delegates representing governments from 25 countries debated two main issues: Should they adopt a system of global standardized time zones, and if so, where should the starting point, or "prime meridian," be? The success of the American experience helped resolve the first issue with dispatch, but just as quickly the second issue hit a geopolitical snag. Britain's longstanding maritime dominance put the imaginary line through its Greenwich Observatory in the lead for prime meridian. The French preferred Paris but suggested a compromise: They would accept Greenwich if the Brits and the Americans adopted the metric system. The Conference approved Greenwich without the metric condition, so feeling snubbed the French went their own way and didn't recognize the prime meridian until 1911.

Private enterprise saw a dilemma as a problem to be solved. Governments dragged their collective feet and politicized it. As Yogi Berra would say, this sounds like "déjà vu all over again."

What time is it? Thanks not to pretentious central planners but to creative entrepreneurs, no matter where you live, there's been a uniform answer to that question for about a century.

—LWR, August 2002

31

Chapter **Thirty-One**

History for Sale: Why Not?

"Sold!" cried the Sotheby's auctioneer on the night of December 18, 2007, as one of history's oldest political documents changed hands. It was Magna Carta, or rather a copy of it that dated to 1297. The buyer was not a government but an individual, a Washington lawyer named David Rubenstein. He paid $21.3 million for it and promptly announced he wanted his newly acquired private property to stay on public view at the National Archives in the nation's capital.

A privately owned Magna Carta? Aren't such important things supposed to be public property? A couple of "educated" American students visiting Britain in mid-December certainly thought so. For a story that aired on CNN about the auction at Sotheby's, they were interviewed at the British Library in London while gazing on another of the great charter's copies on display there.

"I couldn't imagine that there is still a privately owned copy of the Magna Carta floating around the world. It seems really incredible that any one person should actually have that in their possession," one of the young scholars pronounced. "Personally, I hope the government or some charitable foundation gets a hold of it so that everybody can enjoy seeing it," chimed the other. Both assumed that private property and public benefit, at least with regard to historical preservation, were incompatible.

The Magna Carta copy that Rubenstein bought will not be spirited into his closet because it is the new owner's wish that it be preserved for public display. While some might say humanity lucked out in this particular instance, it really is just the latest in a rich heritage of private care of documents, manuscripts, and objects of historical significance. Indeed, the very copy Rubenstein bought was previously owned by businessman Ross Perot's foundation, which in turn had acquired it in 1984 from yet another private owner, the Brudenell family of Britain. Given that record, those students should have sung hosannas to private efforts like that of Rubenstein's.

The content of books from the ancient world appears to have been brought into the digital age largely through private efforts. Through various eras, libraries, scribes, and printers were supported to a great extent through private patronage.

Ecclesiastical institutions were critical in preserving texts that are important to the Western tradition, points out Dr. Ryan Olson, director of education policy at the Mackinac Center for Public Policy and holder of a doctorate in the classics from Oxford University. For example, Olson says, in the sixth century Cassiodorus finished his career as a government official in Ravenna and organized monastic efforts to copy Christian and classical texts. Some work of his monks seems to have ended up in Rome, where it could be more influential. Though the history of transmission can be difficult to trace, scholars have argued that at least one classical work, by Cato, seems to have survived to this day because of Cassiodorus's efforts. "It is our intention," Cassiodorus wrote shortly before his death, "to weave into one fabric and assign to proper usage whatever the ancients have handed down to modern custom."

Borrowing From Cicero

I also learned from Olson that the Roman politician, lawyer, and author Cicero revealed in his letters a network of extensive personal libraries that preserved important books that could be read by members of the public and even borrowed and sent with messengers. Books could be consulted or copied for one's own library and returned to the owner. If one wanted to look at several books, a personal visit to a private library could be arranged.

The Bodleian Library at Oxford, where Olson once studied, was founded by Sir Thomas Bodley and dedicated in 1602. King James I, on entering the library in August 1605, said its founder should be dubbed "Sir Thomas Godly." Bodley had spent his considerable personal wealth acquiring books and early manuscripts that have formed the core of one of the most extensive collections in the world. That collection includes among its innumerable treasures a first edition of Don Quixote, a manuscript of Confucius acquired at a time when few could read its Chinese characters, a fourteenth-century copy of Dante's *Divine Comedy*, as well as first editions of the works of John Milton, who called the library a "most sacred centre," a "glorious treasure-house" of "the best Memorials of Man."

Additional examples of historical preservation through private means are, it turns out, legion. Pittsburgh banker Andrew Mellon acquired a massive assortment of prized artwork. He donated his entire collection (plus $10 million for construction) to start the National Gallery of Art in Washington, D.C. Tens of thousands of historic homes and buildings all across America are owned and maintained privately, many of them refurbished and open for public viewing. Even historic lighthouses, once largely public property, are being preserved today by private owners after decades of neglect by government authorities. On and on it goes.

The more one looks into this, the more apparent it is that private efforts have not just been a sideshow in historical preservation. They have been the centerpiece. And why should it be otherwise? Private owners invest their own resources, acquiring an instant and personal interest in the "capital" value of the historical asset. Being a government employee does not make one more interested in, or better equipped to care for, the things we regard as historically valuable than those many private citizens who put their own resources on the line.

By the way, have you ever noticed that the greatest book-burners in history have been governments, not private individuals?

So what's the problem with a copy of Magna Carta being purchased by a private citizen? Nothing at all. To suggest otherwise is simply to repeat an uninformed and antiquated prejudice. In a civil society of free people, that prejudice should be rare enough to be a museum piece.

—*LWR, May 2008*

Part V

The Negative Power of the Bureaucrat

32

Chapter **Thirty-Two**

John Jacob Astor and the Fur Trade: Testing the Role of Government

What was the first industry in U.S. history to receive a federal subsidy? That dubious honor seems to go to the fur trade. If we study the story of the fur trade, we can see why government-supported companies so often fail and why entrepreneurs tend to provide better products at lower costs.

The buying and selling of furs was a major industry in America throughout its early history. The key animal in the fur trade was the beaver, whose pelt made hats that were in style all over Europe in the 1700s. The fur trade was a worldwide enterprise. It linked fashionable women in Paris to New York exporters, to frontier traders, to Indian trappers. The pelts of beavers, muskrats, otters, and minks went one way and kettles, blankets, axes, and muskets went the other.

At first, fur trading in the United States followed established patterns. The French and British had traded with the Indians for more than a century and the Americans simply picked up where they left off. Trapping methods, river routes, and trading posts were all in place.

The man who confounded the normal development of private enterprise in furs was none other than President George Washington. Washington feared that the many British fur traders along the Canadian border might stir up the Indians, win their loyalties, and thwart U.S. expansion into its own territory.

Private American traders, Washington argued, were too small to compete with larger, more experienced British enterprises. The U.S. government itself was needed to build large trading posts, oust the British, "bring in a small profit, . . . and fix them [the Indians] strongly in our Interest." The Indians especially needed to see evidence of American strength, so Washington recommended that the government build and operate a series of fur factories throughout the American South and West. With Washington's support, Congress appropriated $50,000 for the new factories in 1795 and raised it steadily in later years to a total of $300,000. Such a subsidy was a large expense for a new nation, and one that tested government's ability to act as an entrepreneur.

Here is how the factory system worked. The government created a bureaucracy—the Office of Indian Affairs—to conduct the fur trade. It used the $300,000 from Congress to set up trading posts (usually near military forts), stock them with goods, and pay agents to buy, store, and transfer furs from the trading post to Washington, D. C., where they would be sold at auction. Once the factories were funded, they were supposed to be self-supporting, and perhaps, as Washington said, "bring in a small profit." Agents in the factories would use the first batch of goods to buy furs; then when the furs were sold, the agents could buy more goods and repeat the cycle.

Thomas McKenney and the Office of Indian Affairs

Almost from the start, however, the factory system struggled. Well into the 1800s, the British companies were trading actively throughout the Great Lakes area. So were private American traders. The factories were so poorly run that many Indians held them in contempt and refused to trade there. In 1816, President Monroe appointed Thomas McKenney, a Washington merchant, to take charge of the Office of Indian Affairs and help the factories expand their business.

McKenney worked hard and took his job seriously. He wrote long letters to Indians, invited them to Washington, and tried to expand his staff so he could deal with them more directly. Indians needed to be assimilated into American life, McKenney argued. Schools and farms, not trapping and hunting, were McKenney's vision for future Indian life. Therefore, he stocked the factories with hoes, plows, and other farm equipment. An active government, McKenney believed, was the best means to "amend the heads and hearts of the Indian."

McKenney's ideas proved to be a disaster. Indians wanted rifles and kettles, not hoes and plows. But since McKenney was funded regularly each year by government, regardless of his volume of trade, he had no incentive to change his tactics. Private traders, however, had to please Indians or go broke. As private traders grew in numbers and wealth in the early 1800s, one of them, John Jacob Astor, grew so rich he surpassed the government factories in capital, influence, and volume of business.

John Jacob Astor: **Risk-Taker and World Trader**

Astor, the son of a German butcher, came to the United States in 1784 at age 20 to join his brother in selling violins and flutes. Soon, however, he changed his tune. He became fascinated with the fur trade and studied it day and night. He learned prices, markets, and trade routes for all kinds of pelts. The fur territory—New York, Montreal, and the American Northwest—he traveled and mastered. Astor bought and sold cautiously at first, then with more confidence as the profits rolled in.

He was an odd man to be such a risk-taker. He was quiet, almost secretive, in his business dealings. Astor had a keen mind for enterprise, but he spent years at a time out of the United States, estranged from his wife and fighting bouts of depression. He was both decisive and patient. He had a vision of how America would grow, how the fur trade fit into that growth, and how to market furs around the world. With commanding vision and masterful detail he could profitably buy furs in Michigan, pack them on a boat to New York, ship them to China, and bring tea back home.

Astor separated himself from others through his foresight and perseverance. If the matrons of France wanted beaver hats and otter coats, and if these animals roamed the forests of New York, that was all most traders cared to know. Astor, however, thought more of world trade. Europeans liked to fight each other and wars disrupted markets; why not expand and sell furs to the Chinese—not for fashion, but for warmth in their unheated houses? Besides, he could bring the tea back from China and profit at both ends.

The large market of the Far East prompted Astor to turn his sights west to Michigan. New York and the Atlantic Coast were depleted of furs by the early 1800s. The Great Lakes area—especially the Michigan Territory—then became the heart of the fur trade, yielding thousands of skins for coats and rugs all over the world. Astor founded the American Fur Company in 1808 and made his move to challenge the government factories.

Under Astor, the American Fur Company resembled a modern corporation with specialists, division of labor, and vertical integration. Astor ran the company from his headquarters in New York. Mackinac Island was the center of the actual trading, where most furs were bought, packed on boats, and sent to the East Coast. Astor's agents dotted the rivers throughout the Northwest and they had log cabins well-stocked with goods. They supplied the company's fur traders, who would live with the different Indian tribes and supply them with goods and credit as needed.

Astor's Advantage

In conducting business this way, Astor differed from McKenney and the government factories. McKenney and his predecessors just built trading posts, stocked them with goods, and expected the Indians to come there to trade. Many Indians, however, lived hundreds of miles from a factory and had no supplies to trap with. Even if McKenney had given credit easily, and had known whom to trust, the Indians would have been hampered by distances. Under Astor's system, the fur traders lived with the Indians, learned whom to trust, and bought and sold on the spot. If an Ottawa brave capsized his canoe and lost his musket and powder, he could get replacements from Astor's local trader and avoid the 90-mile walk through swirling snow to see if the government agent in Detroit would give him replacements on credit.

Astor built on this advantage by trading the best supplies he could find at reasonable rates of exchange. Indians wanted guns and blankets, for example, and Astor supplied them at low cost. The best blankets he could find were British-made blue-striped blankets, and Astor bought them at 15 percent less than McKenney paid for lower quality blankets made in America. Astor bought British Tower muskets, the best on the market, for about $10 apiece, but McKenney paid $12.50 apiece for Henry Deringer's muskets made in Philadelphia.

One reason Astor succeeded was that he accepted the Indians as they were, not as he wanted them to be. If they desired axes, kettles, and muskets, he tried to find the best available and sell to them at competitive prices. He respected Indians as shrewd traders and knew he had to have the best goods to get the most business. McKenney, as we have seen, squandered government resources on goods Indians didn't want.

McKenney refused to sell liquor in government factories and urged Indians to be sober, virtuous, and industrious. "The same devotion to the chase, and those irregular habits which have characterized the sons of our forests yet predominate," he lamented.

Liquor was also an item Astor preferred not to supply, even though he knew many Indians wanted it. Not that Astor was a moralist; he was a realist. Drunken trappers gathered no pelts, he discovered. If the factories had been his only competition he probably wouldn't have traded liquor at all. But the traders with Britain's Hudson's Bay Company carried so much liquor they could almost have created another Great Lake with it. Astor thus concluded that for him to be competitive he needed to have some liquor available for trade.

Motivation and Marketing

Trade was not the only area where Astor outmaneuvered the government factories. The motivating of men was another. Astor used a merit system and paid his chief managers good salaries plus a share of the profits. This guaranteed an attention to detail, which Astor needed to stay on top. McKenney and his staff, by contrast, received a standard salary from Congress with no bonuses given in profitable years or cuts given when trade fell.

One final area of Astor's genius was his marketing savvy. He sold his furs at auctions all over the world. If he didn't get the prices he wanted in New York he sent furs to auctions in Montreal, London, Hamburg, and Canton. McKenney, by contrast, had the furs collected in his factories sent to Washington. Then he sold them at auction in nearby Georgetown for whatever price they would bring. He didn't sell in different cities, nor did he withhold any from the market in bad years.

Sometime after 1808, John Jacob Astor surpassed the government factories and emerged as the leading exporter of furs in the United States. He widened his lead after the War of 1812. By the 1820s, the American Fur Company employed over 750 men, not counting the Indians, and collected annual fur harvests of about $500,000, which made it one of the largest companies in America.

McKenney nervously watched the government's share of the fur trade decline year by year. "Why do the factories lose money?" Congress asked when McKenney came before them each year to renew his subsidy. He was embarrassed by Astor's dominance and perplexed at what to do about it. At one point, he urged his agents, or "factors" as they were called, to stir up Indians against private traders. "[A]ll correct means that may be taken to expel those traders," McKenney wrote, would be "of service to humanity and justice."

By 1818, McKenney had reached a dramatic conclusion: the best way to beat Astor was to influence Congress to ban all private fur traders. If this could be done, McKenney could monopolize the fur trade, sell the Indians what he wanted them to have, and pursue his dream of amending their heads and hearts. "Armies themselves," McKenney argued, "would not be so effectual in regulating the native Inhabitants as would a state of dependence on the Government for their *commercial intercourse*." Sure, McKenney admitted, a monopoly "embraces the idea of compulsion. But the power over the Indians is coveted [sic] only for their good—and also to prevent them from doing harm."

John C. Calhoun, Secretary of War and later vice president, was swayed by McKenney's ideas. "The trade should," Calhoun wrote, "as far as practicable, be put effectually under the control of the Government, in order that . . . [the Indians] may be protected against the fraud and the violence to which their ignorance and weakness would, without such protection, expose them."

Even with friends in high places, however, McKenney couldn't muster the support in Congress to ban private fur trading. He therefore presented two backup plans. First, the government should increase his subsidy from $300,000 to $500,000. Second, McKenney wanted to increase the license fees for his competitors. If he couldn't ban private fur traders by law, perhaps he could raise their costs of doing business, and thereby improve the competitive position of his factories.

Astor hated to play politics, but he believed he had to be politically shrewd to survive. He wrote President Monroe and explained how the American Fur Company helped the U.S. economy. Other politicians came to Astor's aid. Governor Ninian Edwards of the Illinois Territory challenged Calhoun: "For my part, I have never been able to discover, and I defy any man to specify, a solitary public advantage that has resulted from it [the factory system] in this country."

From 1816 to 1822, Congress heard from both sides and had frequent debates on the fur trade. For both sides, it was a fight to the death. When McKenney's factories showed a drop in fur sales from $73,305 in 1816 to $28,482 in 1819, his case began to weaken.

Astor then took the offensive and urged Congress to abolish the whole factory system. His first step was to get Congress to see how unpopular the factories were with Indians. Calhoun, McKenney's ally, unwittingly cooperated when, as Secretary of War, he helped authorize Jedidiah Morse, a neutral observer and Congregational minister, to go into Indian country and report on the Indian trade.

Morse visited most of the government factories and interviewed the men who worked in them as well as the private traders nearby. In his report he came down clearly against the factories. "In the first place," Morse wrote, "I have to observe that the Factory system . . . does not appear to me to be productive of any great advantage, either to the Indians themselves, or to the Government." This conclusion was devastating because it revealed that the factory system had failed to do what Washington set it up to do—impress the Indians, gain their respect, and challenge the British in the Northwest Territory. Morse further wrote that "the Indians, who are good judges of the quality of the articles they want, are of the opinion that the Factor's goods are not so cheap, taking into consideration their quality, as those of private traders."

Morse was not completely pleased with private traders. They traded too much whiskey, he wrote, and they gave Indians too much on credit, which weakened their work ethic. But he couldn't deny their success or the "want of confidence in the Government . . . expressed by the Indians in my interviews with them."

Armed with the Morse report, Astor's allies in Congress moved to abolish the factories in 1822. Thomas Hart Benton, the new senator from Missouri, had been a lawyer for Astor and knew the fur trade well. On the Senate floor he ridiculed McKenney's purchases, particularly the eight gross (1,152) jew's harps he had recently sent to the factories. What use, Benton asked, could Indians have for jew's harps? "I know!" he said sarcastically. "They are part of McKenney's schemes to amend the heads and hearts of the Indians, to improve their moral and intellectual faculties, and to draw them from the savage and hunter state, and induct them into the innocent pursuits of civilized life."

The End of the Factory System

Not surprisingly, Benton urged Congress to end the factory system. Most Congressmen agreed. The Senate voted 17 to 11 to end the factories, and the House soon followed. On May 6, 1822, President Monroe signed Benton's bill.

The closing of the factories was a story in itself. The merchandise inside them was to be collected and sold at auctions around the country. The money received would then be returned to the government to offset the $300,000 federal subsidy. The auctions themselves, which became the true test of the market value of the articles in the factories, brought grim news. The government, on its $300,000 investment, received a return of only $56,038.15. As Senator Benton had said, The factory system grew out of a national calamity, and has been one itself.

Many Congressmen were astounded at the waste of government funds revealed by the auctions. If Astor could make millions of dollars trading furs, how could the government lose hundreds of thousands?

Critics demanded answers and Congress formed a committee to investigate the unprofitability of the factories. They sifted through mountains of records and interviewed lines of witnesses. McKenney was on the spot and had to testify, but the committee found no corruption, just inexplicable losses. The factory system just failed, the committee concluded, but it needed to be studied "not only as a matter of curious history, but for the lesson it teaches to succeeding legislators."

Astor, meanwhile, continued to expand and prosper. New companies entered the fur trade during the 1820s and existing ones continued to challenge Astor. The competition was keen and Astor's volume of business varied from place to place. The American Fur Company, however, remained the largest firm in the field after the factories were closed. Astor, better than any American before him, had mastered the complex accounting and organization needed to conduct a worldwide business.

Astor and McKenney: An Epilogue

By the late 1820s and into the 1830s, the fur trade began to decline. Astor always knew the trade couldn't flourish forever—furs were being collected faster than new animals were growing them. Changing tastes slowed down business even more than the scarcity of animals. As Astor noted from Paris in 1832, "they make hats of silk in place of Beaver." Also, the Industrial Revolution and the popularity of cheap, mass-produced clothing shut down markets for furs. "[M]any articles of manufacture which are now very low can be used in place of deer skins & furs," Astor observed in 1823. "[T]hey receive of course the preference." Evidently it didn't occur to Astor to try to get the government to handicap or eliminate his competition.

In 1834, three years before Michigan became a state, Astor quit the fur business and sold the American Fur Company. He was 71 years old and ready to do less strenuous work. The same skills that made him America's largest fur trader also made him profits in New York real estate. For many years, Astor had been buying lots in northern Manhattan, developing the property, and selling it at a profit. This he continued to do. He also invested in the Park Theatre, the Mohawk and

Hudson Railroad Company, and the Astor House Hotel. By the time of his death in 1848, he had accumulated America's largest fortune, about $10 million.

The last years of McKenney's life were not so pleasant. Outside of government, he struggled as a businessman, writer, and lecturer. His wife died, and his son became a wastrel. McKenney lived out of his suitcase, borrowing money and moving from city to city. In 1859 he died, at age 73, destitute, in a Brooklyn boarding house.

—BWF, June 1997

For readers interested in learning more about Astor and McKenney, the author recommends John Denis Haeger, *John Jacob Astor: Business and Finance in the Early Republic* (Detroit: Wayne State University Press, 1991); and Herman J. Viola, *Thomas L. McKenney: Architect of America's Early Indian Policy, 1816–1830* (Chicago: Swallow Press, 1974).

33

Chapter **Thirty-Three**

Why Did the National Road Fail?

"Let's build a national road across the country!" many Americans cried in the early 1800s. The idea of a national road was appealing because it would encourage settlement by connecting the east coast with the interior of the recent Louisiana Purchase.

So popular was the idea that in 1806, Congress voted to fund such a road, and Thomas Jefferson signed the bill. Constitutional arguments were important in this debate. Those who favored the road argued that it was a "post road" for mail delivery, and thus was consistent with Article 1, Section 8, of the Constitution.

But would the national road—which would eventually stretch from Cumberland, Maryland, to Vandalia, Illinois—be economically sound? Put another way, even if the road was a good idea, was government funding the best means to achieve it? After more than 700 miles and $7 million in construction costs, we can answer that question. No, the national road was not sound. Nor was it particularly helpful to westward settlement. By 1850 it was little used, and soon after that it was almost abandoned. What went wrong and why?

173

Three problems inherent in government funding help explain why the national road largely failed.

First, when government money is used to build a road, political decisions, not economic ones, dictate where it is built. In other words, congressmen with political pull will try to draw the road to their districts, whether that route is economically sound or not. As the national road moved north and west from Cumberland to Wheeling, (West) Virginia, it detoured through Union-town and Washington, Pennsylvania. Why? Because Jefferson's treasury secretary, Albert Gallatin, lived in Uniontown, and he persuaded Jefferson to swing the road there. Gallatin also urged Jefferson to run the road on a northern detour into vote-rich Washington County during an election year. "[T]he county of Washington," Gallatin wrote Jefferson, "with which I am well acquainted, having represented it for six years in Congress, gives a uniform majority of about 2000 votes in our favor and that if this be thrown, by reason of this road, in a wrong scale, we will infallibly lose the State of Pennsylvania in the next election." Jefferson responded curtly that "a few towns in that quarter [of Pennsylvania] seem to consider all this expense as undertaken merely for their benefit." But he still sanctioned Gallatin's detours.

Second, when the government builds a road, it will cost more than if entrepreneurs build it. The national road was built with stone (crushed and solid), and it became one of the most expensive roads, if not the most expensive, in the United States in the early 1800s. For example, the privately funded Lancaster Turnpike, also built with stone, cost $7,500 per mile—versus $13,000 per mile for the national road. The builders of the Lancaster Turnpike were spending their own money and had to spend it wisely, or the tolls would not cover their expenses. Those in charge of the national road, by contrast, were political appointees, described by one newspaper editor as being "as numerous as the locusts of Egypt." Funded with taxpayer dollars, the national road never charged tolls, so it never had to turn a profit.

This leads to the final point. Because no one owned the national road, no one had a strong stake in building it well, or preserving it once it was finished. Almost every firsthand account we have suggests that the road was shoddily constructed. Even in its heyday it was never fully paved; it always had gaps and always needed repairing.

For example, Lt. Henry Brewerton of the Corps of Engineers inspected the road in Ohio and found inferior mortar and materials in its construction and tree stumps scattered throughout. Brewerton echoed those who claimed the road fell into disrepair faster than it could be built. Western travelers moaned constantly about the bumpy rides, the steep grades, and the mudslides. David Shriver, the superintendent of the road, complained that travelers stole bridge walls, milestones, and building materials. Lucius Stockton, who traveled the whole of the road and tried to run a passenger service on it, said, "Generally speaking the surface is entirely destroyed, or sunk under the foundation. . . . In one place the foundation itself has been carried away."

R. J. Meigs, the U.S. Postmaster General in the 1820s, found the road almost impassable and the mail, therefore, almost undeliverable. So slow and erratic was federal mail delivery on it that many merchants along the road used private couriers to ensure speedy and reliable mail service.

Express Mail Started

How ironic! Using the national road as a federal post road was the key to making it constitutional—yet privatized mail service regularly outperformed the U.S. Post Office. In desperation, the Post Office added "express mail" service to try to compete with private couriers on the road, but even that often proved to be slower and more irregular than the private couriers. Angry residents along the road and elsewhere sent express-mail letters postage-due to congressmen complaining about the poor service. Reeling from an avalanche of hostile letters, the Postmaster General instructed all postmasters not to deliver any express mail postage-due to "the President or any head of department."

By the 1830s, therefore, many congressmen were having second thoughts about using federal funds for the national road. Some of them, like John Campbell of South Carolina, asked, "Who can suppose that the opening of roads by the government is necessary to attract the farmer to the virgin soil of the West?" Other roads, built by the states or by entrepreneurs, also brought immigrants westward. These roads were clearly constitutional, and they needed no federal tax dollars to operate.

The U.S. government, therefore, began in the 1830s to give pieces of the national road to the states in which they were located. Pennsylvania and Maryland, however, refused to accept their pieces even as gifts until they were repaired and made more usable for travel. By 1840, railroads had emerged, and the national road, even the serviceable parts, was becoming obsolete. But it did serve a useful purpose in teaching Americans this lesson: federally funded transportation is neither a necessary nor a desirable way to fill a continent with settlers.

—BWF, July 2004

34

Chapter **Thirty-Four**

Should Government Build the Railroads?

On July 12, 1831, President Andrew Jackson, who was no prankster, did something that made many people laugh, some curse, and others rub their eyes in disbelief. He appointed 19-year-old Stevens T. Mason to be secretary and acting governor of the Michigan Territory.

Granted, Mason was a very intelligent teenager and his family was nationally prominent. But surely, his critics wondered, this was the worst case of political patronage ever seen. During the next ten years, however, the youthful Mason would often vindicate Jackson's judgment. Mason went from acting governor to elected governor. He plotted the strategy that brought Michigan into the Union, and he made deals that defined Michigan's boundaries on two peninsulas. Unfortunately, he also launched a gigantic scheme of state-run railroads and canals that almost bankrupted the state. As a result, Michigan voters went to the polls en masse to make their state a haven for free enterprise for the rest of the century.

The Mason story begins not in Michigan, but in New York, along a remarkable ditch that was dug in the 1820s. The Erie Canal, an astonishing achievement in engineering, had a big impact on American thinking. Here we had a canal 364 miles long that connected the Great Lakes with the Atlantic coast—and it was built not by entrepreneurs but by the state of New York. Suddenly New York City could trade with farms and cities throughout the midwest. Profits from tolls flowed into the state, and the whole Great Lakes region was open to settlement and trade.

Shortly after 1825, tens of thousands of New Yorkers and New Englanders filtered into Michigan via the Erie Canal. Governor Mason himself used the Erie Canal eagerly when he had to go to Washington to see President Jackson. Almost everyone in Michigan gushed with praise for this new canal, which brought them immigrants and took their exports. The message seemed obvious: states that want to get ahead need active governments to tax their citizens to build a transportation network.

To compete with New York, for example, Pennsylvania spent $14.6 million on its Main Line Canal from Philadelphia to Pittsburgh. Maryland and Massachusetts joined in the rush with a variety of state-supported projects. Illinois and Indiana began elaborate canal networks in 1837, just when Michigan entered the Union. This was when railroads were being built, and some states began to lay track and buy locomotives.

The State as Creator

To Mason this was all exhilarating. Maybe the traditional theory of limited government was wrong. Maybe states could be creators, at least in the area of transportation. And after all, it was state governments, not the one in Washington, that were building these canals.

Even as territorial governor, Mason urged Michigan to lay the foundation for the state to build internal improvements. When delegates met in 1835 to write the Michigan constitution, they—with Mason's encouragement—wrote the following into law:

> Internal improvements shall be encouraged by the government of this state; and it shall be the duty of the legislature, as soon as may be, to make provisions by law for ascertaining the proper objects of improvement, in relation to [roads], Canals, and navigable waters. . . .

In other words, Michigan's constitution almost required the state to fund internal improvements.

After this constitution was adopted, Mason publicly supported an activist state government. "The spirit and enterprise which has arisen among our citizens, if fostered and encouraged by the State, cannot fail to lead to lasting prosperity," Mason said. By 1837, three weeks before Michigan entered the Union, Mason was more urgent: "The period has arrived when Michigan can no longer, without detriment to her standing and importance as a state, delay the action necessary for the development of her vast resources and wealth." He was also optimistic: "we cannot fail soon to reach that high destiny which awaits us. I . . . demand immediate legislative action."

With Mason leading the cheers, the legislature met and almost unanimously passed an elaborate internal improvements bill. Democrats and Whigs alike joined in the public support for it. When the alternate strategy of private ownership came up, Mason recommended that the canals and railroads "should never be beyond at least the partial control of the state." "Extortion from the public" was what Mason called one bill to charter a private railroad. Most Michiganians seemed to agree. *The Detroit Daily Advertiser* noted that "Dewitt Clinton . . . built the [Erie] Canal with the funds of the state. What would be thought of the policy of surrendering that great work to the control of a private corporation[?]"

The example of the Erie Canal had become the ace that trumped all opposing arguments. And if one state subsidy was good, two must be better, and three better yet. Michiganians were so confident that state projects would flourish that they promised to build two railroads from Lake Erie to Lake Michigan, and a couple of major canals across the state as well.

Bad Luck, Bad Judgment

Mason thought the state should spend $5 million to build these projects. Actually, that was just start-up money. As soon as the anticipated tolls started pouring in—as happened with the Erie Canal—the state could then build more. The legislature approved the $5 million. Then the legislature authorized the governor to negotiate a $5 million loan with the lender of his choice under the best terms he could get, as long as he didn't exceed 5¼ percent. The state, in this arrangement, would issue bonds for the $5 million and pay them back as tolls came in from the railroads and canals.

Bad luck was the first problem to strike. The national economy went into a tailspin—the Panic of 1837—and capital was hard to borrow. Then came distractions. While in New York to talk with investors and study the bond market, Mason became sidetracked by Julia Phelps, the daughter of a wealthy leather merchant, Thaddeus Phelps. Mason courted and married her in 1838.

Then came bad judgment. Businesses were failing because of the panic, and most sound investors wanted more than 5¼ percent for their money. Mason finally persuaded the officers of the Morris Canal and Banking Company, a reputable firm, to buy the Michigan bonds. They promised to pay him the $5 million in regular $250,000 installments over several years. Mason gave them the bonds and went back to Michigan with their promise. The Morris Company turned most of the bonds over to the Pennsylvania Bank of the United States, which then sent them to Europe as collateral for its own investments. Within three years, both the Morris Company and the Pennsylvania Bank went broke, leaving Michigan with a $5 million debt scattered among European investors.

The Clinton-Kalamazoo Canal

An even greater disaster were the projects Michigan built. First was a canal that was to begin in Clinton Township near Detroit and extend 216 miles west to Kalamazoo. The Clinton-Kalamazoo Canal began with high hopes and much fanfare. Mason broke ground in Mt. Clemens in 1838 to celebrate the start of digging. Bands, parades, speeches, and a 13-gun salute commemorated the occasion. Then came reality. The Board of Internal Improvements, which Mason appointed to supervise the projects, hired different contractors for each mile of the canal, and these contractors each had different ideas on how to build a canal. One thing they all did wrong was to make the canal only 20 feet wide and four feet deep—too shallow for heavy freight and too narrow for easy passing.

After seven years and only 16 miles of digging, the ledger for the unfinished canal read: "Expenses $350,000, Toll Receipts $90.32." With funding scarce, the board decided sometime around 1843 to cut its losses, abandon the canal, and focus on the two railroads. When construction on the canal stopped, some workers went unpaid and they stole materials from the three locks on the canal. Soon even the completed parts of the canal were ruined.

The Michigan Central Railroad

The two railroads also had problems. The Michigan Central was to go from Detroit west through Ann Arbor, Jackson, and Kalamazoo and on to St. Joseph on Lake Michigan. Boats at St. Joseph could then take freight or passengers to Chicago and back. The route went through prosperous wheat farms and the state's larger cities, but poor construction and management of the road drained most of its profits each year. The Central was built with strap-iron rails, which consisted of thin strips of iron strapped onto wooden rails. These rails were too fragile to carry heavy loads. Rather than switch to the more expensive and durable T-rails, the Board of Internal Improvements chose to run regular heavy shipments over the existing tracks and repair them frequently. Not only was this practice dangerous, it was more costly to the state in the long run.

Robert Parks, who wrote a detailed book on Michigan's railroads, found a deplorable situation on the Central:

> [O]verloaded locomotives were run at twice the recommended safe speed. Under the strain of continuous operation and jarring impact of high speed on strap-iron rails, locomotives and cars were shaken to pieces, and the cost of operation mounted dramatically. Rails were broken and timbers crushed under the heavy loads bouncing over their surface.

By 1846, the Central had been extended only to Kalamazoo. It had technically been profitable each year, but did not earn enough to pay for needed repairs and new rails.

The Michigan Southern

The second railroad, the Michigan Southern, was to parallel the Central in the southern tier of counties from Monroe to New Buffalo. Financially, the Southern was a stunning failure. It had the same problem as the Central, with heavy loads on strap-iron rails. What's worse, the Southern was built poorly: the roadbed was shaky and the curves too sharp for locomotives. Monroe, on Lake Erie, proved to be too shallow a port for heavy freight to enter or exit. Also, the towns west of Monroe were too small to send much traffic on the Southern. By

1846, the road had only reached Hillsdale, about half-way across the state. It had cost over $1.2 million to build that far and its earnings were small. The road did little to move goods or people across the state; it drained capital that could have been used more wisely.

Michigan spent almost $4 million on the Clinton-Kalamazoo Canal, the Michigan Central, and the Michigan Southern. The state spent about $70,000 surveying the Michigan Northern Railroad, from Port Huron to Lake Michigan, before abandoning it. It also spent $47,000 clearing the route for a canal and turnpike near Saginaw. Officials soon quit the project, and the materials "either rotted or were expropriated by local residents."

Many of these problems occurred after Mason's terms as governor, but he received most of the blame because he had touted the projects and signed the loan. In 1837, he had narrowly won re-election, but in 1839 his Whig critics were loud and brutal. Mason chose not to seek a third term. By that year he had begun to consider if the problems with the projects were more than just bad luck or poor management. Maybe the state should never have drifted into economic development. In Mason's final address as governor, he said:

> [T]he error, if error there is, was the emanation of that false spirit of the age, which forced states, as well as individuals, to over-action and extended projects. If Michigan has overtasked her energies and resources, she stands not alone, but has fallen into that fatal policy, which has involved in almost unparalleled embarrassments so many of her sister states. Now, however, the period has arrived, when a corrective should be applied to the dangers which seem to surround her.

A "false spirit of the age," Mason said, may have moved states into the "fatal policy" of funding state projects. Michigan had too many railroads and canals and too few people to pay for them. But, as Mason had begun to realize, in a state-supported system this result would have been hard to avoid. The funding must come through the legislature, and the legislators naturally wanted projects in their districts. Jobs and markets were at stake. Some historians have suggested that if the Michigan Central had been the only project built, the strategy of state funding might have worked. But this was politically impossible. The legislators in the towns along the Central—Detroit, Ann Arbor, and Kalamazoo—needed votes from elsewhere to have their railroads built.

The price for these votes was a commitment to build canals in Mt. Clemens and Saginaw and a railroad in Monroe and Hillsdale.

Political Manipulation

Mason actually saw this problem early and tried to stop it by centralizing power in the Board of Internal Improvements. The board's decisions, however, proved to be just as politically motivated as the legislature's. Many legislators pressured (and possibly bribed) members and some secretly made money from projects.

The story of Levi Humphrey is a case in point. Mason appointed Humphrey, a key Democrat in the state, to the board. When Humphrey took bids for constructing the Michigan Southern, he manipulated the results to assure that his friends in the firm of Cole and Clark won the contracts. Cole and Clark then charged three to four times the market price for supplies. When the complaints reached the legislature, Cole and Clark used some of their profits to bribe witnesses. The Whigs complained loudly, but when they won the governorship in 1839, they did not do much better. In 1840, the board overspent its budget and covered it by falsifying its records.

The problem was not just corruption; it was human nature. Officials did not spend state money as wisely as they would have spent their own. If Mason, for example, had been a wealthy industrialist, would he have invested $5 million of his own money with bankers he hardly knew during a national depression? Would any of the legislators have done so?

The spending policies of the board raise similar questions. In 1838, for example, it had a bridge built over the River Rouge. The problem was that the bridge they decided to build could not carry heavy freight. The Central, not the builders, lost almost $10,000 that year hauling passengers and freight around the bridge. Since no individual owned the bridge, no one had a direct financial stake in building it well—or even protecting it. The next year an arsonist destroyed the bridge.

In another example, the board ordered iron spikes for the Michigan Southern in 1841. The contractors, however, only put one spike in every other hole along the track. They stole the rest of the spikes and, when questioned, they persuaded the board that the unused spikes were defective. The board did not own the spikes or even have to ride on the rickety railroad that resulted; they simply believed the contractors and left the track partly unspiked.

The Boy Governor, no longer a boy, left office in 1840 at age 28. He had served almost nine years as secretary, acting governor, and elected governor. During this time, he had focused so intently on administration that he had left office almost penniless. He decided to leave Michigan for New York City, his wife's home, and make his fortune there in law and business. As he entered Buffalo and made his way across the Erie Canal to New York City, he may have wondered why the experiment with an active government worked so much better in New York than in Michigan. During the next two years, however, if Mason studied local politics, he saw New York repeat Michigan's experience. State legislators in districts outside the Erie Canal area had won eight new canal projects at a cost of $9.4 million. These new canals failed miserably and caused an economic collapse in the state, forcing eight banks to close and new taxes to be imposed.

Pennsylvanians did even worse. They spent $14.6 million on a risky canal from Philadelphia to Pittsburgh. The large losses on it each year helped force the state into default on its bonds. Several other states also defaulted on their internal improvement bonds, which damaged U.S. credit abroad and made Michigan look better. How much attention Mason paid to this we don't know. He died of scarlet fever on January 5, 1843, at age 31.

Mason was gone, but his "false spirit of the age" speech in 1840 had reopened the debate in Michigan on the role of the state in economic development. Right from the start, the government lost money building and operating the state's system of canals and railroads. William Woodbridge, the governor who followed Mason, first suggested selling the railroads to entrepreneurs and getting government out of the internal improvements business. At first, many resisted the idea. Legislators wanted railroads in their districts at taxpayer expense; they worried that entrepreneurs would build them elsewhere.

"The Errors of Our Policy . . ."

As the number of blunders on the projects began to multiply, however, more pressure came for the state to privatize. John Barry, who was elected governor after Woodbridge, echoed Mason and talked about "the spirit of the times unfortunately [becoming] the governing policy of states." Barry argued that "in extraordinary cases only . . . should a state undertake the construction of public works." He continued: "Seeing now the errors of our policy and the evils resulting from a departure from correct principle, let us with the least possible delay correct the one by a return to the other."

Thomas Cooley, Michigan's most prominent lawyer in the 1800s, observed firsthand the way the state ran its railroads. In a history of the state, he wrote, "Doubts were arising in the minds of the people whether the state had been wise in undertaking the construction and management" of internal improvements. "These doubts soon matured into a settled conviction that the management of railroads was in its nature essentially a private business, and ought to be in the hands of individuals. By common consent it came to be considered that the state in entering upon these works had made a serious mistake."

By 1846 Governor Alpheus Felch, who had followed Barry, carried the day for privatization. "The business of transporting passengers and freight by railroad is clearly not within the ordinary design of state government," Felch observed. The legislature finally agreed and voted to sell the state's public works in 1846. The state took bids and sold the Central for $2 million and the Southern for $500,000. As a result, Michigan recovered 90 percent of its investment in the Central and 44 percent in the Southern. If the losses on the canals and other projects are included, the state—through this sale—recaptured about 55 percent of its total investment in internal improvements. This decision helped the state cut its bureaucracy and also avoid bankruptcy.

As a condition of the sale, the new railroad owners had to agree to rebuild both lines with quality rails and extend them to Lake Michigan within three years. It had taken the state nine years to move the lines not much more than half-way across the state; the new entrepreneurs had to rebuild that part and complete the rest in just three years. When they did so, while keeping rates competitive, Michiganians knew they had learned something. They moved quickly to write this discovery into law.

A New Constitution

The next year, 1850, Michigan held a state constitutional convention. The proper role of government was one of the issues. The 1835 constitution, which mandated government support for internal improvements, was changed to include this: "The State shall not subscribe to or be interested in the stock of any company, association, or corporation." Further, "the state shall not be a party to or interested in any work of internal improvement, nor engaged in carrying on any such work" except for the donation of land.

The public debate that followed showed much support for the new constitution. "Looking at it as a whole," said the *Grand Rapids Enquirer*, "we honestly believe that if it had been adopted at the organization of our State Government, our State would now be out of debt, prosperous, and flourishing." In November 1850, the voters of Michigan overwhelmingly accepted the new constitution. Michigan had learned from its history. The building of railroads and the development of resources—lumber, copper, and chemicals—would be done by private enterprise.

—BWF, June 1998

Chapter **Thirty-Five**

Death by Public Works

Almost all historians who write on the New Deal praise Franklin Roosevelt for using government to "solve" economic problems. Often, however, these historians only tell part of the story. One example is Roosevelt's vast public-works program. Here most historians wax eloquent on the dams built by TVA, the roads built by WPA, and the bridges built by FERA and CCC.

What the historians omit are the high taxes levied for these projects, the sometimes inept construction, and the behind-the-scenes politics where votes were traded to bring projects to the districts of powerful congressmen.

In some cases, New Deal programs not only failed, they also had death rates along the way. For example, there's the story of how Roosevelt sent World War I veterans to build bridges in the hurricane country of south Florida. At least 256 of these veterans died in FERA (Federal Emergency Relief Administration) camps in the Florida Keys, where they were sent in hurricane season with poor provisions and no plan of retreat or rescue.

The hurricane tragedy had its origin in a seemingly shrewd political decision by FDR. Unemployed veterans had been difficult to deal with. Ever since World War I they had campaigned in Congress for a special "bonus" for their service. In 1932 they put pressure on President Hoover by traveling to Washington, camping near the White House, and publicizing their demands for immediate payment for their wartime service. In a political blunder, Hoover decided to restore order among the rowdy veterans by sending Douglas MacArthur to confront them with cavalry, infantry, and six tanks. MacArthur decided to fire on them and disperse their camp—and photos blanketed the country showing the fleeing vets under fire from their own government. It was an election year, and when Roosevelt, then the Democrat candidate, saw the pictures and news reports, he reportedly told Felix Frankfurter, "Well, Felix, this will elect me."

Once in office, Roosevelt was determined not to repeat Hoover's mistake. Protesting veterans were not allowed to camp in Washington. They were directed to Ft. Hunt, Virginia, where they received offers to work in CCC (Civilian Conservation Corps) and FERA camps for $1 a day plus food and shelter. Thousands of veterans accepted this offer, and Roosevelt sent them far away from Washington to camps in South Carolina and Florida. In December 1934, over 400 veterans were specifically transferred to the Florida Keys, where they were told to build bridges and roads that would help connect the 90-mile area from Miami to Key West.

Roosevelt's plan to export the contentious vets to Florida was clever, but Harry Hopkins and FERA officials in Washington tended to ignore the veterans once they were out of the capital. In Florida, Fred Ghent, the director in charge of the three camps of 400 veterans, had trouble, first, getting supplies and, second, enlisting help in preparing for hurricanes. The veterans were housed on low land, almost at sea level, in tents and flimsy barracks with poor food, inadequate supplies, and no water for bathing. They had no serious shelter to protect them from a hurricane or even high tides.

In April, three months before hurricane season, Ghent became concerned about the possibility of storms. He wrote FERA in Washington that "this area is subject to hurricanes" and "it is our duty . . . to furnish a safe refuge during a storm." Specifically, he requested that a solid two-story warehouse be built and arrangements be made with the Florida East Coast Railway to transport the men out of the Keys if a hurricane warning should occur. Ghent never received a response from Washington, and in the absence of instructions he took no action.

Trouble began in late August with weather reports of possible hurricanes coming toward Florida. On Sunday, September 1, at 10 a. m. a weather bulletin reached Key West warning of hurricane danger. Residents 20 miles west boarded their houses. The owner of the Hotel Matecumbe, who was within one mile of the veterans' camps, boarded his hotel as well. Ghent was in Miami. The following day he finally sent a Florida East Coast Railway train to the veterans' camps. The railroad was in receivership and many crewmen were unavailable because of the holiday weekend. That day a severe hurricane hit the Keys and knocked the train off the tracks before it ever made it to the FERA camps.

When the full force of the hurricane hit the camps the carnage began. First-hand accounts among the few survivors reveal part of the horror: "There was a big wall of water—15 feet high—20, maybe," reported one veteran. It swept over those shacks and messed them up like they were match boxes." Another reported, "I heard William Clark holler that the roof [of the canteen] was coming down. We all started away in the same direction and the roof came down on us. It must have hit every one of us. After the roof fell all I could hear was the grunting and groaning of the boys. I never saw any of them after that."

After hours of the swirling hurricane one survivor said, "[B]odies were lying all over the roadway and lumber piled on them and some of them had holes in their heads." In the aftermath another said, "I saw bodies with tree stumps smashed through their chests—heads blown off—twisted arms and legs torn off by flying timber that cut like big knives." When the body parts were finally re-assembled the total count was 256 veterans dead. As *Time* magazine reported, "[I]t was slaughter worse than war."

Roosevelt Administration Takes Heat

When the news of the deadly hurricane reached Washington, many newspapers began criticizing the President and FERA. Hopkins denied responsibility, and his assistant, Aubrey Williams, called the tragedy an "act of God." The *Washington Post*, however, disagreed. "In spite of Relief Administrator Hopkins' denial that his organization was negligent in failing to evacuate the veterans on the Florida Keys, there is considerable evidence to support Governor [David] Sholtz's conclusion that 'gross carelessness somewhere' was responsible." D. W. Kennamer, whom the Veterans Administration assigned to investigate the deaths, concluded that "the only extenuating circumstance" for the failure to evacuate the veterans was Ghent's regret "that his letters to the National Emergency Relief Administration regarding this matter were unanswered."

In the search for responsibility, novelist Ernest Hemingway wrote an essay, "Who Murdered the Vets?" "[W]ho sent nearly a thousand war veterans . . . to live in frame shacks on the Florida Keys in hurricane months?" he asked. "Why were the men not evacuated on Sunday, or at latest, Monday morning, when . . . evacuation was their only possible protection?"

Neither President Roosevelt nor Harry Hopkins answered these questions.

The tragic deaths of America's hard-working veterans have almost disappeared from historical memory. Gary Dean Best's *FDR and the Bonus Marchers, 1933–1935*, is an excellent book, but it is the only one ever written on this tragedy. No U.S. history text I have ever seen even mentions the unnecessary deaths of these 256 men in a New Deal project.

This story needs to be remembered and retold. How can students make sound judgments on the proper role of government if they are sheltered from the negative unintended consequences of so many failed government programs?

—BWF, March 2007

36

Chapter **Thirty-Six**

The Origin of American Farm Subsidies

In the United States how did we go from having no role for the federal government in farming to having government intertwined in all aspects of farming from planting to harvesting to selling crops?

The Constitution is clear on the subject. Article 1, Section 8, provides no role for the federal government in regulating American farmers. And that is the way it was (with rare exceptions) until about 1930.

American farmers dominated world markets under the free-enterprise system. They were ever creative in figuring out how to gain larger yields of crops through mechanization or through improving crop strains, such as hybrid corn. Americans have been the best-fed people in the world.

Even during times of economic hardship, the federal government largely stayed out of the farm business. For example, during the mid-1890s, when we had a recession and 18 percent unemployment, the secretary of agriculture, J. Sterling Morton, focused on cutting budgets, not pushing subsidies. He chopped almost 20 percent off his department's budget, which allowed taxpayers to keep and spend more of their cash, rather than sending it to Washington. Morton fired unproductive bureaucrats, starting with a man who held the job of federal rainmaker. He slashed the travel budgets as well.

Furthermore, when beet-sugar producers came to Washington eager for some kind of special help, Morton said, "Those who raise corn should not be taxed to encourage those who desire to raise beets. The power to tax was never vested in a Government for the purpose of building up one class at the expense of other classes."

That philosophy, written in the Constitution by men who were themselves mainly planters and farmers, governed American farming for about 140 years. Even after World War I, when many farmers had to readjust from the high prices commanded during the war, Americans were still determined not to tax one economic group to support another.

One proposal during the 1920s, the McNary-Haugen bill, would have fixed prices of some crops by a complicated bureaucratic system and passed the costs on to American consumers. When Congress, under pressure from some farmers, passed the bill, Coolidge vetoed it.

In his veto message, Coolidge echoed major themes of limited government. "I do not believe," Coolidge said, "that upon serious consideration the farmers of America would tolerate the precedent of a body of men chosen solely by one industry who, acting in the name of the Government, shall arrange for contracts which determine prices, secure the buying and selling of commodities, the levying of taxes on that industry, and pay losses on foreign dumping of any surplus."

Coolidge then added, "There is no reason why other industries— copper, coal, lumber, textiles, and others—in every occasional difficulty should not receive the same treatment by the Government." He concluded, "Such action would establish bureaucracy on such a scale as to dominate not only the economic life but the moral, social, and political future of our people."

The next two presidents, Hoover and Roosevelt, broke the precedents set by Morton, Coolidge, and 140 years of American history. The Great Depression hit the United States, and both men argued that others must be taxed so that some farmers could be subsidized.

Hoover's program was the Farm Board, which fixed price floors for wheat and cotton only. If market prices went below 80 cents a bushel for wheat and 20 cents a pound for cotton, the federal government would step in to buy the crop, pay to store it, and hope to resell it later for a decent price.

The Farm Board had disastrous unintended consequences for almost everyone. For example, many farmers who typically grew other crops shifted to wheat or cotton because they were protected and now provided a secure income. The resulting overproduction forced down the prices of both crops below the price floors, so the government had to buy over 250 million bushels of wheat and 10 million bales of cotton. The costs of buying and storing these crops quickly used up the program's allotted $500 million. After about two years of buying surpluses, the government finally just gave them away or sold them on the world market at huge losses.

When Roosevelt became president, he also intervened in the farm business, but in a different way. He supported the Agricultural Adjustment Act (AAA), which dealt with the problem of oversupply by paying farmers not to produce. As for farm prices, they would be pegged to the purchasing power of farm prices in 1910; millers and processors would pay for much of the cost of the program, which of course meant an increase for consumers in the price of everything from bread to shirts.

Two concepts in the AAA are fascinating. First is the idea that because farmers overproduce some crops the government ought to pay them not to grow on part of their land. Second is the idea of "parity," that farmers ought to be protected from falling prices by fixing them so that they were comparable to the purchasing power of their crop in the excellent years 1909–14.

Let's tackle both of these concepts one at a time. First, Supreme Court Justice Owen Roberts voted with most of the rest of the Court to strike down the AAA as unconstitutional. In doing so, he posed the following analogy:

> Assume that too many shoes are being manufactured throughout the nation; that the market is saturated, the price depressed, the factories running half-time, the employees suffering. Upon the principle of the statute in question Congress might authorize the Secretary of Commerce to enter into contracts with shoe manufacturers providing that each shall reduce his output and that the United States will pay him a fixed sum proportioned to such reduction, the money to make the payments to be raised by a tax on all retail shoe dealers or their customers.

His conclusion echoed that of Coolidge's almost ten years earlier: "A possible result of sustaining the claimed federal power would be that every business group which thought itself under-privileged might demand that a tax be laid on its vendors or vendees, the proceeds to be appropriated to the redress of its deficiency of income."

Parity for Everyone?

In a similar vein, economist Henry Hazlitt challenged the concept of parity by noting that if we gave parity to farmers, why not to other groups? General Motors, for example, was in a deep slump during the Great Depression. Why not a parity price for cars? "A Chevrolet six-cylinder touring car cost $2,150 in 1912," Hazlitt observed, "an incomparably improved six-cylinder Chevrolet sedan cost $907 in 1942; adjusted for 'parity' on the same basis as farm products, however, it would have cost $3,270 in 1942."

Despite temporary resistance from the Supreme Court and American consumers, the farming industry, even after the Great Depression had long vanished, was and is dominated by the ideas of payments to reduce crops and fixing prices at higher-than-market levels. American politicians, under pressure during hard times, sacrificed the Constitution and economic sense for votes at the ballot box.

Once some farmers had their subsidies, they were viewed as entitlements and were hard to take away, even when the farm crisis was over. Perhaps the new Justice Roberts will mark a return to the earlier Justice Roberts, and the Supreme Court will limit the government to its historical role as an enforcer of contracts and a protector of private property.

—BWF, April 2006

37

Chapter **Thirty-Seven**

Lessons from the First Airplane

Mark your calendars! Prepare for commemorative events and feature stories in newspapers all across America. The date is December 17, 2003—the 100th anniversary of the first manned flight at Kitty Hawk, North Carolina, a feat engineered by two brothers named Wright. In one century the airplane went from a dream to a multibillion-dollar industry that transports hundreds of millions of people around the globe every year with speed and convenience that would surely astonish Wilbur and Orville today.

Though most Americans know something of that fateful day in 1903, far fewer are aware of the rivalry between the Wright brothers and another inventor/entrepreneur—one Samuel Pierpont Langley. It's a story that deserves retelling, and there's no better time to tell it than right now. A hundred summers ago, that rivalry was at a fever pitch, and it wasn't at all clear at first that the two bicycle mechanics from Dayton, Ohio, would eventually best the distinguished and better-financed Langley.

By the close of the nineteenth century the possibility of a man-carrying "flying machine" had captivated visionaries in many countries, though the general public regarded the idea as bunk. Nobody knew enough about aerodynamics to build a craft that could generate its own power, get up in the air with a man on board and stay there, and be flown safely and with precision.

In 1878 a simple gift from a father to his two sons—aged 7 and 11—planted the seed that would change history forever. It was a toy helicopter made of cork, bamboo, and paper, and powered by a rubber band. Wilbur and Orville Wright were mesmerized. They built their own copies and versions of it, fostering a lifelong fascination with flight. Twenty-one years later, in 1899, they took time out from their modest bicycle shop to begin the work that would lead to the world's first successful airplane.

Langley, meantime, was already way ahead of the Wrights. Born in 1834, he earned an international reputation for his work in physics and astronomy and by publishing a book on aerodynamics. He was secretary of the respected Smithsonian Institution in Washington, D.C. As early as 1896, he had even built and flown an unmanned "aerodrome"—a tandem-wing aircraft that used a lightweight steam engine for propulsion. He was sure he would be the man to invent the airplane, and probably deemed it unthinkable that young whippersnappers from small-town America could come out of nowhere with little money and beat him to it.

Both Langley and the Wright brothers had Smithsonian connections but with a huge and perhaps decisive difference. For Langley the Smithsonian was the conduit for a $50,000 federal grant, matched by the Institution, to finance his experiments (equivalent to about a million dollars in today's purchasing power). As for the Wrights, in 1899 Wilbur wrote a letter to the Smithsonian asking for nothing more than a reading list on flight. He and Orville would finance their dream not with government money, but with the nickels and dimes they could scrape from the profits in their private business.

During the summer and fall of 1903 Langley worked feverishly at his Washington home base. Because he felt it safest to fly over water, he spent half his money building a houseboat with a catapult to launch his newest craft with a man, Charles Manly, aboard. A catapult launch meant that the plane would have to go from a dead stop to a flying speed of 60 mph in just 70 feet, a feat that would prove beyond the reach of his craft's capabilities.

Meanwhile back in Dayton, Wilbur and Orville Wright worked on propeller design, a lightweight engine, and wings that mimicked the way pigeons flew, as the brothers observed them. What they put together solved the problem of controlling flight, which Langley's craft would never have achieved even if it had taken to the air.

On October 7, 1903, Langley's plane, with Manly aboard, was ready to go. At least that's what Langley and Manly thought. But the stress of the catapult launch badly damaged the front wing, and the plane tumbled over and disappeared in 16 feet of water. A reporter present wrote that it flew "like a handful of mortar." The hapless "pilot" was unharmed.

A second launch set for December 8 proved even more disastrous. The rear wing and tail collapsed at the moment of launch, and the plane dove right into the icy Potomac River. This time poor Manly nearly drowned. Financially, for both Langley and American taxpayers, it was a total loss.

Flying Money

Critics went wild. James Tobin, author of *To Conquer the Air: The Wright Brothers and the Great Race for Flight* (2003), quotes one congressman as saying at the time, "You tell Langley for me that the only thing he ever made fly was Government money." The War Department concluded that "we are still far from the ultimate goal, and it would seem as if years of constant work and study by experts, together with the expenditure of thousands of dollars, would still be necessary before we can hope to produce an apparatus of practical utility along these lines."

But just nine days after Langley's second spectacular flight to the bottom of the Potomac, Wilbur and Orville Wright took turns flying their carefully designed plane for as long as 59 seconds over the Outer Banks of North Carolina. The craft cost them about $1,000. It cost American taxpayers nothing. Within a year, they were making flights of five miles at a time; within two years, they were flying distances of 20 to 25 miles.

In November 1904 the Wrights offered to sell planes to the War Department. They weren't seeking a subsidy; they wanted to sell planes for military reconnaissance and communication. But they received the same form-letter refusal that the War Department routinely sent to "flying machine" cranks.

Now what on earth could be the lesson in this remarkable story? Could it be that government, as some argue, is more farsighted than the private sector and therefore subsidies are needed to spur new inventions? Or that government quickly sees the error of its ways and corrects its mistakes? Or that the pursuit of profit just adds another layer of cost and makes new inventions more expensive than necessary?

If you think any of those "lessons" apply, then the textbooks you've been reading belong right where Samuel Pierpont Langley's plane landed.

—*LWR, July 2003*

38

Chapter **Thirty-Eight**

Subsidies Hurt Recipients, Too

More than ever, historians need to study the economic consequences of government programs. Only by analyzing the results of past government intervention can we calculate the impact of future government intervention.

The Tennessee Valley Authority (TVA) provides a useful example. Established as part of the New Deal in the 1930s, it was a favorite program of Franklin Roosevelt's. Under the TVA the federal government built dams and generated hydroelectric power for residents of the Tennessee Valley. In the 1920s President Calvin Coolidge vetoed a TVA bill twice, and President Hoover vetoed it once. Both men believed that federal funding was unconstitutional, but FDR disagreed and signed it into law in 1933.

Many historians have praised the TVA as a centerpiece of the New Deal. "The TVA," wrote William Leuchtenburg, dean of New Deal historians, "was the most spectacularly successful of the New Deal agencies, not only because of its achievements in power and flood control, but because of its pioneering in areas from malaria control to library bookmobiles, from recreational lakes to architectural design."

Most historians have agreed.

But as TVA grew, some observers noticed problems. Standard bureaucratic inefficiency was one. Second were the Tennesseans who had to be relocated because of the flooding of land and destruction of property. Third were the existing private companies, such as the Tennessee Electric Light and Power Company, that had to compete with the taxpayer-subsidized TVA.

In fact, the taxpayer subsidy for TVA created what economist Henry Hazlitt called an "optical illusion." "Here is a mighty dam, a stupendous arc of steel and concrete . . . ." Hazlitt observed, "[a]nd it is all presented . . . as a net economic gain without offsets."

But 98 percent of the American population was subsidizing the 2 percent in the Tennessee Valley. "Again," Hazlitt concluded, "we must make an effort of the imagination to see the private power plants, the private homes, the typewriters and television sets that were never allowed to come into existence because of the money that was taken from people all over the country to build the photogenic Norris Dam."

What appeared to some Tennesseans to be an "economic miracle" was merely a transfer of wealth. But the voters in Tennessee made sure that they protected the TVA subsidy, and it has persisted and increased over time.

The case for the TVA (voters improving their lives through a federal subsidy) and the case against the TVA (bureaucratic inefficiencies plus the drain of taxpayer dollars) became standard arguments used to support or oppose other federal subsidies—both during and after the New Deal years.

Then came William U. Chandler with a devastating book, *The Myth of TVA*, written in 1983. Chandler said the problem was more complicated than that of the whole nation subsidizing a small part. He said the Tennessee Valley's prosperity was actually being held back by the TVA.

Chandler's evidence was astonishing. For example, Georgia, which had nothing equivalent to the TVA, and Tennessee had nearly identical levels of income before the TVA, but during the 1940s and 1950s Georgia (and other states nearby) began pulling ahead of Tennessee. "Among the nine states of the southeastern United States," Chandler concluded, "there has been essentially an inverse relationship between income per capita and the extent to which the state was served by TVA. . . ."

How can receiving a giant dam and reduced costs of electricity stymie economic development? Chandler concluded that the cheap electricity gave farmers in Tennessee incentives to remain in small-scale agriculture rather than move into more promising areas of manufacturing, industry, and services. Meanwhile, many farmers in Georgia and North Carolina improved their education and moved to Atlanta, Raleigh, or Charlotte to start or work for businesses.

Chandler further discovered that people in the TVA area were even slower to adopt and use electricity than were people just outside the TVA area. With their ever-increasing incomes, Georgians and North Carolinians could afford more electricity than the more stagnant population in the Tennesse Valley

Chandler's research should make all students of government intervention pause. The massive subsidy for the TVA hindered economic growth in the exact area targeted for federal help. If the TVA example is repeated elsewhere, that is a powerful argument against government subsidies—perhaps the strongest argument that can be made (outside the constitutional argument).

In fact, the TVA lesson does have widespread applicability. One of America's first large subsidies was a multimillion-dollar gift to Edward Collins in the 1840s to build and operate four steamships to and from England to deliver passengers, freight, and mail. With the cushion of federal aid, Collins had no incentive to innovate with steel hulls or engine technology. Like the farmers of the Tennessee Valley, he could make do with federal help so why try something different? Within ten years Collins had lost the competitive race to Cornelius Vanderbilt, who had no federal subsidy but showed great innovation in steamship design and the economics of steamship operation.

The Union Pacific received tens of millions of dollars in federal aid and millions of acres of land to build a transcontinental railroad that was not as straight, not as well built, and not as stable as the Great Northern Railroad, which received not a cent of federal aid. The builders of the Union Pacific constructed their line to receive subsidies, not to transport passengers in the long run. James J. Hill had to compete with the Union Pacific, and he built the Great Northern piece by piece with the best track and over the best terrain possible. During the Panic of 1893, the Union Pacific went broke, but the Great Northern made profits each year. In some ways, the federal subsidy was actually the undoing of the Union Pacific.

Subsidies Change Behavior

Subsidies change the way the recipients behave, and these changes often work against, not for, them. That is the neglected argument against opening the door to federal aid in the first place; but it is an argument that needs to be studied and forcefully made.

The idea that recipients of subsidies are damaged by subsidies applies to individuals as well as businesses. The example of the rise of the welfare state is pertinent here. Americans naturally have compassion for people who are poor but who are trying to improve their lives. Federal aid, however, can stifle individual initiative. That is one reason charity was a private function in the United States so long. Private givers can more easily determine the quantity and duration of aid needed to restore broken lives.

During the 1960s, under the Aid to Families with Dependent Children program, money to unwed mothers increased substantially. As a result, recipients had an incentive not to get married or go to work because those activities would cause them to lose their federal assistance. Thus American taxpayers were not the only losers in the program. Recipients who never developed their talents were losers as well.

Most students of government intervention know that federal subsidies are a drain on those who pay for them. What needs more emphasis is that sometimes the recipients of tax dollars become worse off as well.

—BWF, October 2007

39

Chapter **Thirty-Nine**

A Tribute to the Jitney

No person shall operate or cause to be operated any jitney upon any street, avenue, boulevard or other public place within the City of Detroit whether such jitney operates wholly within the City of Detroit, or from some point within the City of Detroit or to some point outside of the City of Detroit to some point within the City of Detroit.

So reads the official ban on one of the oldest illegal businesses that still operate openly in Detroit, Michigan. The rather emphatic language says, in effect, "We don't want any part of this!" And yet on public bulletin boards at grocery, drug, and department stores all over the city, one can find notices that announce, "For Jitney Service, Call This Number."

Just what is this "jitney" thing that the City of Detroit, in the name of protecting the public, officially declares *verboten*? It's a very popular business in which mostly retired autoworkers, church deacons, widowers, and otherwise idle but able citizens charge a small fee to give poor people a ride from where they shop to where they live.

The crime is that jitneys do their good work without a taxi license from the city government—the same city government that wouldn't authorize a single additional taxicab for 50 years. Getting a license to do just about anything in Detroit means endless delays, lengthy waiting lists, mounds of paperwork, and senseless rigmarole.

Thriving Business

Fortunately, the cops in Detroit look the other way and the jitney business is thriving. According to the *Detroit Free Press*, no one has filed a complaint against a jitney in at least 26 years and no jitney driver in recent memory has had to face the stipulated fine of $500 and 90 days in jail. Nearly a third of Detroit's households don't have cars, and the city has one of the lowest per capita incomes of any urban area in the nation, so it's likely that thousands of technically illegal jitney rides occur there every week. The drivers charge much less than the taxicabs (which many of their customers cannot afford), often carry their clients' bags from the store to the vehicle, are easily accessible in any neighborhood, and are the primary means of transportation for Detroit's poor.

The spontaneous order that Detroit's jitney system has produced is elaborate as well as efficient. According to a report from the Washington, D.C.-based Institute for Justice:

> Although the jitney drivers in Detroit do not at first seem to be organized, the structure of jitney service is actually quite complex. While there is little camaraderie and no formal organization of jitney drivers, the market produces a structure of needs and services. . . . [They] operate mostly out of strip mall shopping centers. . . . Most jitney drivers will not service the whole shopping center but will attach themselves to one store. Thus, each driver has his territory. Well-known jitney drivers often will transport the store's employees to and from work as well.

Assurance of driver reliability is handled nicely by the market itself. Word of mouth directs store employees and customers to particular drivers, who tend to live in the areas they serve. Owners of stores vouch for certain drivers by issuing them cards that are placed prominently in windshields. Drivers seem to prefer this private certification of competence to licensing. "When asked about the possibility of jitney licenses," says the Institute for Justice, "many drivers are suspicious of what it would mean to have to deal with the bureaucracy at the City/County Building."

Jitneys aren't special to Detroit. They operate in most major American cities in direct but illegal competition with both the government-sanctioned taxi monopolies and government-run bus systems. In some places, they face a lot more harassment from the authorities than they do in Detroit.

In New York City, the police bust jitney drivers all the time. Writing in the *New York Times Magazine* of August 10, 1997, John Tierney tells the story of an immigrant from Barbados who spent years trying to go the legal route and get a license to transport residents around the city in his van. His application included more than 900 supporting statements from riders, business groups, and church leaders. He was approved by the City Taxi and Limousine Commission and supported by Mayor Rudy Giuliani. But in the end, the city council did what it has done with almost every such request: it rejected his application. Now this outlaw entrepreneur and thousands just like him in the Big Apple dodge the cops every day as they earn a living and their customers' approval.

Jitneys have a long and honorable tradition in America. According to two California economic historians writing in the October 1972 *Journal of Law and Economics*, the first one appeared in 1914 in Los Angeles, when L. P. Draper accepted a fare from a stranger in exchange for a brief ride in Draper's Ford Model T. The fare was a "jitney"—slang for a nickel—and it became the industry's standard fee for many years thereafter. By the autumn of 1915, a thriving jitney industry was providing inexpensive and reliable transportation in cities from San Francisco to Portland, Maine.

It didn't take long, however, for public officials and their friends in the electric streetcar industry to start piling on regulations with the aim of running the jitney competition out of business. The *Electric Railway Journal* called the jitneys "a menace," "a malignant growth," and "this Frankenstein of transportation."

During World War I, the American Electric Railway Association even suggested that jitney drivers be drafted into the military. It called for the War Industries Board to "suppress entirely all useless competition with existing electric railways" and argued that "men engaged in nonessential automobile service of this nature should be forced to obtain some useful occupations or compelled to enter the service."

Electric railways aren't around much anymore, but taxicab and city bus monopolies have taken their place in the war against jitneys. Laws against jitneys and the victimless crime of helping people get around town without a license, whether fully enforced or not, represent a cynical use of the police power of government by special interests. They are evidence of corrupt and stupid politicians who often express sympathy for the poor at the same time they make war on poor entrepreneurs.

The persistence of jitneys on America's streets is an inspiration, a testimony to the power of the profit motive that fires up people to help people even when it's illegal to do so. As to the war against them, Mr. Bumble's famous line from Dickens's *Oliver Twist* comes to mind: "The law is a ass."

—LWR, January 2000

40

Chapter **Forty**

In the Grip of Madness

"Thank God we had the federal government last week to bail out the private sector!" That is what a rather statist friend of mine declared a year ago as the economy tanked, almost gleeful that the financial crisis seemed to be proving how much we all need a massive federal establishment to both regulate and rescue us.

Never mind the federal government's own indispensable role as an enabler in the crisis, from its reckless monetary policy to its jawboning banks into making dubious mortgage loans. Never mind the long-term danger of its assumption of colossal new obligations and the moral hazard in the message its intervention sends. My response to my friend was of a more narrow focus. "Thank God we have the private sector to bail out the federal government not just last week, but every week!" I exclaimed.

Think about it. Taxes on the private sector pay a majority of the federal government's bills. For most of the rest, the government borrows by selling its debt obligations, mostly to private-sector entities–including banks, insurance companies, and individuals.

The federal government is the world's biggest taxer and the world's biggest debtor. If those of us in the private sector didn't pay our taxes or didn't buy Washington's paper, the feds would have gone belly-up decades ago. We've rescued Washington to the tune of tens of trillions of dollars over the years. A big difference between Washington's bailing out the private sector and the private sector's bailing out Washington is that the private sector has to work, invest, employ people, and produce goods to come up with the cash. It can't create it out of thin air like Ben Bernanke can.

Our friends in Washington have blessed us with future burdens almost too astronomical to comprehend. In the name of taking care of us in our old age, we are saddled with no less than $6 trillion in Social Security payouts over the next 75 years–for which there are no presently earmarked funding streams. According to Brian Riedl of the Heritage Foundation, the unfunded obligations for the new federal prescription drug program, enacted under President Bush, total another $8 trillion.

On and on it goes. The private sector has an awful lot of bailing out to do in the coming decades. I shudder to think how deeply we taxpayers will have to dig in the not-too-distant future to pay the bills of our benevolent, compassionate, and forward-thinking government.

Since Barack Obama took office in January 2009, the federal government has spent a full billion dollars every single hour. Before his term is half over, federal spending will have doubled in just a decade. The deficit in one year's budget is now as large as the entire budget in George W. Bush's first year as president, 2001–and I thought not very long ago that the spending spree he and the Republicans gave us would be tough to beat! The flood of red ink is now adding to the national debt to the tune of about $4 billion every day. At well over $11 trillion, that debt amounts to $37,000 for every living American.

Too Big to Succeed?

We're told by the wise planners in Washington that certain private firms are "too big to fail." So we're handing big chunks of them over to the government.

The question we all should be asking ourselves is this: Are we trusting our economy and our lives to a government that is too big to succeed?

Once upon a time in America, most citizens expected government to keep the peace and otherwise leave them alone. We built a vibrant, self-reliant, entrepreneurial culture with strong families and solid values. We respected property and largely kept the spirit of the Eighth and Tenth Commandments against coveting and stealing. We understood that government didn't have anything to give anybody except what it first took from somebody and that a government big enough to give us everything we want would be big enough to take away everything we've got. We practiced fiscal discipline in our personal lives and expected nothing less from the people in the government we elected, or we threw them out.

But somewhere along the way we lost our moral compass. And just like the Roman Republic that rose on integrity and collapsed in turpitude, we thought the "bread and circuses" the government could provide us would buy us comfort and security.

We gave the government the responsibility to educate our children, though government can never be counted on to teach well the main ingredients of a free society—liberty and character—or just about anything else, for that matter. We asked the government to give us health care, wel-fare, pensions, college education, and farm subsidies, and now our politicians are bankrupting the country to pay the bills. This welfare state of ours has become one big circle of 305 million people, each with his hand in the next fellow's pocket.

This is a government whose reach even before the financial crisis scarcely left an aspect of American life untouched, from the cradle to the grave and the volume of our toilet-bowl water in between. As a portion of our personal income, its tax and regulatory burden consumes at least five times what it did just a century ago. But to the majority on the Potomac, government is nowhere yet big enough. This is madness writ large.

Stick to the Knitting

Remember *In Search of Excellence*, the 1982 best-selling management book by Tom Peters and Robert Waterman? One of its salient points is that an organization gets off track when it no longer "sticks to the knitting." When it allows its mission to blur and stretch far beyond its founding design, when it becomes distracted by endless and dubious new responsibilities, its core competency evaporates. It will fail to do what it is supposed to do, because it's doing too much of what it's not supposed to do.

It may come as a surprise to those who see aspirin made in Washington as the cure for every ailment, but the federal government is not God. It can't even be a good Santa Claus. It's no Mother Teresa either, because on those occasions when it does some good it usually costs an arm and a leg and sends a big part of the bill to generations yet unborn. The fact is, the bigger government gets, the more it starts to look like Moe, Larry, and Curly.

Accentuating the madness of the present day, the cover of *Newsweek* declared last March, "We are all socialists now." Pardon me, but I'm not about to sign on to a proven flop.

—*LWR, September 2009*

Part VI

Depressions, Poverty and Inequality

41

Chapter **Forty-One**

Great Myths of the Great Depression

Many volumes have been written about the Great Depression of 1929–1941 and its impact on the lives of millions of Americans. Historians, economists and politicians have all combed the wreckage searching for the "black box" that will reveal the cause of the calamity. Sadly, all too many of them decide to abandon their search, finding it easier perhaps to circulate a host of false and harmful conclusions about the events of seven decades ago. Consequently, many people today continue to accept critiques of free-market capitalism that are unjustified and support government policies that are economically destructive.

How bad was the Great Depression? Over the four years from 1929 to 1933, production at the nation's factories, mines and utilities fell by more than half. People's real disposable incomes dropped 28 percent. Stock prices collapsed to one-tenth of their pre-crash height. The number of unemployed Americans rose from 1.6 million in 1929 to 12.8 million in 1933. One of every four workers was out of a job at the Depression's nadir, and ugly rumors of revolt simmered for the first time since the Civil War.

The terror of the Great Crash has been the failure to explain it," writes economist Alan Reynolds. "People were left with the feeling that massive economic contractions could occur at any moment, without warning, without cause. That fear has been exploited ever since as the major justification for virtually unlimited federal intervention in economic affairs.[31]

Old myths never die; they just keep showing up in economics and political science textbooks. With only an occasional exception, it is there you will find what may be the 20th century's greatest myth: *Capitalism and the free-market economy were responsible for the Great Depression, and only government intervention brought about America's economic recovery.*

A Modern Fairy Tale

According to this simplistic perspective, an important pillar of capitalism, the stock market, crashed and dragged America into depression. President Herbert Hoover, an advocate of "hands-off," or laissez-faire, economic policy, refused to use the power of government and conditions worsened as a result. It was up to Hoover's successor, Franklin Delano Roosevelt, to ride in on the white horse of government intervention and steer the nation toward recovery. The apparent lesson to be drawn is that capitalism cannot be trusted; government needs to take an active role in the economy to save us from inevitable decline.

But those who propagate this version of history might just as well top off their remarks by saying, "And Goldilocks found her way out of the forest, Dorothy made it from Oz back to Kansas, and Little Red Riding Hood won the New York State Lottery." The popular account of the Depression as outlined above belongs in a book of fairy tales and not in a serious discussion of economic history.

The Great, Great, Great, Great Depression

To properly understand the events of the time, it is factually appropriate to view the Great Depression as not one, but *four* consecutive downturns rolled into one. These four "phases" are:[32]

I. Monetary Policy and the Business Cycle

---

[31] Alan Reynolds, "What Do We Know About the Great Crash?" *National Review,* November 9, 1979, p. 1416.

[32] Hans F. Sennholz, "The Great Depression," *The Freeman,* April 1975, p. 205.

II. The Disintegration of the World Economy

III. The New Deal

IV. The Wagner Act

The first phase covers why the crash of 1929 happened in the first place; the other three show how government intervention worsened it and kept the economy in a stupor for over a decade. Let's consider each one in turn.

Phase I: The Business Cycle

The Great Depression was not the country's first depression, though it proved to be the longest. Several others preceded it.

A common thread woven through all of those earlier debacles was disastrous intervention by government, often in the form of political mismanagement of the money and credit supply. None of these depressions, however, lasted more than four years and most of them were over in two. The calamity that began in 1929 lasted at least three times longer than any of the country's previous depressions because the government compounded its initial errors with a series of additional and harmful interventions.

Central Planners Fail at Monetary Policy

A popular explanation for the stock market collapse of 1929 concerns the practice of borrowing money to buy stock. Many history texts blithely assert that a frenzied speculation in shares was fed by excessive "margin lending." But Marquette University economist Gene Smiley, in his 2002 book *Rethinking the Great Depression*, explains why this is not a fruitful observation:

> There was already a long history of margin lending on stock exchanges, and margin requirements—the share of the purchase price paid in cash—were no lower in the late twenties than in the early twenties or in previous decades. In fact, in the fall of 1928 margin requirements began to rise, and borrowers were required to pay a larger share of the purchase price of the stocks.

The margin lending argument doesn't hold much water. Mischief with the money and credit supply, however, is another story.

Most monetary economists, particularly those of the "Austrian School," have observed the close relationship between money supply and economic activity. When government inflates the money and credit supply, interest rates at first fall. Businesses invest this "easy money" in new production projects and a boom takes place in capital goods. As the boom matures, business costs rise, interest rates readjust upward, and profits are squeezed. The easy-money effects thus wear off and the monetary authorities, fearing price inflation, slow the growth of, or even contract, the money supply. In either case, the manipulation is enough to knock out the shaky supports from underneath the economic house of cards.

One prominent interpretation of the Federal Reserve System's actions prior to 1929 can be found in *America's Great Depression* by economist Murray Rothbard. Using a broad measure that includes currency, demand and time deposits, and other ingredients, he estimated that the Fed bloated the money supply by more than 60 percent from mid-1921 to mid-1929.[33] Rothbard argued that this expansion of money and credit drove interest rates down, pushed the stock market to dizzy heights, and gave birth to the "Roaring Twenties."

Reckless money and credit growth constituted what economist Benjamin M. Anderson called "the beginning of the New Deal"[34]—the name for the better-known but highly interventionist policies that would come later under President Franklin Roosevelt. However, other scholars raise doubts that Fed action was as inflationary as Rothbard believed, pointing to relatively flat commodity and consumer prices in the 1920s as evidence that monetary policy was not so wildly irresponsible.

Substantial cuts in high marginal income tax rates in the Coolidge years certainly helped the economy and may have ameliorated the price effect of Fed policy. Tax reductions spurred investment and real economic growth, which in turn yielded a burst of technological advancement and entrepreneurial discoveries of cheaper ways to produce goods. This explosion in productivity undoubtedly helped to keep prices lower than they would have otherwise been.

Regarding Fed policy, free-market economists who differ on the extent of the Fed's monetary expansion of the early and mid-1920s are

---

[33] Murray Rothbard, *America's Great Depression* (Kansas City: Sheed and Ward, Inc., 1975), p. 89.

[34] Benjamin M. Anderson, *Economics and the Public Welfare: A Financial and Economic History of the United States*, 1914-46, 2nd edition (Indianapolis: Liberty Press, 1979), p. 127.

of one view about what happened next: The central bank presided over a dramatic contraction of the money supply that began late in the decade. The federal government's responses to the resulting recession took a bad situation and made it far, far worse.

The Bottom Drops Out

By 1928, the Federal Reserve was raising interest rates and choking off the money supply. For example, its discount rate (the rate the Fed charges member banks for loans) was increased four times, from 3.5 percent to 6 percent, between January 1928 and August 1929. The central bank took further deflationary action by aggressively selling government securities for months after the stock market crashed. For the next three years, the money supply shrank by 30 percent. As prices then tumbled throughout the economy, the Fed's higher interest rate policy boosted *real* (inflation-adjusted) rates dramatically.

The most comprehensive chronicle of the monetary policies of the period can be found in the classic work of Nobel Laureate Milton Friedman and his colleague Anna Schwartz, *A Monetary History of the United States, 1867–1960*. Friedman and Schwartz argue conclusively that the contraction of the nation's money supply by one-third between August 1929 and March 1933 was an enormous drag on the economy and largely the result of seismic incompetence by the Fed. The death in October 1928 of Benjamin Strong, a powerful figure who had exerted great influence as head of the Fed's New York district bank, left the Fed floundering without capable leadership—making bad policy even worse.[35]

At first, only the "smart" money—the Bernard Baruchs and the Joseph Kennedys who watched things like money supply and other government policies—saw that the party was coming to an end. Baruch actually began selling stocks and buying bonds and gold as early as 1928; Kennedy did likewise, commenting, "only a fool holds out for the top dollar."[36]

The masses of investors eventually sensed the change at the Fed and then the stampede began. In a special issue commemorating the

---

[35] Milton Friedman and Anna Jacobson Schwartz, *A Monetary History of the United States, 1867–1960* (New York: National Bureau of Economic Research, 1963; ninth paperback printing by Princeton University Press, 1993), pp. 411-415.

[36] Lindley H. Clark, Jr., "After the Fall," *The Wall Street Journal*, October 26, 1979, p. 18.

50th anniversary of the stock market collapse, *U.S. News & World Report* described it this way:

> Actually the Great Crash was by no means a one-day affair, despite frequent references to Black Thursday, October 24, and the following week's Black Tuesday. As early as September 5, stocks were weak in heavy trading, after having moved into new high ground two days earlier. Declines in early October were called a "desirable correction." *The Wall Street Journal*, predicting an autumn rally, noted that "some stocks rise, some fall."
>
> Then, on October 3, stocks suffered their worst pummeling of the year. Margin calls went out; some traders grew apprehensive. But the next day, prices rose again and thereafter seesawed for a fortnight.
>
> The real crunch began on Wednesday, October 23, with what one observer called "a Niagara of liquidation." Six million shares changed hands. The industrial average fell 21 points. "Tomorrow, the turn will come," brokers told one another. Prices, they said, had been carried to "unreasonably low" levels.
>
> But the next day, Black Thursday, stocks were dumped in even heavier selling. The ticker fell behind more than 5 hours, and finally stopped grinding out quotations at 7:08 p.m. [37]

At their peak, stocks in the Dow Jones Industrial Average were selling for 19 times their earnings—somewhat high, but hardly what stock market analysts regard as a sign of inordinate speculation. The distortions in the economy promoted by the Fed's monetary policy had set the country up for a recession, but other impositions to come would soon turn the recession into a full-scale disaster. As stocks took a beating, Congress was playing with fire: On the very morning of Black Thursday, the nation's newspapers reported that the political forces for higher trade-damaging tariffs were making gains on Capitol Hill.

The stock market crash was only a reflection—not the direct cause—of the destructive government policies that would ultimately produce the Great Depression: The market rose and fell in almost direct synchronization with what the Fed and Congress were doing. And what they did in the 1930s ranks way up there in the annals of history's greatest follies.

---

[37] "Tearful Memories That Just Won't Fade Away," *U. S. News & World Report*, October 29, 1979, pp. 36-37.

Buddy, Can You Spare $20 Million?

Black Thursday shook Michigan harder than almost any other state. Stocks of auto and mining companies were hammered. Auto production in 1929 reached an all-time high of slightly more than 5 million vehicles, then quickly slumped by 2 million in 1930. By 1932, near the deepest point of the Depression, they had fallen by another 2 million to just 1,331,860—down an astonishing 75 percent from the 1929 peak.

Thousands of investors everywhere, including many well-known people, were hit hard in the 1929 crash. Among them was Winston Churchill. He had invested heavily in American stocks before the crash. Afterward, only his writing skills and positions in government restored his finances.

Clarence Birdseye, an early developer of packaged frozen foods, had sold his business for $30 million and put all his money into stocks. He was wiped out.

William C. Durant, founder of General Motors, lost more than $40 million in the stock market and wound up a virtual pauper. (GM itself stayed in the black throughout the Depression under the cost-cutting leadership of Alfred P. Sloan.)

Phase II: Disintegration of the World Economy

Though modern myth claims that the free market "self-destructed" in 1929, government policy was the debacle's principal culprit. If this crash had been like previous ones, the hard times would have ended in two or three years at the most, and likely sooner than that. But unprecedented political bungling instead prolonged the misery for over 10 years.

Unemployment in 1930 averaged a mildly recessionary 8.9 percent, up from 3.2 percent in 1929. It shot up rapidly until peaking out at more than 25 percent in 1933. Until March of 1933, these were the years of President Herbert Hoover—a man often depicted as a champion of noninterventionist, laissez-faire economics.

"The Greatest Spending Administration In All Of History"

Did Hoover really subscribe to a "hands-off-the-economy," free-market philosophy? His opponent in the 1932 election, Franklin

Roosevelt, didn't think so. During the campaign, Roosevelt blasted Hoover for spending and taxing too much, boosting the national debt, choking off trade, and putting millions on the dole. He accused the president of "reckless and extravagant" spending, of thinking "that we ought to center control of everything in Washington as rapidly as possible," and of presiding over "the greatest spending administration in peacetime in all of history." Roosevelt's running mate, John Nance Garner, charged that Hoover was "leading the country down the path of socialism." [38] Contrary to the conventional view about Hoover, Roosevelt and Garner were absolutely right.

The crowning folly of the Hoover administration was the Smoot-Hawley Tariff, passed in June 1930. It came on top of the Fordney-McCumber Tariff of 1922, which had already put American agriculture in a tailspin during the preceding decade. The most protectionist legislation in U.S. history, Smoot-Hawley virtually closed the borders to foreign goods and ignited a vicious international trade war. Professor Barry Poulson describes the scope of the act:

> The act raised the rates on the entire range of dutiable commodities; for example, the average rate increased from 20 percent to 34 percent on agricultural products; from 36 percent to 47 percent on wines, spirits, and beverages; from 50 to 60 percent on wool and woolen manufactures. In all, 887 tariffs were sharply increased and the act broadened the list of dutiable commodities to 3,218 items. A crucial part of the Smoot-Hawley Tariff was that many tariffs were for a specific amount of money rather than a percentage of the price. As prices fell by half or more during the Great Depression, the effective rate of these specific tariffs doubled, increasing the protection afforded under the act.[39]

Smoot-Hawley was as broad as it was deep, affecting a multitude of products. Before its passage, clocks had faced a tariff of 45 percent; the act raised that to 55 percent, plus as much as another $4.50 per clock. Tariffs on corn and butter were roughly doubled. Even sauerkraut was tariffed for the first time. Among the few remaining tariff-free goods, strangely enough, were leeches and skeletons (perhaps as a political sop to the American Medical Association, as one wag wryly remarked).

---

[38] "FDR's Disputed Legacy," *Time*, February 1, 1982, p. 23.

[39] Barry W. Poulson, *Economic History of the United States* (New York: Macmillan Publishing Co., Inc., 1981), p. 508.

Tariffs on linseed oil, tungsten, and casein hammered the U.S. paint, steel and paper industries, respectively. More than 800 items used in automobile production were taxed by Smoot-Hawley. Most of the 60,000 people employed in U.S. plants making cheap clothing out of imported wool rags went home jobless after the tariff on wool rags rose by 140 percent.[40]

Officials in the administration and in Congress believed that raising trade barriers would force Americans to buy more goods made at home, which would solve the nagging unemployment problem. But they ignored an important principle of international commerce: Trade is ultimately a two-way street; if foreigners cannot sell their goods here, then they cannot earn the dollars they need to buy here. Or, to put it another way, government cannot shut off imports without simultaneously shutting off exports.

You Tax Me, I Tax You

Foreign companies and their workers were flattened by Smoot-Hawley's steep tariff rates and foreign governments soon retaliated with trade barriers of their own. With their ability to sell in the American market severely hampered, they curtailed their purchases of American goods. American agriculture was particularly hard hit. With a stroke of the presidential pen, farmers in this country lost nearly a third of their markets. Farm prices plummeted and tens of thousands of farmers went bankrupt. A bushel of wheat that sold for $1 in 1929 was selling for a mere 30 cents by 1932.

With the collapse of agriculture, rural banks failed in record numbers, dragging down hundreds of thousands of their customers. Nine thousand banks closed their doors in the United States between 1930 and 1933. The stock market, which had regained much of the ground it had lost since the previous October, tumbled 20 points on the day Hoover signed Smoot-Hawley into law, and fell almost without respite for the next two years. (The market's high, as measured by the Dow Jones Industrial Average, was set on Sept. 3, 1929, at 381. It hit its 1929 low of 198 on Nov. 13, then rebounded to 294 by April 1930. It declined again as the tariff bill made its way toward Hoover's desk in June and did not bottom out until it reached a mere 41 two years later. It would be a quarter-century before the Dow would climb to 381 again.)

---

[40] Reynolds, p. 1419.

The shrinkage in world trade brought on by the tariff wars helped set the stage for World War II a few years later. In 1929, the rest of the world owed American citizens $30 billion. Germany's Weimar Republic was struggling to pay the enormous reparations bill imposed by the disastrous Treaty of Versailles. When tariffs made it nearly impossible for foreign businessmen to sell their goods in American markets, the burden of their debts became massively heavier and emboldened demagogues like Adolf Hitler. "When goods don't cross frontiers, armies will," warns an old but painfully true maxim.

Free Markets or Free Lunches?

Smoot-Hawley by itself should lay to rest the myth that Hoover was a free market practitioner, but there is even more to the story of his administration's interventionist mistakes. Within a month of the stock market crash, he convened conferences of business leaders for the purpose of jawboning them into keeping wages artificially high even though both profits and prices were falling. Consumer prices plunged almost 25 percent between 1929 and 1933 while nominal wages on average decreased only 15 percent—translating into a substantial increase in wages in real terms, a major component of the cost of doing business. As economist Richard Ebeling notes, "The 'high-wage' policy of the Hoover administration and the trade unions . . . succeeded only in pricing workers out of the labor market, generating an increasing circle of unemployment."[41]

Hoover dramatically increased government spending for subsidy and relief schemes. In the space of one year alone, from 1930 to 1931, the federal government's share of GNP soared from 16.4 percent to 21.5 percent.[42] Hoover's agricultural bureaucracy doled out hundreds of millions of dollars to wheat and cotton farmers even as the new tariffs wiped out their markets. His Reconstruction Finance Corporation ladled out billions more in business subsidies. Commenting decades later on Hoover's administration, Rexford Guy Tugwell, one of the architects of Franklin Roosevelt's policies of the 1930s, explained, "We didn't admit

---

[41] Richard M. Ebeling, "Monetary Central Planning and the State-Part XI: The Great Depression and the Crisis of Government Intervention," *Freedom Daily* (Fairfax, Virginia: The Future of Freedom Foundation, November 1997), p. 15.

[42] Paul Johnson, *A History of the American People* (New York: HarperCollins Publishers, 1997), p. 740.

it at the time, but practically the whole New Deal was extrapolated from programs that Hoover started."[43]

Though Hoover at first did lower taxes for the poorest of Americans, Larry Schweikart and Michael Allen in their sweeping *A Patriot's History of the United States: From Columbus's Great Discovery to the War on Terror* stress that he "offered no incentives to the wealthy to invest in new plants to stimulate hiring." He even taxed bank checks, "which accelerated the decline in the availability of money by penalizing people for writing checks."[44]

In September 1931, with the money supply tumbling and the economy reeling from the impact of Smoot-Hawley, the Fed imposed the biggest hike in its discount rate in history. Bank deposits fell 15 percent within four months and sizable, deflationary declines in the nation's money supply persisted through the first half of 1932.

Compounding the error of high tariffs, huge subsidies and deflationary monetary policy, Congress then passed and Hoover signed the Revenue Act of 1932. The largest tax increase in peacetime history, it doubled the income tax. The top bracket actually more than doubled, soaring from 24 percent to 63 percent. Exemptions were lowered; the earned income credit was abolished; corporate and estate taxes were raised; new gift, gasoline and auto taxes were imposed; and postal rates were sharply hiked.

Can any serious scholar observe the Hoover administration's massive economic intervention and, with a straight face, pronounce the inevitably deleterious effects as the fault of free markets? Schweikart and Allen survey some of the wreckage:

By 1933, the numbers produced by this comedy of errors were staggering: national unemployment rates reached 25 percent, but within some individual cities, the statistics seemed beyond comprehension. Cleveland reported that 50 percent of its labor force was unemployed; Toledo, 80 percent; and some states even averaged over 40 percent. Because of the dual-edged sword of declining revenues and increasing welfare demands, the burden on the cities pushed many municipalities to the brink. Schools in New York shut down, and teachers in Chicago were owed some $20

---

[43] Ibid., p. 741.
[44] Larry Schweikart and Michael Allen, *A Patriot's History of the United States: From Columbus's Great Discovery to the War on Terror* (New York: Sentinel, 2004), p. 553.

million. Private schools, in many cases, failed completely. One government study found that by 1933 some fifteen hundred colleges had gone belly-up, and book sales plummeted. Chicago's library system did not purchase a single book in a year-long period.[45]

Phase III: The New Deal

Franklin Delano Roosevelt won the 1932 presidential election in a landslide, collecting 472 electoral votes to just 59 for the incumbent Herbert Hoover. The platform of the Democratic Party, whose ticket Roosevelt headed, declared, "We believe that a party platform is a covenant with the people to be faithfully kept by the party entrusted with power." It called for a 25 percent reduction in federal spending, a balanced federal budget, a sound gold currency "to be preserved at all hazards," the removal of government from areas that belonged more appropriately to private enterprise and an end to the "extravagance" of Hoover's farm programs. This is what *candidate* Roosevelt promised, but it bears no resemblance to what *President* Roosevelt actually delivered.

Washington was rife with both fear and optimism as Roosevelt was sworn in on March 4, 1933—fear that the economy might not recover and optimism that the new and assertive president just might make a difference. Humorist Will Rogers captured the popular feeling toward FDR as he assembled the new administration: "The whole country is with him, just so he does *something*. If he burned down the Capitol, we would all cheer and say, well, we at least got a fire started anyhow."[46]

"Nothing To Fear But Fear Itself"

Roosevelt did indeed make a difference, though probably not the sort of difference for which the country had hoped. He started off on the wrong foot when, in his inaugural address, he blamed the Depression on "unscrupulous money changers." He said nothing about the role of the Fed's mismanagement and little about the follies of Congress that had contributed to the problem. As a result of his efforts, the economy would linger in depression for the rest of the decade. Adapting a phrase from 19th century writer Henry David Thoreau, Roosevelt famously declared in his address that, "We have nothing to fear but fear itself."

---

[45] Ibid., p. 554.
[46] "FDR's Disputed Legacy," p. 24.

But as Dr. Hans Sennholz of Grove City College explains, it was FDR's policies to come that Americans had genuine reason to fear:

> In his first 100 days, he swung hard at the profit order. Instead of clearing away the prosperity barriers erected by his predecessor, he built new ones of his own. He struck in every known way at the integrity of the U.S. dollar through quantitative increases and qualitative deterioration. He seized the people's gold holdings and subsequently devalued the dollar by 40 percent.[47]

Frustrated and angered that Roosevelt had so quickly and thoroughly abandoned the platform on which he was elected, Director of the Bureau of the Budget Lewis W. Douglas resigned after only one year on the job. At Harvard University in May 1935, Douglas made it plain that America was facing a momentous choice:

> Will we choose to subject ourselves—this great country—to the despotism of bureaucracy, controlling our every act, destroying what equality we have attained, reducing us eventually to the condition of impoverished slaves of the state? Or will we cling to the liberties for which man has struggled for more than a thousand years? It is important to understand the magnitude of the issue before us. . . . If we do not elect to have a tyrannical, oppressive bureaucracy controlling our lives, destroying progress, depressing the standard of living . . . then should it not be the function of the Federal government under a democracy to limit its activities to those which a democracy may adequately deal, such for example as national defense, main-taining law and order, protecting life and property, preventing dis-honesty, and . . . guarding the public against . . . vested special interests?[48]

New Dealing from the Bottom of the Deck

Crisis gripped the banking system when the new president assumed office on March 4, 1933. Roosevelt's action to close the banks and declare a nationwide "banking holiday" on March 6 (which did not completely end until nine days later) is still hailed as a decisive and necessary action by Roosevelt apologists. Friedman and Schwartz, however, make it plain that this supposed cure was "worse than the

---

[47] Sennholz, p. 210.

[48] From *The Liberal Tradition: A Free People and a Free Economy* by Lewis W. Douglas, as quoted in "Monetary Central Planning and the State, Part XIV: The New Deal and Its Critics," by Richard M. Ebeling in *Freedom Daily*, February 1998, p. 12.

disease." The Smoot-Hawley tariff and the Fed's unconscionable monetary mischief were primary culprits in producing the conditions that gave Roosevelt his excuse to temporarily deprive depositors of their money, and the bank holiday did nothing to alter those fundamentals. "More than 5,000 banks still in operation when the holiday was declared did not reopen their doors when it ended, and of these, over 2,000 never did thereafter," report Friedman and Schwartz.
[49]

Economist Jim Powell of the Cato Institute authored a splendid book on the Great Depression in 2003, titled *FDR's Folly: How Roosevelt and His New Deal Prolonged the Great Depression.* He points out that "Almost all the failed banks were in states with unit banking laws"—laws that prohibited banks from opening branches and thereby diversifying their portfolios and reducing their risks. Powell writes: "Although the United States, with its unit banking laws, had thousands of bank failures, Canada, which permitted branch banking, didn't have a single failure . . ."[50] Strangely, critics of capitalism who love to blame the market for the Depression never mention that fact.

Congress gave the president the power first to seize the private gold holdings of American citizens and then to fix the price of gold. One morning, as Roosevelt ate eggs in bed, he and Secretary of the Treasury Henry Morgenthau decided to change the ratio between gold and paper dollars. After weighing his options, Roosevelt settled on a 21 cent price hike because "it's a lucky number." In his diary, Morgenthau wrote, "If anybody ever knew how we really set the gold price through a combination of lucky numbers, I think they would be frightened."[51] Roosevelt also single-handedly torpedoed the London Economic Conference in 1933, which was convened at the request of other major nations to bring down tariff rates and restore the gold standard.

Washington and its reckless central bank had already made mincemeat of the gold standard by the early 1930s. Roosevelt's rejection of it removed most of the remaining impediments to limitless currency and credit expansion, for which the nation would pay a high price in later years in the form of a depreciating currency. Sen. Carter

---

[49] Friedman and Schwartz, p. 330.

[50] Jim Powell, *FDR's Folly: How Roosevelt and His New Deal Prolonged the Great Depression* (New York: Crown Forum, 2003), p. 32.

[51] John Morton Blum, *From the Morgenthau Diaries: Years of Crisis, 1928–1938* (Boston: Houghton Mifflin Company, 1959), p. 70.

Glass put it well when he warned Roosevelt in early 1933: "It's dishonor, sir. This great government, strong in gold, is breaking its promises to pay gold to widows and orphans to whom it has sold government bonds with a pledge to pay gold coin of the present standard of value. It is breaking its promise to redeem its paper money in gold coin of the present standard of value. It's dishonor, sir."[52]

Though he seized the country's gold, Roosevelt did return booze to America's bars and parlor rooms. On his second Sunday in the White House, he remarked at dinner, "I think this would be a good time for beer."[53] That same night, he drafted a message asking Congress to end Prohibition. The House approved a repeal measure on Tuesday, the Senate passed it on Thursday and before the year was out, enough states had ratified it so that the 21st Amendment became part of the Constitution. One observer, commenting on this remarkable turn of events, noted that of two men walking down the street at the start of 1933—one with a gold coin in his pocket and the other with a bottle of whiskey in his coat—the man with the coin would be an upstanding citizen and the man with the whiskey would be the outlaw. A year later, precisely the reverse was true.

In the first year of the New Deal, Roosevelt proposed spending $10 billion while revenues were only $3 billion. Between 1933 and 1936, government expenditures rose by more than 83 percent. Federal debt skyrocketed by 73 percent.

FDR talked Congress into creating Social Security in 1935 and imposing the nation's first comprehensive minimum wage law in 1938. While to this day he gets a great deal of credit for these two measures from the general public, many economists have a different perspective. The minimum wage law prices many of the inexperienced, the young, the unskilled and the disadvantaged out of the labor market. (For example, the minimum wage provisions passed as part of another act in 1933 threw an estimated 500,000 blacks out of work). [54] And current studies and estimates reveal that Social Security has become such a long-term actuarial nightmare that it will either have to be privatized or the already high taxes needed to keep it afloat will have to be raised to the stratosphere.

---

[52] Anderson, p. 315.
[53] "FDR's Disputed Legacy," p. 24.
[54] Anderson, p. 336.

Roosevelt secured passage of the Agricultural Adjustment Act, which levied a new tax on agricultural processors and used the revenue to supervise the wholesale destruction of valuable crops and cattle. Federal agents oversaw the ugly spectacle of perfectly good fields of cotton, wheat and corn being plowed under (the mules had to be convinced to trample the crops; they had been trained, of course, to walk between the rows). Healthy cattle, sheep and pigs were slaughtered and buried in mass graves. Secretary of Agriculture Henry Wallace personally gave the order to slaughter 6 million baby pigs before they grew to full size. The administration also paid farmers for the first time for not working at all. Even if the AAA had helped farmers by curtailing supplies and raising prices, it could have done so only by hurting millions of others who had to pay those prices or make do with less to eat.

Blue Eagles, Red Ducks

Perhaps the most radical aspect of the New Deal was the National Industrial Recovery Act, passed in June 1933, which created a massive new bureaucracy called the National Recovery Administration. Under the NRA, most manufacturing industries were suddenly forced into government-mandated cartels. Codes that regulated prices and terms of sale briefly transformed much of the American economy into a fascist-style arrangement, while the NRA was financed by new taxes on the very industries it controlled. Some economists have estimated that the NRA boosted the cost of doing business by an average of *40 percent—* not something a depressed economy needed for recovery.

The economic impact of the NRA was immediate and powerful. In the five months leading up to the act's passage, signs of recovery were evident: factory employment and payrolls had increased by 23 and 35 percent, respectively. Then came the NRA, shortening hours of work, raising wages arbitrarily and imposing other new costs on enterprise. In the six months after the law took effect, industrial production dropped 25 percent. Benjamin M. Anderson writes, "NRA was not a revival measure. It was an antirevival measure. . . . Through the whole of the NRA period industrial production did not rise as high as it had been in July 1933, before NRA came in." [55]

The man Roosevelt picked to direct the NRA effort was General Hugh "Iron Pants" Johnson, a profane, red-faced bully and professed

---

[55] Ibid., pp. 332-334.

admirer of Italian dictator Benito Mussolini. Thundered Johnson, "May Almighty God have mercy on anyone who attempts to interfere with the Blue Eagle" (the official symbol of the NRA, which one senator derisively referred to as the "Soviet duck"). Those who refused to comply with the NRA Johnson personally threatened with public boycotts and "a punch in the nose."

There were ultimately more than 500 NRA codes, "ranging from the production of lightning rods to the manufacture of corsets and brassieres, covering more than 2 million employers and 22 million workers." [56] There were codes for the production of hair tonic, dog leashes, and even musical comedies. A New Jersey tailor named Jack Magid was arrested and sent to jail for the "crime" of pressing a suit of clothes for 35 cents rather than the NRA-inspired "Tailor's Code" of 40 cents.

In *The Roosevelt Myth*, historian John T. Flynn described how the NRA's partisans sometimes conducted "business":

> The NRA was discovering it could not enforce its rules. Black markets grew up. Only the most violent police methods could procure enforcement. In Sidney Hillman's garment industry the code authority employed enforcement police. They roamed through the garment district like storm troopers. They could enter a man's factory, send him out, line up his employees, subject them to minute interrogation, take over his books on the instant. Night work was forbidden. Flying squadrons of these private coat-and-suit police went through the district at night, battering down doors with axes looking for men who were committing the crime of sewing together a pair of pants at night. But without these harsh methods many code authorities said there could be no compliance because the public was not back of it. [57]

The Alphabet Commissars

Roosevelt next signed into law steep income tax increases on the higher brackets and introduced a 5 percent withholding tax on corporate dividends. He secured another tax increase in 1934. In fact, tax hikes became a favorite policy of Roosevelt for the next 10 years, culminating in a top income tax rate of 90 percent. Sen. Arthur

---

[56] "FDR's Disputed Legacy," p. 30.
[57] John T. Flynn, *The Roosevelt Myth* (Garden City, N.Y.: Garden City Publishing Co., Inc., 1949), p. 45.

Vandenberg of Michigan, who opposed much of the New Deal, lambasted Roosevelt's massive tax increases. A sound economy would not be restored, he said, by following the socialist notion that America could "lift the lower one-third up" by pulling "the upper two-thirds down." [58] Vandenberg also condemned "the congressional surrender to alphabet commissars who deeply believe the American people need to be regimented by powerful overlords in order to be saved."[59]

Alphabet commissars spent the public's money like it was so much bilge. They were what influential journalist and social critic Albert Jay Nock had in mind when he described the New Deal as "a nation-wide, State-managed mobilization of inane buffoonery and aimless commotion."[60]

Roosevelt's Civil Works Administration hired actors to give free shows and librarians to catalog archives. It even paid researchers to study the history of the safety pin, hired 100 Washington workers to patrol the streets with balloons to frighten starlings away from public buildings, and put men on the public payroll to chase tumbleweeds on windy days.

The CWA, when it was started in the fall of 1933, was supposed to be a short-lived jobs program. Roosevelt assured Congress in his State of the Union message that any new such program would be abolished within a year. "The federal government," said the president, "must and shall quit this business of relief. I am not willing that the vitality of our people be further stopped by the giving of cash, of market baskets, of a few bits of weekly work cutting grass, raking leaves, or picking up papers in the public parks." Harry Hopkins was put in charge of the agency and later said, "I've got four million at work but for God's sake, don't ask me what they are doing." The CWA came to an end within a few months but was replaced with another temporary relief program that evolved into the Works Progress Administration, or WPA, by 1935. It is known today as the very government program that gave rise to the new term, "boondoggle," because it "produced" a lot more than the

---

[58] C. David Tompkins, *Senator Arthur H. Vandenberg: The Evolution of a Modern Republican, 1884–1945* (East Lansing, MI: Michigan State University Press, 1970), p. 157.

[59] Ibid., p. 121.

[60] Albert J. Nock, *Our Enemy, the State* (www.barefootsworld.net/nockoets1.html), Chapter 1, Section IV.

77,000 bridges and 116,000 buildings to which its advocates loved to point as evidence of its efficacy.[61]

With good reason, critics often referred to the WPA as "We Piddle Around." In Kentucky, WPA workers catalogued 350 different ways to cook spinach. The agency employed 6,000 "actors" though the nation's actors' union claimed only 4,500 members. Hundreds of WPA workers were used to collect campaign contributions for Democratic Party candidates. In Tennessee, WPA workers were fired if they refused to donate 2 percent of their wages to the incumbent governor. By 1941, only 59 percent of the WPA budget went to paying workers anything at all; the rest was sucked up in administration and overhead. The editors of *The New Republic* asked, "Has [Roosevelt] the moral stature to admit now that the WPA was a hasty and grandiose political gesture, that it is a wretched failure and should be abolished?"[62] The last of the WPA's projects was not eliminated until July of 1943.

Roosevelt has been lauded for his "job-creating" acts such as the CWA and the WPA. Many people think that they helped relieve the Depression. What they fail to realize is that it was the rest of Roosevelt's tinkering that prolonged the Depression and which largely prevented the jobless from finding real jobs in the first place. The stupefying roster of wasteful spending generated by these jobs programs represented a diversion of valuable resources to politically motivated and economically counterproductive purposes.

A brief analogy will illustrate this point. If a thief goes house to house robbing everybody in the neighborhood, then heads off to a nearby shopping mall to spend his ill-gotten loot, it is not assumed that because his spending "stimulated" the stores at the mall he has thereby performed a national service or provided a general economic benefit. Likewise, when the government hires someone to catalog the many ways of cooking spinach, his tax-supported paycheck cannot be counted as a net increase to the economy because the wealth used to pay him was simply diverted, not created. Economists today must still battle this "magical thinking" every time more government spending is proposed—as if money comes not from productive citizens, but rather from the tooth fairy.

"An Astonishing Rabble Of Impudent Nobodies"

---

[61] Martin Morse Wooster, "Bring Back the WPA? It Also Had A Seamy Side," *The Wall Street Journal*, September 3, 1986, p. A26.
[62] Ibid.

Roosevelt's haphazard economic interventions garnered credit from people who put high value on the appearance of being in charge and "doing something." Meanwhile, the great majority of Americans were patient. They wanted very much to give this charismatic polio victim and former New York governor the benefit of the doubt. But Roosevelt always had his critics, and they would grow more numerous as the years groaned on. One of them was the inimitable "Sage of Baltimore," H. L. Mencken, who rhetorically threw everything but the kitchen sink at the president. Paul Johnson sums up Mencken's stinging but often-humorous barbs this way:

> Mencken excelled himself in attacking the triumphant FDR, whose whiff of fraudulent collectivism filled him with genuine disgust. He was the 'Fuhrer,' the 'Quack,' surrounded by 'an astonishing rabble of impudent nobodies,' 'a gang of half-educated pedagogues, nonconstitutional lawyers, starry-eyed uplifters and other such sorry wizards.' His New Deal was a 'political racket,' a 'series of stupendous bogus miracles,' with its 'constant appeals to class envy and hatred,' treating government as 'a milch-cow with 125 million teats' and marked by 'frequent repudiations of categorical pledges.'[63]

Signs of Life

The American economy was soon relieved of the burden of some of the New Deal's worst excesses when the Supreme Court outlawed the NRA in 1935 and the AAA in 1936, earning Roosevelt's eternal wrath and derision. Recognizing much of what Roosevelt did as unconstitutional, the "nine old men" of the Court also threw out other, more minor acts and programs which hindered recovery.

Freed from the worst of the New Deal, the economy showed some signs of life. Unemployment dropped to 18 percent in 1935, 14 percent in 1936, and even lower in 1937. But by 1938, it was back up to nearly 20 percent as the economy slumped again. The stock market crashed nearly 50 percent between August 1937 and March 1938. The "economic stimulus" of Franklin Delano Roosevelt's New Deal had achieved a real "first": *a depression within a depression!*

Phase IV: The Wagner Act

---

[63] Johnson, p. 762.

The stage was set for the 1937–38 collapse with the passage of the National Labor Relations Act in 1935—better known as the "Wagner Act" and organized labor's "Magna Carta." To quote Sennholz again:

> This law revolutionized American labor relations. It took labor disputes out of the courts of law and brought them under a newly created Federal agency, the National Labor Relations Board, which became prosecutor, judge, and jury, all in one. Labor union sympathizers on the Board further perverted this law, which already afforded legal immunities and privileges to labor unions. The U.S. thereby abandoned a great achievement of Western civilization, equality under the law.

> The Wagner Act, or National Labor Relations Act, was passed in reaction to the Supreme Court's voidance of NRA and its labor codes. It aimed at crushing all employer resistance to labor unions. Anything an employer might do in self-defense became an "unfair labor practice" punishable by the Board. The law not only obliged employers to deal and bargain with the unions designated as the employees' representative; later Board decisions also made it unlawful to resist the demands of labor union leaders.[64]

Armed with these sweeping new powers, labor unions went on a militant organizing frenzy. Threats, boycotts, strikes, seizures of plants and widespread violence pushed productivity down sharply and unemployment up dramatically. Membership in the nation's labor unions soared: By 1941, there were two and a half times as many Americans in unions as had been the case in 1935. Historian William E. Leuchtenburg, himself no friend of free enterprise, observed, "Property-minded citizens were scared by the seizure of factories, incensed when strikers interfered with the mails, vexed by the intimidation of nonunionists, and alarmed by flying squadrons of workers who marched, or threatened to march, from city to city."[65]

An Unfriendly Climate for Business

From the White House on the heels of the Wagner Act came a thunderous barrage of insults against business. Businessmen, Roosevelt fumed, were obstacles on the road to recovery. He blasted them as "economic royalists" and said that businessmen as a class were

---

64 Sennholz, pp. 212-213.
65 William E. Leuchtenburg, *Franklin D. Roosevelt and the New Deal, 1932–1940* (New York: Harper and Row, 1963), p. 242.

"stupid."[66] He followed up the insults with a rash of new punitive measures. New strictures on the stock market were imposed. A tax on corporate retained earnings, called the "undistributed profits tax," was levied. "These soak-the-rich efforts," writes economist Robert Higgs, "left little doubt that the president and his administration intended to push through Congress everything they could to extract wealth from the high-income earners responsible for making the bulk of the nation's decisions about private investment."[67]

During a period of barely two months during late 1937, the market for steel—a key economic barometer—plummeted from 83 percent of capacity to 35 percent. When that news emblazoned headlines, Roosevelt took an ill-timed nine-day fishing trip. *The New York Herald-Tribune* implored him to get back to work to stem the tide of the renewed Depression. What was needed, said the newspaper's editors, was a reversal of the Roosevelt policy "of bitterness and hate, of setting class against class and punishing all who disagreed with him."[68]

Columnist Walter Lippmann wrote in March 1938 that "with almost no important exception every measure he [Roosevelt] has been interested in for the past five months has been to reduce or discourage the production of wealth."[69]

As pointed out earlier in this essay, Herbert Hoover's own version of a "New Deal" had hiked the top marginal income tax rate from 24 to 63 percent in 1932. But he was a piker compared to his tax-happy successor. Under Roosevelt, the top rate was raised at first to 79 percent and then later to 90 percent. Economic historian Burton Folsom notes that in 1941 Roosevelt even proposed a whopping 99.5-percent marginal rate on all incomes over $100,000. "Why not?" he said when an advisor questioned the idea.[70]

After that confiscatory proposal failed, Roosevelt issued an executive order to tax all income over $25,000 at the astonishing rate of

---

[66] Ibid., pp. 183-184.

[67] Robert Higgs, "Regime Uncertainty: Why the Great Depression Lasted So Long and Why Prosperity Resumed After the War," *The Independent Review*, Volume I, Number 4: Spring 1997, p. 573.

[68] Gary Dean Best, *The Critical Press and the New Deal: The Press Versus Presidential Power, 1933–1938* (Westport, Connecticut: Praeger Publishers, 1993), p. 130.

[69] Ibid., p. 136.

[70] Burton Folsom, "What's Wrong With The Progressive Income Tax?", *Viewpoint on Public Issues*, No. 99-18, May 3, 1999, Mackinac Center for Public Policy, Midland, Michigan.

100 percent. He also promoted the lowering of the personal exemption to only $600, a tactic that pushed most American families into paying at least some income tax for the first time. Shortly thereafter, Congress rescinded the executive order, but went along with the reduction of the personal exemption.[71]

Meanwhile, the Federal Reserve again seesawed its monetary policy in the mid-1930s, first up then down, then up sharply through America's entry into World War II. Contributing to the economic slide of 1937 was this fact: From the summer of 1936 to the spring of 1937, the Fed doubled reserve requirements on the nation's banks. Experience has shown time and again that a roller-coaster monetary policy is enough by itself to produce a roller-coaster economy.

Still stinging from his earlier Supreme Court defeats, Roosevelt tried in 1937 to "pack" the Supreme Court with a proposal to allow the president to appoint an additional justice to the Court for every sitting justice who had reached the age of 70 and did not retire. Had this proposal passed, Roosevelt could have appointed six new justices favorable to his views, increasing the members of the Court from 9 to 15. His plan failed in Congress, but the Court later began rubber-stamping his policies after a number of opposing justices retired. Until Congress killed the packing scheme, however, business fears that a Court sympathetic to Roosevelt's goals would endorse more of the old New Deal prevented investment and confidence from reviving.

Economic historian Robert Higgs draws a close connection between the level of private investment and the course of the American economy in the 1930s. The relentless assaults of the Roosevelt administration—in both word and deed—against business, property, and free enterprise guaranteed that the capital needed to jump-start the economy was either taxed away or forced into hiding. When FDR took America to war in 1941, he eased up on his anti-business agenda, but a great deal of the nation's capital was diverted into the war effort instead of into plant expansion or consumer goods. Not until both Roosevelt and the war were gone did investors feel confident enough to "set in motion the postwar investment boom that powered the economy's return to sustained prosperity."[72]

---

[71] Ibid.
[72] Higgs, p. 564.

This view gains support in these comments from one of the country's leading investors of the time, Lammot du Pont, offered in 1937:

> Uncertainty rules the tax situation, the labor situation, the monetary situation, and practically every legal condition under which industry must operate. Are taxes to go higher, lower or stay where they are? We don't know. Is labor to be union or non-union? . . . Are we to have inflation or deflation, more government spending or less? ... Are new restrictions to be placed on capital, new limits on profits? . . . It is impossible to even guess at the answers."[73]

Many modern historians tend to be reflexively anti-capitalist and distrustful of free markets; they find Roosevelt's exercise of power, constitutional or not, to be impressive and historically "interesting." In surveys, a majority consistently rank FDR near the top of the list for presidential greatness, so it is likely they would disdain the notion that the New Deal was responsible for prolonging the Great Depression. But when a nationally representative poll by the American Institute of Public Opinion in the spring of 1939 asked, "Do you think the attitude of the Roosevelt administration toward business is delaying business recovery?" the American people responded "yes" by a margin of more than 2-to-1. The business community felt even more strongly so.[74]

In his private diary, FDR's very own Treasury Secretary, Henry Morgenthau, seemed to agree. He wrote: "We have tried spending money. We are spending more than we have ever spent before and it does not work. . . . We have never made good on our promises. ... I say after eight years of this Administration we have just as much unemployment as when we started . . . and an enormous debt to boot!"[75]

At the end of the decade and 12 years after the stock market crash of Black Thursday, 10 million Americans were jobless. The unemployment rate was in excess of 17 percent. Roosevelt had pledged in 1932 to end the crisis, but it persisted two presidential terms and countless interventions later.

Whither Free Enterprise?

---

[73] Quoted in Herman E. Kroos, *Executive Opinion: What Business Leaders Said and Thought on Economic Issues, 1920s–1960s* (Garden City, N.Y.: Doubleday and Co., 1970), p. 200.
[74] Higgs, p. 577.
[75] Blum, pp. 24-25.

How was it that FDR was elected four times if his policies were deepening and prolonging an economic catastrophe? Ignorance and a willingness to give the president the benefit of the doubt explain a lot. Roosevelt beat Hoover in 1932 with promises of less government. He instead gave Americans more government, but he did so with fanfare and fireside chats that mesmerized a desperate people. By the time they began to realize that his policies were harmful, World War II came, the people rallied around their commander-in-chief, and there was little desire to change the proverbial horse in the middle of the stream by electing someone new.

Along with the holocaust of World War II came a revival of trade with America's allies. The war's destruction of people and resources did not help the U.S. economy, but this renewed trade did. A reinflation of the nation's money supply counteracted the high costs of the New Deal, but brought with it a problem that plagues us to this day: a dollar that buys less and less in goods and services year after year. Most importantly, the Truman administration that followed Roosevelt was decidedly less eager to berate and bludgeon private investors and as a result, those investors re-entered the economy and fueled a powerful postwar boom. The Great Depression finally ended, but it should linger in our minds today as one of the most colossal and tragic failures of government and public policy in American history.

The genesis of the Great Depression lay in the irresponsible monetary and fiscal policies of the U.S. government in the late 1920s and early 1930s. These policies included a litany of political missteps: central bank mismanagement, trade-crushing tariffs, incentive-sapping taxes, mind-numbing controls on production and competition, senseless destruction of crops and cattle and coercive labor laws, to recount just a few. It was not the free market that produced 12 years of agony; rather, it was political bungling on a grand scale.

Those who can survey the events of the 1920s and 1930s and blame free-market capitalism for the economic calamity have their eyes, ears and minds firmly closed to the facts. Changing the wrong-headed thinking that constitutes much of today's conventional wisdom about this sordid historical episode is vital to reviving faith in free markets and preserving our liberties.

The nation managed to survive both Hoover's activism and Roosevelt's New Deal quackery, and now the American heritage of freedom awaits a rediscovery by a new generation of citizens. This time we have nothing to fear but myths and misconceptions.

Postscript: Have We Learned Our Lessons?

Eighty years after the Great Depression began, the literature on this painful episode of American history is undergoing an encouraging metamorphosis. The conventional assessment that so dominated historical writings for decades argued that free markets caused the debacle and that FDR's New Deal saved the country. Surely, there are plenty of poorly-informed partisans, ideologues and quacks that still make these superficial claims. Serious historians and economists, however, have been busy chipping away at the falsehoods. The essay you have just read cites many recent works worth careful reading in their entirety.

At the very moment this latest edition of *Great Myths of the Great Depression* was about to go to press, Simon & Schuster published a splendid new volume I strongly recommend. Authored by the Foundation for Economic Education's senior historian and Hillsdale College professor, Dr. Burton W. Folsom, the book is provocatively titled *New Deal or Raw Deal?—How FDR's Economic Legacy Has Damaged America*. It's one of the most illuminating works on the subject. It will help mightily to correct the record and educate our fellow citizens about what really happened in the 1930s.

Another great addition to the literature, appearing in 2007, is *The Forgotten Man: A New History of the Great Depression* by Amity Shlaes. The fact that it has been a *New York Times* bestseller suggests there is a real hunger for the truth about this period of history.

While Americans may be unlearning some of what they thought they knew about the Great Depression, that's not the same as saying we have learned the important lessons well enough to avoid making the same mistakes again. Indeed, today we are no closer to fixing the primary cause of the business cycle—monetary mischief—than we were 80 years ago.

The financial crisis that gripped America in 2008 ought to be a wake-up call. The fingerprints of government meddling are all over it.

From 2001 to 2005, the Federal Reserve revved up the money supply, expand-ing it at a feverish double-digit rate. The dollar plunged in overseas markets and commodity prices soared. With the banks flush with liquidity from the Fed, interest rates plummeted and risky loans to borrowers of dubious merit ballooned. Politicians threw more fuel on the fire by jawboning banks to lend hundreds of billions of dollars for subprime mortgages.

When the bubble burst, some of the very culprits who promoted the policies that caused it postured as our rescuers while endorsing new interventions, bigger government, more inflation of money and credit and massive taxpayer bailouts of failing firms. Many of them are also calling for higher taxes and tariffs, the very nonsense that took a recession in 1930 and made it a long and deep depression.

The taxpayer bailouts of agencies such as Fannie Mae and Freddie Mac, as well as a growing number of private firms in the early fall of 2008, represent more folly with a monumental price tag. Not only will we and future generations be paying those bills for decades, the very process of throwing good money after bad will pile moral hazard on top of moral hazard, fostering more bad decisions and future bailouts. This is the stuff that undermines both free enterprise and the soundness of the currency. Much more inflation to pay these bills is more than a little likely, sooner or later.

"Government," observed the renowned Austrian economist Ludwig von Mises, "is the only institution that can take a valuable commodity like paper, and make it worthless by applying ink." Mises was describing the curse of inflation, the process whereby government expands a nation's money supply and thereby erodes the value of each monetary unit—dollar, peso, pound, franc or whatever. It often shows up in the form of rising prices, which most people confuse with the inflation itself. The distinction is an important one because, as economist Percy Greaves explained so eloquently, "Changing the definition changes the responsibility."

Define inflation as rising prices and, like the clueless Jimmy Carter of the 1970s, you'll think that oil sheiks, credit cards and private bus-inesses are the culprits, and price controls are the answer. Define inflation in the classic fashion as an increase in the supply of money and credit, with rising prices as a consequence, and you then have to ask the revealing question, "Who increases the money supply?" Only one entity can do that legally; all others are called "counterfeiters" and go to jail.

Nobel laureate Milton Friedman argued indisputably that inflation is always and everywhere a monetary matter. Rising prices no more cause inflation than wet streets cause rain.

Before paper money, governments inflated by diminishing the precious-metal content of their coinage. The ancient prophet Isaiah reprimanded the Israelites with these words: "Thy silver has become dross, thy wine mixed with water." Roman emperors repeatedly melted down the silver denarius and added junk metals until the denarius was less than one percent silver. The Saracens of Spain clipped the edges of their coins so they could mint more until the coins became too small to circulate. Prices rose as a mirror image of the currency's worth.

Rising prices are not the only consequence of monetary and credit expansion. Inflation also erodes savings and encourages debt. It undermines confidence and deters investment. It destabilizes the economy by fostering booms and busts. If it's bad enough, it can even wipe out the very government responsible for it in the first place and then lead to even worse afflictions. Hitler and Napoleon both rose to power in part because of the chaos of runaway inflations.

All this raises many issues economists have long debated: Who or what should determine a nation's supply of money? Why do governments so regularly mismanage it? What is the connection between fiscal and monetary policy? Suffice it to say here that governments inflate because their appetite for revenue exceeds their willingness to tax or their ability to borrow. British economist John Maynard Keynes was an influential charlatan in many ways, but he nailed it when he wrote, "By a continuing process of inflation, governments can confiscate, secretly and unobserved, an important part of the wealth of their citizens."

So, you say, inflation is nasty business but it's just an isolated phenomenon with the worst cases confined to obscure nooks and crannies like Zimbabwe. Not so. The late Frederick Leith-Ross, a famous authority on international finance, observed: "Inflation is like sin; every government denounces it and every government practices it." Even Americans have witnessed hyperinflations that destroyed two currencies—the ill-fated continental dollar of the Revolutionary War and the doomed Confederate money of the Civil War.

Today's slow-motion dollar depreciation, with consumer prices rising at persistent but mere single-digit rates, is just a limited version of the same process. Government spends, runs deficits and pays some of its bills through the inflation tax. How long it can go on is a matter of speculation, but trillions in national debt and politicians who make misers of drunken sailors and get elected by promising even more are not factors that should encourage us.

Inflation is very much with us but it must end someday. A currency's value is not bottomless. Its erosion must cease either because govern-ment stops its reckless printing or prints until it wrecks the money. But surely, which way it concludes will depend in large measure on whether its victims come to understand what it is and where it comes from. Meanwhile, our economy looks like a roller coaster because Congresses, Presidents and the agencies they've empowered never cease their monetary mischief.

Are you tired of politicians blaming each other, scrambling to cover their behinds and score political points in the midst of a crisis, and piling debts upon debts they audaciously label "stimulus packages"? Why do so many Americans want to trust them with their health care, education, retirement and a host of other aspects of their lives? It's madness writ large. The antidote is the truth. We must learn the lessons of our follies and resolve to fix them now, not later.

To that end, I invite the reader to join the education process. Support organizations like FEE that are working to inform citizens about the proper role of government and how a free economy operates. Help distribute copies of this essay and other good publications that promote liberty and free enterprise. Demand that your representatives in govern-ment balance the budget, conform to the spirit and letter of the Consti-tution and stop trying to buy your vote with other people's money.

Everyone has heard the sage observation of philosopher George Santayana: "Those who cannot remember the past are condemned to repeat it." It's a warning we should not fail to heed.

—LWR, 2010

Chapter **Forty-Two**

The 1932 Bait-and-Switch

Harry Truman once said, "The only thing new in the world is the history you don't know." That observation applies especially well to what tens of millions of Americans have been taught about Franklin Delano Roosevelt, the man under whom Truman served as vice president for about a month. Recent scholarship (including a highly acclaimed book, *New Deal or Raw Deal*, by FEE senior historian Burton Folsom) is thankfully disabusing Americans of the once-popular myth that FDR saved us from the Great Depression.

Another example is a 2004 article by two UCLA economists—Harold L. Cole and Lee E. Ohanian—in the important mainstream *Journal of Political Economy*. They observed that Franklin Roosevelt extended the Great Depression by seven long years. "The economy was poised for a beautiful recovery," the authors show, "but that recovery was stalled by these misguided policies."

In a commentary on Cole and Ohanian's research, Loyola University economist Thomas DiLorenzo pointed out that six years after FDR took office, unemployment was almost six times the pre-Depression level.

Per capita GDP, personal consumption expenditures, and net private investment were all lower in 1939 than they were in 1929.

"The fact that it has taken 'mainstream' neoclassical economists so long to recognize [that FDR's policies exacerbated the disaster]," notes DiLorenzo, "is truly astounding," but still "better late than never."

Part of the Great FDR Myth is the notion that he won the presidency in 1932 with a mandate for central planning. My own essay on this period (*Great Myths of the Great Depression*) argued otherwise, based on the very platform and promises on which FDR ran. But until a few months ago I was unaware of a long-forgotten book that makes the case as well as any.

Hell Bent for Election was written by James P. Warburg, a banker who witnessed the 1932 election and the first two years of Roosevelt's first term from the inside. Warburg, the son of prominent financier and Federal Reserve cofounder Paul Warburg, was no less than a high-level financial adviser to FDR himself. Disillusioned with the President, he left the administration in 1934 and wrote his book a year later.

Warburg voted for the man who said this on March 2, 1930, as governor of New York:

> The doctrine of regulation and legislation by "master minds," in whose judgment and will all the people may gladly and quietly acquiesce, has been too glaringly apparent at Washington during these last ten years. Were it possible to find "master minds" so unselfish, so willing to decide unhesitatingly against their own personal interests or private prejudices, men almost godlike in their ability to hold the scales of justice with an even hand, such a government might be to the interests of the country; but there are none such on our political horizon, and we cannot expect a complete reversal of all the teachings of history.

What Warburg and the country actually elected in 1932 was a man whose subsequent performance looks little like the platform and promises on which he ran and a lot like those of that year's Socialist Party candidate, Norman Thomas.

Who campaigned for a "drastic" reduction of 25 percent in federal spending, a balanced federal budget, a rollback of government intrusion into agriculture, and restoration of a sound gold currency? Roosevelt did. Who called the administration of incumbent Herbert Hoover "the greatest spending administration in peace time in all our history" and assailed it for raising taxes and tariffs? Roosevelt did. FDR's running mate, John Nance Garner, even declared that Hoover "was leading the country down the road to socialism."

Copying Hoover and the Socialists

It was socialist Norman Thomas, not Franklin Roosevelt, who proposed massive increases in federal spending and deficits and sweeping interventions into the private economy—and he barely mustered 2 percent of the vote. When the dust settled, Warburg shows, we got what Thomas promised, more of what Hoover had been lambasted for, and almost nothing that FDR himself had pledged. FDR employed more "master minds" to plan the economy than perhaps all previous presidents combined.

After detailing the promises and the duplicity, Warburg offered this assessment of the man who betrayed him and the country:

> Much as I dislike to say so, it is my honest conviction that Mr. Roosevelt has utterly lost his sense of proportion. He sees himself as the one man who can save the country, as the one man who can "save capitalism from itself," as the one man who knows what is good for us and what is not. He sees himself as indispensable. And when a man thinks of himself as being indispensable . . . that man is headed for trouble.

Was FDR an economic wizard? Warburg reveals nothing of the sort, observing that FDR was "undeniably and shockingly superficial about anything that relates to finance." He was driven not by logic, facts, or humility but by "his emotional desires, predilections, and prejudices."

"Mr. Roosevelt," wrote Warburg, "gives me the impression that he can really believe what he wants to believe, really think what he wants to think, and really remember what he wants to remember, to a greater extent than anyone I have ever known." Less charitable observers might diagnose the problem as "delusions of grandeur."

"I believe that Mr. Roosevelt is so charmed with the fun of brandishing the band leader's baton at the head of the parade, so pleased with the picture he sees of himself, that he is no longer capable of recognizing that the human power to lead is limited, that the 'new ideas' of leadership dished up to him by his bright young men in the Brain Trust are nothing but old ideas that have been tried before, and that one cannot uphold the social order defined in the Constitution and at the same time undermine it," Warburg lamented.

So if Warburg was right (and I believe he was), Franklin Delano Roosevelt misled the country with his promises in 1932 and put personal ambition and power lust in charge—not a very uncommon thing as politicians go. In any event, the country got a nice little bait-and-switch deal, and the economy languished as a result.

In the world of economics and free exchange, the rule is that you get what you pay for. The 1932 election is perhaps the best example of the rule that prevails all too often in the political world: You get what you voted against.

—LWR, June 2010

43

Chapter **Forty-Three**

Child Labor and the British Industrial Revolution

Everyone agrees that in the 100 years between 1750 and 1850 there took place in Great Britain profound economic changes. This was the age of the Industrial Revolution, complete with a cascade of technical innovations, a vast increase in industrial production, a renaissance of world trade, and rapid growth of urban populations.

Where historians and other observers clash is in the interpretation of these great changes. Were they "good" or "bad"? Did they represent improvement to the citizens, or did these events set them back? Perhaps no other issue within this realm has generated more intellectual heat than the one concerning the labor of children. The enemies of freedom—of capitalism—have successfully cast this matter as an irrefutable indictment of the capitalist system as it was emerging in nineteenth-century Britain.

The many reports of poor working conditions and long hours of difficult toil make harrowing reading, to be sure. William Cooke Taylor wrote at the time about contemporary reformers who, witnessing children at work in factories, thought to themselves, "How much more delightful would have been the gambol of the free limbs on the hillside;

the sight of the green mead with its spangles of buttercups and daisies; the song of the bird and the humming of the bee." [76]

Of those historians who have interpreted child labor in industrial Britain as a crime of capitalism, none have been more prominent than J. L. and Barbara Hammond. Their many works, including *Lord Shaftesbury* (1923), *The Village Labourer* (1911), *The Town Labourer* (1917), and *The Skilled Labourer* (1919) have been widely promoted as "authoritative" on the issue.

The Hammonds divided the factory children into two classes: "apprentice children" and "free-labour children." It is a distinction of enormous significance, though one the authors themselves failed utterly to appreciate. Once having made the distinction, the Hammonds proceeded to treat the two classes as though no distinction between them existed at all. A deluge of false and misleading conclusions about capitalism and child labor has poured forth for years as a consequence.

Opportunity or Oppression?

"Free-labour" children were those who lived at home but worked during the days in factories at the insistence of their parents or guardians. British historian E. P. Thompson, though generally critical of the factory system, nonetheless quite properly conceded that "it is perfectly true that the parents not only needed their children's earnings, but expected them to work."[77]

Professor Ludwig von Mises, the great Austrian economist; put it well when he noted that the generally deplorable conditions extant for centuries before the Industrial Revolution, and the low levels of productivity which created them, caused families to embrace the new opportunities the factories represented: "It is a distortion of facts to say that the factories carried off the housewives from the nurseries and the kitchens and the children from their play. These women had nothing to cook with and to feed their children. These children were destitute and starving. Their only refuge was the factory. It saved them, in the strict sense of the term, from death by starvation."[78]

---

[76][76] William Cooke Taylor, *The Factory System* (London, 1844), pp. 2.3-24.

[77] E. P Thompson, *The Making of the English Working Class* (New York: Random House, 1964), p. 339.

[78] Ludwig von Mises, *Human Action* (New Haven, Connecticut: Yale University Press, 1949). p. 615.

Private factory owners could not forcibly subjugate "free-labour" children; they could not compel them to work in conditions their parents found unacceptable. The mass exodus from the socialist Continent to increasingly capitalist, industrial Britain in the first half of the 19th century strongly suggests that people did indeed find the industrial order an attractive alternative. And no credible evidence exists which argues that parents in these early capitalist days were any less caring of their offspring than those of pre-capitalist times.

The situation, however, was much different for "apprentice" children, and close examination reveals that it was *these* children on whom the critics were focusing when they spoke of the "evils" of capitalism's Industrial Revolution. These youngsters, it turns out, were under the direct authority and supervision not of their parents in a free labor market, but of government officials. Many were orphans; a few were victims of negligent parents or parents whose health or lack of skills kept them from earning sufficient income to care for a family. All were in the custody of "parish authorities." As the Hammonds wrote, ". . . the first mills were placed on streams, and the necessary labour was provided by the importation of cartloads of pauper children from the workhouses in the big towns. London was an important source, for since the passing of Hanway's Act in 1767 the child population in the workhouses had enormously increased, and the parish authorities were anxious to find relief from the burden of their maintenance . . . . To the parish authorities, encumbered with great masses of unwanted children, the new cotton mills in Lancashire, Derby, and Notts were a godsend."[79]

The Hammonds proceed to report the horrors of these mills with descriptions like these: "crowded with overworked children," "hotbeds of putrid fever," "monotonous toil in a hell of human cruelty," and so forth. Page after page of the Hammonds' writings—as well as those of many other anti-capitalist historians—deal in this manner with the condition of these parish apprentices. Though consigned to the control of a government authority, these children are routinely held up as victims of the "capitalist order."

Historian Robert Hessen is one observer who has taken note of this historiographical mischief and has urged others to acknowledge the error. The parish apprentice children, he writes, were "sent into virtual

---

[79] J. L and Barbara Hammond, *The Town Labourer* (London: Longmans, Green, and Co., 1917), pp. 144.45.

slavery by the parish authorities, *a government body*: they were deserted or orphaned pauper children who were legally under the custody of the poor-law officials in the parish, and who were bound by these officials into long terms of unpaid apprenticeship in return for a bare subsistence."[80] Indeed, Hessen points out, the first Act in Britain that applied to factory children was passed to protect these very parish apprentices, not "free-labour" children.

The Role of the State

It has not been uncommon for historians, including many who lived and wrote in the 19th century, to report the travails of the apprentice children without ever realizing they were effectively indicting *government*, not the economic arrangement of free exchange we call capitalism. In 1857, Alfred Kydd published a two-volume work entitled *The History of the Factory Movement*. He speaks of "living bodies caught in the iron grip of machinery in rapid motion, and whirled in the air, bones crushed, and blood cast copiously on the floor, because of physical exhaustion." Then, in a most revealing statement, in which he refers to the children's "owners," Kydd declares that "The factory apprentices have been *sold* by auction as 'bankrupt's effects."[81] [Emphasis added.]

A surgeon by the name of Philip Gaskell made extensive observations of the physical condition of the manufacturing population in the 1830s. He published his findings in a book in 1836 entitled *Artisans and Machinery*. The casual reader would miss the fact that, in his revelations of ghastly conditions for children, he was referring to the parish apprentices: "That glaring mismanagement existed in numberless instances there can be no doubt; and that these unprotected creatures, thus thrown entirely into the power of the manufacturer, were overworked, often badly-fed, and worse treated. No wonder can be felt that these glaring mischiefs attracted observation, and finally, led to the passing of the Apprentice Bill, a bill intended to regulate these matters."[82]

---

[80] Robert Hessen, "The Effects of the Industrial Revolution on Women and Children," in Ayn Rand, *Capitalism: The Unknown Ideal* (New York: New American Library, 1967), p, 106.

[81] Alfred Kydd, *The History of the Factory Movement* (New York: Burr Franklin, n.d.), pp. 21-22.

[82] Philip Gaskell, *Artisans and Machinery* (New York: Augustus M. Kelley, 1968), p. 141.

The Apprentice Bill that Gaskell mentioned was passed in 1802, the first of the much-heralded factory legislation, the very one Hessen stresses was aimed at the abuse by the parish officials. It remains that capitalism is not a system of compulsion. The lack of physical force, in fact, is what distinguishes it from pre-capitalist, feudal times. When feudalism reigned, men, women, and children were indeed "sold" at auction, forced to work long hours at arduous manual labor, and compelled to toil under whatever conditions and for whatever compensation pleased their masters. This was the system of serfdom, and the deplorable system of parish apprenticeship was a remnant of Britain's feudal past.

The emergence of capitalism was sparked by a desire of Englishmen to rid themselves of coercive economic arrangements. The free laborer increasingly supplanted the serf as capitalism blossomed. It is a gross and most unfortunate distortion of history for anyone to contend that capitalism or its industrialization was to blame for the agony of the apprentice children.

Though it is inaccurate to judge capitalism guilty of the sins of parish apprenticeship, it would also be inaccurate to assume that free-labor children worked under ideal conditions in the early days of the Industrial Revolution. By today's standards, their situation was clearly bad. Such capitalist achievements as air conditioning and high levels of productivity would, in time, substantially ameliorate it, however. The evidence in favor of capitalism is thus compellingly suggestive: From 1750 to 1850, when the population of Great Britain nearly tripled, the exclusive choice of those flocking to the country for jobs was to work for private capitalists.

The Sadler Report

A discussion of child labor in Britain would be incomplete without some reference to the famous Sadler Report. Written by a Member of Parliament in 1832 and filled with stories of brutality, degradation, and Oppression against factory workers of all ages and status, it became the bible for indignant reformers well into the 20th century. The Hammonds described it as "one of the main sources of our knowledge of the conditions of factory life at the time. Its pages bring before the reader in the vivid form of dialogue the kind of life that was led by the victims of the new system." [83] Two other historians, B. L. Hutchins and A. Harrison, describe it as "one of the most valuable collections of evidence on industrial conditions that we possess."[84]

W. H. Hutt, in his essay, "The Factory System of the Early Nineteenth Century," reveals that bad as things were, they were never nearly so bad as the Sadler Report would have one believe. Sadler, it turns out, had been agitating for passage of the Ten Hours' Bill, and in doing so he employed every cheap political trick in the book, including the falsification of evidence.[85] The report was part of those tactics.

Hutt quotes R. H. Greg (author of *The Factory Question*, 1837), who accused Sadler of giving to the world "such a mass of ex-parte statements, and of gross falsehoods and calumnies . . . as probably never before found their way into any public document."[86]

This view is shared by no less an anti-capitalist than Friedrich Engels, partner of Karl Marx. In his book, *The Condition of the Working Classes in England*, Engels says this of the Sadler Report: "This is a very partisan document, which was drawn up entirely by enemies of the factory system for purely political purposes. Sadler was led astray by his passionate sympathies into making assertions of a most misleading and erroneous kind. He asked witnesses questions in such a way as to elicit answers which, although correct, nevertheless were stated in such a form as to give a wholly false impression."[87]

As already explained, the first of the factory legislation was an act of mercy for the enslaved apprentice children. Successive acts between 1819 and 1846, however, placed greater and greater restrictions on the employment of free-labor children. Were they necessary to correct alleged "evils of industrialization"?

The evidence strongly suggests that whatever benefits the legislation may have produced by preventing children from going to work (or raising the cost of employing them) were marginal, and probably were outweighed by the harm the laws actually caused.

---

[83] J. L. and Barbara Hammond, *Lord Shaftesbury* (London: Constable, 1923), p. 16.

[84] B. L. Hutchins and A. Harrison, *A History of Factory Legislation* (New York: Augustus M. Kelley, 1966), p. 34.

[85] W. H. Hurt, "The Factory System of the Early Nineteenth Century," in F. A. Hayek ed., *Capitalism and the Historians* (Chicago: University of Chicago Press, 1954), pp. 15684.

[86] Ibid., p. 158.

[87] Friedrich Engels, *The Condition of the Working Classes in England* (New York: Macmillan; 1958), p. 192.

Gaskell admitted a short time after one of them had passed that it "caused multitudes of children to be dismissed, but it has only increased the evils it was intended to remedy, and must of necessity be repealed."[88]

Hurt believes that "in the case of children's labor the effects [of restrictive laws] went further than the mere loss of their work; they lost their training and, consequently, theft skill as adults."[89]

Conditions of employment and sanitation were best, as the Factory Commission of 1833 documented, in the larger and newer factories. The owners of these larger establishments, which were more easily and frequently subject to visitation and scrutiny by inspectors, increasingly chose to dismiss children from employment rather than be subjected to elaborate, arbitrary, and ever-changing rules on how they might run a factory employing youths. The result of legislative intervention was that these dismissed children, most of whom needed to work in order to survive, were forced to seek jobs in smaller, older, and more out-of-the-way places where sanitation, lighting, and safety were markedly inferior.[90] Those who could not find new jobs were reduced to the status of their counterparts a hundred years before, that is, to irregular and grueling agricultural labor, or worse—in the words of Mises— "infested the country as vagabonds, beggars, tramps, robbers, and prostitutes."[91]

So it is that child labor was relieved of its worst attributes not by legislative fiat, but by the progressive march of an ever more productive, capitalist system. Child labor was virtually eliminated when, for the first time in history, the productivity of parents in free labor markets rose to the point that it was no longer economically necessary for children to work in order to survive. The emancipators and benefactors of children were not legislators or factory inspectors, but factory owners and financiers. Their efforts and investments in machinery led to a rise in real wages, to a growing abundance of goods at lower prices, and to an incomparable improvement in the general standard of living.

Of all the interpretations of industrial history, it would be difficult to find one more perverse than that which ascribes the suffering of

---

[88] Gaskell, p. 67.
[89] Hutt, p. 182.
[90] Hessen. p. 106.
[91] Mises, p. 614.

children to capitalism and its Industrial Revolution. The popular critique of child labor in industrial Britain is unwarranted, misdirected propaganda. The Hammonds and others should have focused on the activities of government, not capitalists, as the source of the children's plight. It is a confusion which has unnecessarily taken a heavy toll on the case for freedom and free markets. On this issue, it is long overdue for the friends of capitalism to take the ideological and historiographical offensive.

—LWR, April 1991

44

Chapter **Forty-Four**

Government, Poverty and Self-Reliance: Wisdom From 19th Century Presidents

I can hardly give a speech about presidents without citing a witty remark from an old friend of mine from Tennessee, humorist Tom Anderson. He once said, back in the 1970s, "Franklin Roosevelt proved a man could be president a lifetime; Harry Truman proved any man could be president; Dwight Eisenhower proved we really didn't need one; and every president since proved that it was dangerous to have one." Funny, but there's a kernel of truth there!

Here's a quotation from an American president. Who do you think it was?

The lessons of history, confirmed by the evidence immediately before me, show conclusively that continued dependence upon relief induces a spiritual and moral disintegration fundamentally destructive to the national fiber. To dole out relief in this way is to administer a narcotic, a subtle destroyer of the human spirit. It is inimical to the dictates of sound policy. It is in violation of the traditions of America.

Those were not the words of a 19th century president. They came from the lips of our 32nd chief executive, Franklin Delano Roosevelt, in his State of the Union Address on Jan. 4, 1935. A moment later, he declared, "The Federal Government must and shall quit this business of relief."

We all know that it didn't. Indeed, 30 years later Lyndon Johnson would take "this business of relief" to new and expensive heights in an official "War on Poverty." Another 30 years and more than $5 trillion in federal welfare later, a Democratic president in 1996 would sign a bill into law that ended the federal entitlement to welfare. As Ronald Reagan, a far wiser man, observed long before it dawned on Bill Clinton, "We fought a war on poverty, and poverty won."

What Reagan instinctively knew, Bill Clinton finally admitted and FDR preached but didn't practice was that government poverty programs are themselves poverty-stricken. We have paid an awful price in lives and treasure to learn some things that the vast majority of Americans of the 19th century—and the chief executives they elected—could have plainly told us: Government welfare or "relief" programs encouraged idleness, broke up families, produced intergenerational dependency and hopelessness, cost taxpayers a fortune and yielded harmful cultural pathologies that may take generations to cure.

The failure of the dole was so complete that one journalist a decade ago posed a question to which just about everybody knows the answer and the lesson it implies. "Ask yourself," wrote John Fund of *The Wall Street Journal*, "if you had a financial windfall and wanted to help the poor, would you even *think* about giving time or a check to the government?"

The pre-eminent beneficiaries of the whole 20th century experiment in federal poverty-fighting were not those whom the programs ostensibly were intended to help. Rather, those beneficiaries were primarily two other groups:

1. Politicians who got elected and re-elected as champions of the needy and downtrodden. Some were sincere and well-meaning. Others were cynical, ill-informed, short-sighted and opportunistic. All were deluded into traveling paths down which not a single administration of the 19th century ever ventured—the use of the public treasury for widespread handouts to the needy.

The problem was neatly summarized once again by Tom Anderson, whose vignette on recent presidents I cited earlier. Anderson said the "welfare state" got its name because, "The politicians get well, while everybody else pays the fare."

2. The bureaucracy—the armies of professional poverty fighters whose jobs and empires always seemed secure regardless of the actual effects of the programs they administered. Economist Walter Williams put it well when he described this as "feeding the sparrows through the horses." Williams also famously observed, "A lot of people went to Washington (D.C.) to do good, and apparently have done very well."

Liberty: The Real War on Poverty

An unabashed, unrepentant welfare statist would probably survey the men who held the highest office in the land during the 19th century and dismiss them as heartless, uncaring and hopelessly medieval. Even during the severe depressions of the 1830s and the 1890s, Presidents Martin Van Buren and Grover Cleveland never proposed that Washington, D.C., extend its reach to the relief of private distress broadly speaking, and they opposed even the smallest suggestions of that kind.

Welfare statists make a crucial error, however, when they imply that it was left to presidents of a more enlightened 20th century to finally care enough to help the poor. The fact is, our leaders in the 1800s did mount a war on poverty—the most comprehensive and effective ever mounted by any central government in world history. It just didn't have a gimmicky name like "Great Society," nor did it have a public relations office and elitist poverty conferences at expensive seaside resorts. If you could have pressed them then for a name for it, most if not all of those early chief executives might well have said their anti-poverty program was, in a word, liberty. This word meant things like self-reliance, hard work, entrepreneurship, the institutions of civil society, a strong and free economy, and government confined to its constitutional role as protector of liberty by keeping the peace.

James Madison

In hindsight, it's a little amazing that the last great president of the 19th century, Grover Cleveland, was just about as faithful to that legacy of liberty as the first great one of that century, Thomas Jefferson. When

Cleveland left office in March 1897, the federal government was still many years away from any sort of national program for public payments to the indigent.

To be sure, the Washington, D.C., establishment was bigger than Jefferson had left it in many other respects—alarmingly so, in most cases. But it was not yet even remotely a welfare state. Regardless of political party, the presidents of that period did not read into the Constitution any of the modern-day welfare-state assumptions. They understood these essential verities: Government has nothing to give anybody except what it first takes from somebody, and a government big enough to give the people everything they want is big enough to take away everything they've got. These chief executives had other things going for them, too—notably, a humbling faith in Divine Providence, and a healthy confidence in what a free and compassionate people could do without federal help.

And what a poverty program liberty proved to be! In spite of a horrendous civil war, half a dozen economic downturns and wave after wave of impoverished immigrants, America progressed from near-universal poverty at the start of the century to within reach of the world's highest per-capita income at the end of the century. The poverty that remained stood out like the proverbial sore thumb because it was now the exception, no longer the rule. In the absence of stultifying government welfare programs, our free and self-reliant citizenry spawned so many private, distress-relieving initiatives that American generosity became one of the marvels of the world. This essentially spontaneous, non-centrally-planned "war on poverty" stands in stark contrast to Lyndon Johnson's "Great Society" because it actually worked.

My assistant in preparing this paper, a Grove City College senior named Christopher Haberman, expressed in an e-mail to me a little frustration at what he was not finding as he researched the papers of Thomas Jefferson and James Madison. He wrote: "I was disappointed to find that there were not many direct references to poverty. It seems that (they) were more concerned with Barbary pirates. They had no concept of (direct) government aid to the impoverished."

Haberman was right. Consider Jefferson—the author of the Declaration of Independence, America's third president, and someone who exerted enormous intellectual influence during this country's formative years. His were the first two presidential terms of America's first full century as a nation. His election in 1800 marked a turning point from 12 years of Federalist Party rule and set the tone for decades to follow.

In his first Inaugural Address in 1801, Jefferson gave us a splendid summation of what government should do. It did not describe welfare programs, but rather, "A wise and frugal government, which shall restrain men from injuring one another, shall leave them otherwise free to regulate their own pursuits of industry and improvement, and shall not take from the mouth of labor the bread it has earned. This is the sum of good government."

A similar view was held by James Madison, a key figure in the construction of the Constitution, a prime defender of it in *The Federalist Papers* and our fourth president. Madison vetoed bills for so-called "internal improvements," such as roads, at federal expense, so it would have been inconceivable to Madison that it was constitutional to use the power of government to take from some people and give to others because the others were poor and needed it. While there might be a reasonable, even constitutional, case for certain federal road-building projects for national defense purposes (or at least the benefit of everyone), for Madison and Jefferson there was no constitutional case to be made for assistance to individuals in poverty.

In a speech in the U.S. House of Representatives years before he became president, Madison declared: "The government of the United States is a definite government, confined to specified objects. It is not like state governments, whose powers are more general. Charity is no part of the legislative duty of the government."

Honoring the Rules

Why didn't Jefferson, Madison and other American presidents of the 19th century simply stretch the Constitution until it included poverty assistance to individuals? Why does it seem to have hardly ever occurred to them? Many factors and reasons explain this, but this one was paramount: Such power was not to be found in the rule book.

Let me elaborate. Imagine playing a game—baseball, gin rummy, Monopoly or whatever—in which there is only one rule: anything goes.

What kind of a game would this be? Chaotic, frustrating, unpredictable, impossible. Eventually, the whole thing would degenerate into a free-for-all. And while simple games would be intolerable if played this way, the consequences for the many deadly serious things humans engage in—from driving on the highways to waging war—would be almost too frightful to imagine.

The most profound political and philosophical trend of our time is a serious erosion of any consensus about what government is supposed to do and what it is not supposed to do. But this was not so in Jefferson and Madison's day. The "instruction books" at that time were America's founding documents, namely the Declaration of Independence and the Constitution, including the Bill of Rights. In the spirit of those great works, most Americans shared a common view of "the sum of good government"—the protection of life and property.

Today, far too many people think that government exists to do anything for anybody at any time they ask for it, from children's day care to handouts for artists. Texas congressman Ron Paul is noted for blowing the whistle whenever a bill is proposed that violates the spirit or the letter of the Constitution, but quite often he does so all by himself. How are his appeals received by the great majority of other members of Congress? "Like water off a duck's back," he once told me.

I once gave a series of lectures to high school seniors, and I asked the students what they thought the responsibilities of government were. I heard "provide jobs" or "take care of the poor" far more often than I heard anything like "safeguard our freedoms." (In fact, I think the only time I heard the latter was when I said it myself.)

A while back, an organization called the Communitarian Network made news when it called for the federal government to make organ donations mandatory, so that each citizen's body after death could be "harvested" for the benefit of sick people. Like ending poverty, helping sick people is a good cause, but is it really a duty of government to take your kidneys?

You can imagine how Jefferson and Madison might have answered such a question. In their day, Americans appreciated the concept of individual rights and entertained very little of this nonsense. But there is no consensus today even on what a right *is*, let alone which ones free citizens have.

Years ago when the Reagan administration proposed abolishing subsidies to Amtrak, the nationalized passenger rail service, I was struck by a dissenter who phrased her objection on national television this way: "I don't know how those people in Washington expect us to get around out here. We have a right to this service."

Once when Congress voted to stop funding the printing of Playboy magazine in Braille, the American Council of the Blind filed suit in federal court, charging that the congressional action constituted censorship and *denial of a basic right.*

The lofty notion that individuals possess certain rights—definable, inalienable and sacred—has been cheapened beyond anything our Founders and early presidents would recognize. When those gifted thinkers asserted rights to "freedom of speech," "freedom of the press" or "freedom of assembly," they did not mean to say that one has a right to be given a microphone, a printing press, a lecture hall or a Playboy magazine at someone else's expense.

Indeed, their concept of rights did not require the initiation of force against others, or the elevation of any "want" to a lawful lien on the life or property of any other citizen. Each individual was deemed a unique and sovereign being, who required only that other citizens deal with him honestly and voluntarily or not at all. It was this notion of rights that became an important theme of America's founding documents and early presidencies. It is the only notion of rights that does not produce an unruly mob in which each person has his hands in someone else's pocket.

This wisdom prompted early Americans to add a Bill of Rights to a Constitution that already contained a separation of government powers, checks and balances, and numerous "thou-shalt-nots" directed at government itself. They knew—unlike tens of millions of Americans today—that a government that lacks narrow rules and strict boundaries, that robs Peter to pay Paul, that confuses rights with wants, will yield financial ruin at best and political tyranny at worst.

Jefferson, Madison and almost all of the succeeding 20 presidents of the 19th century were constrained by this view of the federal government, and most of them were happy to comply with it. When doing so, they were faithful to their charge. They were true poverty fighters, because they knew that if liberty were not preserved, poverty would be the least of our troubles. They had read the rule book, and they knew the importance of following the rules.

"Plain and Simple Duties"

Andrew Jackson, whose tenure stretched from 1829 to 1837, was our seventh president and an exceedingly popular one. He, too, reminded Congress frequently in Jeffersonian terms what the federal role was. In his fourth annual message on Dec. 4, 1832, he wrote:

"Limited to a general superintending power to maintain peace at home and abroad, and to prescribe laws on a few subjects of general interest not calculated to restrict human liberty, but to enforce human rights, this government will find its strength and its glory in the faithful discharge of these plain and simple duties."

In his second Inaugural Address three months later, Jackson again underscored the federal government's limited mission. He said:

> (I)t will be my aim to inculcate by my official acts the necessity of exercising by the General Government those powers only that are clearly delegated; to encourage simplicity and economy in the expenditures of the Government; to raise no more money from the people than may be requisite for these objects, and in a manner that will best promote the interests of all classes of the community and of all portions of the Union.

As if to head off any misunderstandings about the role of the federal government, Jackson went on to say, "To suppose that because our Government has been instituted for the benefit of the people it must therefore have the power to do what ever may seem to conduce to the public good is an error into which even honest minds are too apt to fall."

Compared to giants like Jefferson, Madison and Jackson, Franklin Pierce of New Hampshire is often thought of as a mere cipher. But he was another in a long string of 19th century American presidents who had their heads on straight when it came to the matter of federal poverty assistance. Among his nine vetoes was one in 1854 that nixed a bill to help the mentally ill. Here's what Pierce said:

> It can not be questioned that if Congress has power to make provision for the indigent insane . . . it has the same power to provide for the indigent who are not insane, and thus to transfer to the Federal Government the charge of all the poor in all the States. It has the same power to provide hospitals and other local establishments for the care and cure of every species of human infirmity, and thus to assume all that duty of either public philanthropy, or public necessity to the dependent, the orphan, the sick, or the needy which is now discharged by the States themselves or by corporate institutions or private endowments existing under the legislation of the States. The whole field of public beneficence is thrown open to the care and culture of the Federal Government. . . . If Congress may and ought to provide for any one of these objects, it may and ought to provide for them all.

It is a testament to the lack of federal welfare-style programs during more than 60 years under our first 13 presidents that Pierce, our 14th, termed as "novel" the very idea of "providing for the care and support of all those among the people of the United States who by any form of calamity become fit objects of public philanthropy."

Meanwhile, the poor of virtually every other nation on the planet were poor because of what governments were doing to them, often in the name of doing something for them: taxing and regulating them into penury; seizing their property and businesses; persecuting them for their faith; torturing and killing them because they held views different from those in power; and squandering their resources on official luxury, mindless warfare and wasteful boondoggles. America was about government not doing such things to people—and that one fact was, all by itself, a powerfully effective anti-poverty program.

"The Art of Associating Together"

Americans of all colors pulled themselves out of poverty in the 19th century by creating wealth through invention and enterprise. As they did so, they generously gave much of their income—along with their time and personal attention—to the aid of their neighbors and communities. When the French social commentator Alexis de Tocqueville visited a young, bustling America during the Jackson administration in the 1830s, he cited the vibrancy of this "civil society" as one of our greatest assets.

De Tocqueville was amazed that Americans were constantly forming "associations" to advance the arts, build libraries and hospitals, and meet social needs of every kind. If something good needed to be done, it didn't occur to Andrew Jackson or his fellow citizens to expect politicians and bureaucrats, who were distant in both space and spirit, to do it for them. "Among the laws that rule human societies," wrote de Tocqueville in "Democracy in America," "there is one which seems to be more precise and clear than all others. If men are to remain civilized or to become so, the art of associating together must grow and improve. . . ."

Indeed, this "art of associating together" in the 19th century produced the most remarkable flowering of private charitable assistance ever seen. This era saw the founding of many of America's most notable, lasting private associations—from the Salvation Army to the Red Cross.

For many reasons, such groups are far more effective in solving social problems—poverty, homelessness and illiteracy, for instance— than are government programs. They are more likely to get to the root of problems that stem from spiritual, attitudinal and behavioral deficiencies. They are also more inclined to demand accountability, which means they won't simply cut a check every two weeks without expecting the recipient to do something in return and change destructive patterns of behavior. Ultimately, private associations also tend to promote self-reliance, instead of dependency.

And if these groups don't produce results, they usually wither; the parishioners or others who voluntarily support them will put their money elsewhere. In contrast, when a government program fails to perform, its lobbyists make a case for more funding. Worse, they usually get it.

From start to finish, what private charities do represents a manifestation of free will. No one is compelled to provide assistance. No one is coerced to pay for it. No one is required to accept it. All parties come together of their own volition.

And therein lies the magic of it all! The link between the giver, the provider and the receiver is strong precisely because each knows he can walk away from it at the slightest hint of insincerity, broken promises or poor performance. Because each party gives his own time or resources voluntarily, he tends to focus on the mission and doesn't get bogged down in secondary agendas, like filling out the proper paperwork or currying favor with those in power.

Management expert Peter Drucker summed it up well when he said that private charities, both faith-based and secular, "spend far less for results than governments spend for failure."

Men and women of faith—whether Christian, Jewish, Muslim or something else—should be the first to argue that God doesn't need federal funds to do His work. When they get involved in charitable work, it's usually with the knowledge that a change of heart will often do more to conquer poverty than a welfare check. They focus on changing hearts, one heart at a time.

That's the way most Americans thought and behaved in the 19th century. They would have thought it a cop-out of the first order to pass these responsibilities on to politicians. Instead, Americans became the most generous people on earth. Christians specifically viewed personal, charitable involvement as "servanthood" commanded of them by Christ.

"No More Were Needed"

Consider a story that I first learned from the eminent Hillsdale College historian Burton Folsom, a good friend of mine.

In 1881, a raging fire swept through the state of Michigan's "Thumb" area, killing nearly 200 people and destroying more than 1 million acres of timberland. "The flames ran faster than a horse could gallop," said one survivor of the devastating blaze. Its hurricane-like fury uprooted trees, blew away buildings and destroyed millions of dollars of property across four counties.

This disaster produced an outpouring of generosity from Americans everywhere. In fact, the Michigan fire became the first disaster relief effort of Clara Barton and the newly formed American Red Cross. As the smoke billowed eastward across the nation, Barton's hometown of Dansville, N.Y., became a focal point of relief. According to the officers of the Dansville Red Cross, a call from Clara Barton "rallied us to our work."

"Instantly," they said, "we felt the help and strength of our organization (the Red Cross), young and untried as it was." Men, women and children throughout western New York brought food, clothing and other gifts. Before the Red Cross would send them to Michigan, a committee of ladies inspected each item and restitched garments or replaced food when necessary.

Speed was important, not only because many were hungry, but also because winter was approaching. Bedding and heavy clothing were in demand. Railroads provided the shipping. People left jobs and homes and trekked to Michigan to get personally involved in the rebuilding. Soon, the Red Cross in New York and the local relief committees in Michigan were working together to distribute supplies until "no more were needed," according to the final report from the Red Cross.

The Red Cross' assistance was much appreciated. And it made disaster relief faster, more efficient and national in scope.

But even if such help had not come, Michiganians were prepared to organize relief voluntarily within the state. During an 1871 fire that left nearly 3,000 Michigan families homeless, Gov. Henry Baldwin personally organized the relief efforts and gave about $150,000 out of his own pockets—a sum equivalent to more than $3 million today. Few, if any, thought it necessary to create a federal relief bureaucracy.

Baldwin and the Red Cross met the true definition of compassion. They suffered with the fire victims and worked personally to reduce their pain. Baldwin, the Red Cross and the fire victims themselves might even have felt that aid from Washington, D.C., might dampen the enthusiasm of the volunteers who gave their energy and resources out of a sense of duty and brotherly love. And this was in a year when the federal budget had a $100 million surplus, not the $400 billion deficit of today!

Government relief is in fact pre-emptive. There is little reason to believe that politicians are more compassionate or caring than the population that elects them. There is little reason to believe that politicians who are not on the scenes of either poverty or disaster and don't know the families affected will be more knowledgeable about how best to help them than those who are present and personally know the victims. There is even less reason to believe that politicians spend other people's money more effectively than those people to whom it belongs in the first place. Instead, when government gets involved, there is good reason to believe that much of its effort simply displaces what private people and groups would do better and more cost-effectively if government stayed home.

"Government Should Not Support the People"

All of which leads me to a few words about a president who happens to be among my personal favorites: Grover Cleveland—our 22nd and 24th president (the only one to serve two nonconsecutive terms), and the humble son of a Presbyterian minister.

Cleveland said what he meant and meant what he said. He did not lust for political office, and he never felt he had to cut corners, equivocate or connive in order to get elected. He was so forthright and plainspoken that he makes Harry Truman seem indecisive by comparison.

This strong streak of honesty led him to the right policy conclusion again and again. H.L. Mencken, who was known for cutting politicians down to size, even wrote a nice little essay on Cleveland titled "A Good Man in a Bad Trade."

Cleveland thought it was an act of fundamental dishonesty for some to use government for their own benefit at everyone else's expense. Accordingly, he took a firm stand against some early stirrings of an American welfare state.

In *The American Leadership Tradition: Moral Vision from Washington to Clinton*, Marvin Olasky noted that when Cleveland was mayor of Buffalo, N.Y., in the early 1880s, his "willingness to resist demands for government handouts made his name known throughout New York State," catapulting him to the governorship in 1882 and the presidency in 1884.

Indeed, frequent warnings against using the government to redistribute income were characteristic of Cleveland's tenure. He regarded as a "serious danger" the notion that government should dispense favors and advantages to individuals or their businesses. This conviction led him to veto a wagonload of bills—414 in his first term and 170 in his second—far more than all the previous 21 presidents com-bined. "I ought to have a monument over me when I die," he once said, "not for anything I have ever done, but for the foolishness I have put a stop to."

In vetoing a bill in 1887 that would have appropriated $10,000 in aid for Texas farmers struggling through a drought, Cleveland wrote:

> I can find no warrant for such an appropriation in the Constitution; and I do not believe that the power and duty of the General Government ought to be extended to the relief of individual suffering which is in no manner properly related to the public service or benefit. A prevalent tendency to disregard the limited mission of this power and duty should, I think, be steadfastly resisted, to the end that the lesson should be constantly enforced that, though the people support the Government, the Government should not support the people.

Cleveland went on to point out, "The friendliness and charity of our countrymen can always be relied upon to relieve their fellow-citizens in misfortune." Americans proved him right. Those Texas farmers eventually received in private aid more than 10 times what the vetoed bill would have provided.

As a devoted Christian, Cleveland saw the notion of taking from some to give to others as a violation of the Eighth and Tenth Commandments, which warn against theft and envy. He noticed what 20th century welfare statists did not, namely, that there was a *period* after the word "steal" in the Eighth, with no added qualifications. It does not say, "Thou shalt not steal unless the other guy has more than you do, or unless a government representative does it for you, or unless you can't find anyone who will give it to you freely, or unless you're totally convinced you can spend it better than the guy to whom it belongs."

Cleveland had been faithful to the Founders and to what he believed were God's commandments, common sense and historical experience. I can't say the same for certain of his successors who, in more recent times, cast wisdom to the winds and set America on a very different course.

"Slaves to the System"

For the first 150 years of American history, government at all levels played little role in social welfare. In a 1995 Heritage Foundation document titled "America's Failed $5.4 Trillion War on Poverty," Robert Rector and William Lauber point out, "As late as 1929, before the onset of the Great Depression, federal, state, and local welfare expenditures were only $90 million." In inflation-adjusted dollars, that would be under $1 billion today. By 1939, welfare spending was almost 50 times that amount, but at least the politicians of the day thought of it as a temporary bridge for its recipients. Welfare spending then fell and wouldn't return to the 1939 levels until Lyndon Johnson's "War on Poverty" in the mid-1960s.

And now we know, after $5.4 trillion and a series of catastrophic fiscal and social consequences, those old-fashioned virtues and principles generally embraced by America's 19th century presidents were right on the mark.

More than 100 years ago, the great intellectual and crusader for liberty Auberon Herbert offered a cogent observation from his native Britain. His remarks neatly summarize the views of the men I've discussed here:

No amount of state education will make a really intelligent nation; no amount of Poor Laws will place a nation above want; no amount of Factory Acts will make us better parents. . . . To have our wants sup-plied from without by a huge state machinery, to be regulated and inspected by great armies of officials, who are themselves slaves of the system which they administer, will in the long run teach us nothing, (and) will profit us nothing.

In March 2005, an international commission called on wealthy countries like the United States to dramatically increase their foreign aid. Many of the governments of Europe are in full support.

But what would American presidents of the 19th century have had to say about that? I can imagine Cleveland, Johnson, Pierce, Van Buren, Jackson, Madison or Jefferson reacting in disbelief at the very suggestion. Cleveland might have said, "Aid to foreign countries? We don't even dispense aid to Americans." And he would have had a century of unprecedented progress against poverty to point to as his example.

For the benefit of welfare statists here and abroad, I think Cleveland and the others I've spoken of today would be very comfortable echoing the sentiments of the 19th century French economist and statesman Frederic Bastiat:

> And now that the legislators and do-gooders have so futilely inflicted so many systems upon society, may they finally end where they should have begun: May they reject all systems, and try liberty; for liberty is an acknowledgment of faith in God and His works.

—*LWR, April 2005*

Note: The above was first delivered as a speech at the inaugural conference of the Center for Vision and Values on the campus of Mr. Reed's undergraduate alma mater, Grove City College, in April 2005.

45

Chapter **Forty-Five**

The Silver Panic

"History is little more than the register of the crimes, follies, and misfortunes of mankind," in the opinion of historian Edward Gibbon. While it may be argued that there are numerous triumphs in human affairs to write about, Gibbon's observation seems to be true. If the typical history text were to be stripped of any mention of war, depression, famine, coercion, tragedy, genocide, scandal, rivalry, and mayhem, the remains could probably be reprinted in a leaflet.

Strangely, the awesome Panic of 1893 seems to have escaped the careful scrutiny and exhaustive research of historians. Though it occurred only a little more than a century ago, it remains an obscure episode in American history. It signaled the beginning of a deep depression. Businesses collapsed by the thousands. Banks closed their doors in record numbers. Unemployment soared and idle millions roamed the streets and countryside seeking jobs or alms. And the country witnessed a spectacular display of political fireworks, now all but forgotten.

For the believer in the free economy, the story of the Panic of 1893 offers a treasure chest of empirical support. The lessons of this tragedy add up to a compelling indictment of government's ability to "manage" a nation's money.

Charles Albert Collman observed that "Money trouble was the manifest peculiarity of the long, drawn out Panic of '93."[92] Indeed, a break down of the monetary system and national bankruptcy were narrowly averted in that year. But money is that great invention which permits the development of a modern exchange economy. How could something so vital to commerce become so troublesome?

Everyone knows that fingerprints are a great aid in placing a suspect at the scene of a crime. The distinguishing characteristics of each individual's skin patterns make this possible. In the case of the Panic of 1893, the tragedy is smothered with the fingerprints of politicians. "I deem it proper at the outset to state," wrote Charles S. Smith in the October, 1893 *North American Review*, "that the recent panic was not the result of over-trading, undue speculation or the violation of business principles throughout the country. In my judgment it is to be attributed to unwise legislation with respect to the silver question; it will be known in history as 'the Silver Panic,' and will constitute a reproach and an accusation against the common sense, if not the common honesty, of our legislators who are responsible for our present monetary laws."[93]

Early Interventions

Contrary to popular impression, government in America has never been totally aloof from the monetary scene. Article I, Section 8, of the Constitution grants Congress the power "to coin money, regulate the value thereof, and of foreign coin, and fix the standard of weights and measures." In the century preceding 1893, Congress experimented with two central banks, a national banking system, paper money issues, and fixed ratios of gold and silver.

America's first cyclical depression occurred in 1819, after three wild years of currency inflation caused by the Second Bank of the United States. When that "money monster" was eliminated by hard money man Andrew Jackson, the economy slumped into depression again and all

---

[92] Charles Albert Collman, *Our Mysterious Panics*, 1830–1930 (New York: Greenwood Press, 1968), p. 88.

[93] Charles S. Smith, "The Business Outlook," *North American Review*, October 1893, p. 386.

the maladjustments of the Bank era had to be liquidated. In 1857 the economy had to retrench after a decade of credit expansion on behalf of state governments that had forced their obligations on the state banking systems. In 1873 the post-Civil War readjustment finally corrected the excesses of the government's rampant greenback inflation. The back-ground of the 1893 debacle is equally interventionist and has some uniquely interesting features which give rise to the label, "The Silver Panic."

Gold and silver rose to prominence as the monies of the civilized world through a process of free and natural selection in the marketplace of exchange. Both circulated as money, though gold was far more valuable. The market ratio between the metals had been roughly 15 to 1 (15 ounces of silver trading for 1 ounce of gold) for centuries. Gold was preferred for large transactions and silver for small ones. The free market had established "parallel standards" of gold and silver, each freely fluctuating within a narrow range in relation to market supplies and demands. Before long, though, government decided it would "help out" the market by interfering to "simplify" matters. The result was another of the many well-intentioned blunders imposed on a populace by force of law: the official "fixing" of the gold/silver ratio. This became the policy of bimetallism.

Under the direction of Alexander Hamilton, the federal government adopted an official ratio of 15 to 1 in 1792. If the market ratio had been the same and had stayed the same for as long as the fixed ratio was in effect, then the fixed ratio would have been superfluous. But the market ratio, like all market prices, changed over time as supply and demand conditions changed. As these changes occurred, the fixed bimetallic ratio became obsolete and "Gresham's Law" came into operation.

Gresham's Law

Gresham's Law holds that bad money drives out good money *when government fixes the ratio between the two circulating monies*. "Bad money" refers to the money which is artificially over-valued by the government's ratio. "Good money" is the one which is artificially undervalued. Gresham's Law began working soon after Hamilton fixed the ratio at 15 to 1, as the market ratio stood at, roughly, 15½ to 1. This meant that if one had an ounce of gold, one could get 15½ ounces of silver on the bullion market, but only 15 ounces for it at the government's mint. Conversely, if one had 15 ounces of silver, one could get an ounce of gold at the mint but less than an ounce on the market. So silver flowed into the mint and was coined while gold disappeared, went into hiding, or was shipped overseas. The country was thus put on a de facto silver standard, even though it was the declared policy of the government to maintain both metals in circulation.

Congress in 1834 changed the ratio to 16 to 1, but the market ratio had not changed much, and this time gold was over-valued and silver under-valued. Gold flowed into the mint, silver disappeared, and the country found itself on a de facto gold standard.

With the end of the Civil War inflation, and subsequent readjustment in the depression of 1873, the story of the Panic of 1893 begins to unfold. It opens with the inflationist agitation of the 1870s.

In 1875, the newly-formed National Greenback Party called for currency inflation. The proposal attracted widespread support in the West and South where many farmers joined associations to lobby for inflation. They demanded at first that the government balloon the paper money supply in the belief that such a policy would guarantee prosperity. It was a demand that finds a less shrill but no less potent voice among many economists today. An eloquent refutation of the idea that the printing press can create economic wealth can be found in the words of Benjamin Bristow, President Grant's Secretary of the Treasury. In his annual message of 1874, Bristow declared:

> The history of irredeemable paper currency repeats itself whenever and wherever it is used. It increases present prices, deludes the laborer with the idea that he is getting higher wages, and brings a fictitious prosperity from which follow inflation of business and credit and excess of enterprise in ever-increasing ratio, until it is dis-covered that trade and commerce have become fatally diseased, when confidence is destroyed, and then comes the shock to credit, followed by disaster and depression, and a demand for relief by further issues. . . . The universal use of, and reliance on, such a currency tends to blunt the moral sense and impair the natural self-dependence of the people, and trains them to the belief that the Government must directly assist their individual fortunes and business, help them in their personal affairs, and enable them to discharge their debts by partial payment. This inconvertible paper currency begets the delusion that the remedy for private pecuniary distress is in legislative measures, and makes the people unmindful of the fact that the true remedy is in greater production and less

spending, and that real prosperity comes only from individual effort and thrift.[94]

The greenback inflation of the Civil War era left an indelible impression on many Americans. They were suspicious of plans to revive a policy of deliberate paper money expansion on behalf of any special interest group. In 1875, Congress passed the Specie Resumption Act, declaring it the policy of the government to redeem the Civil War greenbacks at par in gold on January 1, 1879. It was regarded from this point on that in order to protect the redemption of the greenbacks, the Treasury would be obliged to maintain a minimum of $100,000,000 in gold on reserve. The most that the inflationists got was a government pledge not to cancel the greenbacks once redeemed, but to reissue them so that the total number outstanding would remain the same.

Turning to Silver

The attention of the inflationists was then directed at another medium: silver. Robert F. Hoxie, in the *Journal of Political Economy* in 1893, wrote that the inflationists focused their demands on a silver inflation as a matter of expediency. "They had no love for silver as such," revealed Hoxie, "but it was the cheapest and most abundant substance for which they could gain support, its use would result in more legal tender currency, and its metallic character would in a measure shield the advocates from being stigmatized as inflationists."[95]

The inflationists now became "silverites" and their rallying cry became "Free Silver at 16 to 1." Their influence was sufficient to secure passage of the Bland-Allison Act in February, 1878—the first of the acts putting the government in the business of purchasing quantities of silver for coinage. The Act provided for the purchase by the Treasury of not less than two, nor more than four, million dollars' worth of silver bullion per month, to be coined into dollars each containing 371¼ grains of pure silver (which coincided with the lawful ratio of 16 to 1, since the gold dollar still contained 23.22 grains of pure gold). These dollars were to be legal tender at their nominal value for all debts and

---

[94] James A. Barnes, *John G. Carlisle, Financial Statesman* (New York: Dodd, Mead and Co., 1931; reprint ed., Gloucester, Mass.: Peter Smith, 1967), pp. 32-33.

[95] Robert F. Hoxie, "The Silver Debate of 1890," *Journal of Political Economy* 1 (1892–1893): 561.

dues, public and private. Paper silver certificates were to be issued upon deposit of the bulky silver dollars in the Treasury.

The free silver forces were dissatisfied with Bland-Allison because it did not go far enough—it did not provide for the free and unlimited government purchase and coinage of silver at 16 to 1. The only silver to be coined would be the two to four million dollars' worth that the government purchased each month, and the Treasury, while the law was on the books, rarely bought more than the minimum amount.

Silver producers in particular had a vested interest in the state of affairs, for the market price of silver had begun a long-term decline in the1870s. Securing a government pledge to buy silver at a higher price than could be obtained in the free market was an obviously lucrative arrangement. As the market ratio of silver to gold steadily rose above 16 to 1, the profit potential became enormous.

Bland-Allison Passed Over President's Veto

Bland-Allison was passed over the veto of President Rutherford B. Hayes. The president, in his veto message, noted that minting silver coins at the ratio of sixteen ounces of silver to one ounce of gold would drive gold out of circulation. The decline of the market price of silver had raised the *market* ratio at the time of passage of the act to nearly 18¼ to 1. If the mint offered to pay one ounce of gold for just sixteen ounces of silver, then only silver would be minted and the country would be on the road back to a de facto silver standard. In Hayes' belief, "A currency worth less than it purports to be worth will in the end defraud not only creditors, but all who are engaged in legitimate business, and none more surely than those who are dependent on their daily labor for their daily bread."[96]

When money is left to the free market, its supply is restricted by its scarcity and costs of production. Its value is thus preserved. The declining price of silver on the free market would have erased the profitability of many mines and hence would have prevented a drastic increase in silver currency. But when the government stepped in and bought large quantities of silver bullion for coinage, and paid more for it in gold than was offered in the market, it forced the quantity of the white metal in circulation to exceed its true demand. The government

---

[96] Herman E. Krooss, ed., *Documentary History of Banking and Currency in the United States*, vol. 2 (New York: Chelsea House Publishers, 1969), pp. 1921–1922.

does much the same thing today when it subsidizes peanuts or wheat. The result of this political interference is a chronic surplus of these commodities.

The silverites' drive for favorable legislation culminated in the Sherman Silver Purchase Act of 1890, which replaced the Bland-Allison Act. The Sherman Act stipulated that the Treasury had to purchase 4.5 million ounces of silver per month, or roughly twice the amount the Treasury had been purchasing under Bland-Allison. Payment was to be made in a new legal tender paper currency, the so-called Treasury notes of 1890, redeemable in either gold or silver at the discretion of the Treasury. The 4.5 million ounces of silver mandated by the law represented almost the entire output of American silver mines. This continuing subsidy to silver producers meant that the government was engaged in a full-blown force-feeding of the American economy. It was only a matter of time before the patient would suffer the pangs of indigestion.

U.S. Out of Step

The action of the United States government in 1878 and 1890 with respect to silver was especially peculiar in light of world monetary events. Germany, immediately after the Franco-Prussian War in the early 1870s, had withdrawn her silver from circulation and adopted a single gold standard. France, Belgium, Switzerland, Italy, and Greece followed by first restricting the coinage of silver and then eliminating it altogether. Denmark, Norway, and Sweden adopted the single gold standard, making silver subsidiary by 1875. In that year, the government of Holland closed its mints to the coinage of silver. A year later, the Russian government suspended the coinage of silver except for use in the Chinese trade. In 1879, Austria-Hungary ceased to coin silver for individuals, except for a special trade coin. This rapid worldwide transition from silver to gold prompted the United States Treasury Department in 1879 to note that "since the monetary disturbance of 1873–78 not a mint of Europe has been open to the coinage of silver for individuals."[97] Yet the United States government, at a time when the value of silver was falling dramatically and when the nation's trading partners were abandoning the white metal, stepped in to promote silver against gold at the unrealistic ratio of 16 to 1!

---

[97] Ibid., p. 1934.

One way of looking at silver's depreciation is to consider the annual average market value of the 371 ¼ grain silver dollar. In 1878, the bullion value of that much silver was about 890; by 1890 it dropped to 810; by 1893, it was worth 600; and by 1895 it plummeted to a mere 500. A climate of uncertainty pervaded the world of finance. As Professor J. Laurence Laughlin wrote, "No one could know that contracts entered into when a dollar stood for 100 cents in gold might not be paid off in silver which stood for 50 cents on a dollar. That was the predicament in which every investor found himself who had an obligation payable only in 'coin' and not in gold." [98]

In an article entitled "Thou Shalt Not Steal," Isaac L. Rice penned an eloquent repudiation of the government's silver coinage policy. His argument evoked the moral side of the question and eighty years later is still a forceful indictment of monetary dishonesty:

> Of the various classes of crime that come under the category of theft none is more odious and despicable than the use of false weights and measures. Stamping a coin containing 3711/4 grains of silver as of the weight of one hundred cents, while in truth it is of the weight of fifty-three cents, is a falsification of weights morally not distinguishable from stamping any other kind of weight as of two pounds which in truth is only of one pound. Only the methods by which fraud is to be made are different. The thievish individual depends upon secret deceit, the qualities of the sneak thief; the Government on coercion, the qualities of the highwayman.[99]

In accordance with inexorable economic law, the Bland-Allison and Sherman Acts caused a drain of gold from the Treasury and an inflow of silver. This tampering with the fixity of the standard threatened the Treasury's declared policy of redeeming greenbacks and other government obligations in gold. And, the disappearance of gold from circulation and from the reserves of the nation's banks threatened the sanctity of all contracts made in gold. Professor Laughlin observed that no producer "could feel so entirely sure of the standard of payments that he could, without fear or hesitation, make his estimates a few years ahead."[100]

---

[98] J. Laurence Laughlin, *The History of Bimetallism in the United States*, 4th ed. (New York: D. Appleton and Co., 1900), p. 274.

[99] Isaac L. Rice, "Thou Shalt Not Steal," *Forum* 22 (September 1896—February 1897): 1.

[100] Laughlin, p. 269.

The Flight of Capital

The silver purchases noticeably affected the confidence of foreigners in the American economy. Many British and French investors expected devaluation of the dollar at the least, with complete financial collapse predicted by some. Capital flowed out of the country as these foreigners sold American securities. Even Americans, in increasing numbers after 1890, began exporting funds for investment in Canada, Europe, and some of the Latin American countries, all of which seemed stronger than the United States.

The inflationary impact of the Bland-Allison and Sherman Acts was particularly important in paving the way for panic and depression. A. D. Noyes, writing in *Political Science Quarterly*, stated that "The coinage of over-valued silver dollars since 1878, and the issue of Treasury notes on silver bullion since 1890, have actually increased the country's silver and paper circulation, between 1879 and 1894, by seventy-five per cent."[101]

W. Jett Lauck, in his study entitled *The Causes of the Panic of 1893*, found that the Sherman Act inflation produced an "absence of the usual stringency in the New York money market" in the fall of 1891. Call loans ranged from two to four per cent, a significant decline from earlier levels.[102]

In 1910 the National Monetary Commission requested 0. M. W. Sprague to report on the nation's finances since the Civil War. In his authoritative report, *History of Crises Under the National Banking System*, Sprague found that from January, 1891 to June, 1893, "there was an increase of $68,000,000 in the estimated amount of money in circulation." The effect on bank credit was typical of any "easy money" policy: "During 1892 the low rates for loans were a clear indication that the banks would have been glad to lend more than the demand of borrowers made possible." The classic symptoms of currency inflation were evident, a situation which Sprague found to be unsustainable. He felt that "a situation which demands increasing credits to prevent

---

[101] A. D. Noyes, "The Banks and the Panic of 1893," Political Science Quarterly 9 (No. 1): p. 15

[102] W. Jett Lauck, *The Causes of the Panic of 1893* (Boston: Houghton, Mifflin and Co., 1907), p. 80.

collapse is certain to arrive at that state in any case, and delay can hardly be expected to improve matters."[103]

End of the Boom

The economy, drugged by easy money, was showing outward signs of prosperity. Unemployment, which had been above 5 per cent in 1890 and 1891, fell to 3.7 per cent in 1892. Crop failures in Europe coupled with exceptional harvests here in the United States boosted agriculture. President Harrison told Congress, "There has never been a time in our history when work was so abundant, or when wages were as high."[104] The boom was, however, only temporary. The twin evils of inflation and uncertainty as to the fixity of the standard were eating at the vitals of the nation's commerce. Late in January, 1893, prices of staples such as wheat and iron, previously on the rise, began to recede. Price declines across the board foreshadowed a general cyclical contraction. "General business activity," according to Charles Hoffman, "suffered a severe check that was recognized at once in the business journals. The stock market gave ominous signs of falling prices before any sharp drop took place."[105] Banks became apprehensive over the Treasury's loss of gold (as well as their own) and began to contract the pyramid of credit. Loans declined almost 10 per cent from February to the beginning of May. An article in the February, 1893 issue of *Forum* spoke of "a dangerous state of uneasiness in financial circles," and warned that "Fear is an element in monetary conditions which may be as serious in its effects as reason."[106]

A dramatic event took place on February 20. The Philadelphia and Reading Railroad, a chronic invalid which nonetheless had paid its usual bond dividend the month before, collapsed into bankruptcy. "When the end came," writes Rendigs Fels, "it had a floating debt of $18.5 million

---

[103] O. M. W. Sprague, *History of Crises Under the National Banking System* (Washington, D.C.: Government Printing Office, 1910; reprint ed., New York: Augustus M. Kelley, 1968), p. 158.

[104] Robert Sobel, *Panic on Wall Street: A History of America's Financial Disasters* (New York: Macmillan Co., 1968), p. 243.

[105] Charles Hoffman, *The Depression of the Nineties: An Economic History*, Contributions in Economics and Economic History, no. 2 (Westport, Conn.: Greenwood Press, 1970), p. 107.

[106] Geo. Fred Williams, "Imminent Danger From the Silver Purchase Act," *Forum* 14 (September 1892–February 1893): 789.

compared to cash and bills receivable of little more than $100,000."[107]
The failure of the Philadelphia and Reading, a firm supported by
powerful Wall Street financial houses, caused many businessmen to
question the conditions of other railroads and the financial institutions
behind them.

When President Harrison left office on March 4, 1893, the
Treasury's gold reserve stood at the historic low of $100,982,410—an
eyelash above the $100 million minimum deemed necessary for
protecting the redemption of greenbacks. Merchants increasingly
refused to accept silver in violation of the law and ugly threats of strikes
echoed in the nation's factories.

On April 22 the Treasury's gold reserve fell below the $100 million
minimum for the first time since the resumption of specie payments in
1879. Bankers and investors realized that the Treasury could not
indefinitely continue drawing upon the remaining gold reserve to
redeem the Treasury notes of 1890 in the attempt to maintain their
value. Banks had to brake their easy money habits and began calling in
their loans at a frantic pace. More and more investors began to fear that
before securities could be sold and realized upon, depreciated silver
would take the place of gold as the standard of payments.

By Wednesday, May 3, tension in the commercial community
triggered a massive wave of selling on the stock market. *The New York
Times* recorded the events the next day:

> Not since 1884 had the stock market had such a break in prices as
> occurred yesterday, and few days in its history were more exciting.
> In the industrial shares particularly, there was a smashing of values
> almost without precedent. In the last thirty minutes the brokers on
> the floor of the Exchange found the quotations on the board of little
> use.

Figures posted at one moment were valueless the next. In the
industrials which were receiving the most punishment prices were
dropping a point at a time. The crowds trading in them were made up of
shouting men, who struggled about the floor like football players in a
scrimmage.[108]

---

[107] Rendigs Fels, *American Business Cycles: 1865–1897* (Raleigh: University of North
Carolina Press, 1959; reprint ed., Westport, Conn.: Greenwood Press, 1973), p. 185.
[108] Industrials Were Hit Hard," *New York Times*, 4 May 1893, p. 1.

The Panic of 1893 had begun! On May 4 a stock market favorite, National Cordage Trust, went into receivership. Shortly before the panic, Cordage common stock had sold for $70 per share. The plunge was precipitous, as Charles Albert Collman vividly explains:

> In the Cordage Trust circle of the New York Stock Exchange, hats were being smashed, coats torn, cravats ruined. Here was an agony that meant financial life or death to many. Cordage common had gone off 18 points. The preferred had lost 22. Suddenly howls went up from the floor. Those who could distinguish the words, heard the ominous cry: "Nineteen for Cordage!"

The shares, a few moments later, went down to $12.[109]

The Cordage Crash

The Cordage crash was taken as, in Collman's words, "some occult signal for the halting of enterprise."[110] Plants closed their gates and went quickly into receivership. Unemployment rocketed to 9.6 per cent before year-end, nearly three times the rate for 1892. In 1894, an estimated 16.7 per cent of industrial wage-earners were idle.

From January to July, 1893, mercantile failures totaled a remarkable 3,401, with liabilities totaling $169,000,000. The bulk of the losses came after the first week of May. Sprague revealed that the "failures exceeded both in number and in amount of liabilities those which had occurred in any other period of equal length in our history."[111]

Bank failures and suspensions were the greatest on record. Most occurred in the South and West, where the evils of a vicious currency expansion had taken root far more extensively than in the rest of the country.

The economy was going through the pains of liquidation. The malinvestments fostered by the Bland-Allison Act and Sherman Act inflation were being sloughed off. The threat to the de facto gold standard was a factor which no doubt complicated things, heightened uncertainty, determined the timing of the panic, and exacerbated the depression, but the chief responsibility for the crisis rested with the attempted force-feeding of the nation's money supply by government

---

[109] Collman, p. 164.
[110] Ibid, p. 165.
[111] Sprague, p. 169.

policy. The *Commercial and Financial Chronicle* said as much on July 8, 1893:

> The country is struggling with disturbed credit and the general derangement of commercial and financial affairs which a forced and over-valued currency has developed. . . . Nothing but corrective legislation which shall remove the disturbing law, can afford any measure of real relief.[112]

With the economy in depression, the necessity for eliminating the legislation which precipitated the tragedy became increasingly apparent. On June 30, President Grover Cleveland called for a special session of Congress to repeal the Sherman Silver Purchase Act of 1890. "The present perilous condition," he declared, "is largely the result of a financial policy which the Executive branch of the government finds embodied in unwise laws which must be executed until repealed by Congress."[113] The ensuing debate in the Congress was a splendid contest, pitting the forces of sound, honest money against the forces of inflation, in which the sound money men calmly answered the question, "What would you put in place of the silver purchases?" with the single, solitary word, "Nothing!"

Cockran Favors Repeal

On August 26, Congressman Bourke Cockran of New York rose to deliver a memorable address in favor of repeal. The speech has been called the most eloquent and scholarly of the entire debate. The congressman advised his colleagues:

> I think it safe to assert that every commercial crisis can be traced to an unnecessary inflation of the currency, or to an improvident expansion of credit. The operation of the Sherman Law has been to flood this country with paper money without providing any method whatever for its redemption. The circulating medium has become so redundant that the channels of commerce have overflowed and gold has been expelled.[114]

Cockran proceeded to trace the history of coinage in England and explained how debasing the currency led to recurrent depressions.

---

[112] Hoffman, p. 229.

[113] "Congress to Meet August 7," *New York Times*, 1 July 1893, p. 1.

[114] James McGurrin, *Bourke Cockran* (New York: Charles Scribner's Sons, 1948), p. 135.

James McGurrin, Cockran's biographer, believes that the subsequent vote in the House of Representatives in favor of repeal "was due in no small measure to Bourke Cockran's matchless eloquence and sagacious leadership."[115]

The repeal bill passed the House on August 28 by a wide margin. President Cleveland's forceful leadership prompted the Senate to do likewise in October. The *New York Times* heralded the occasion: "The Treasury is released from this day from the necessity of purchasing a commodity it does not require, out of a money chest already depleted, and at the risk of dangerous encroachment upon the gold reserve." [116]

An indispensable pre-condition to recovery was accomplished with the repeal of the Sherman Silver Purchase Act. The derangement of the nation's money was a big step closer to solution, though the road to recovery was long and hard. Not until 1897 did depression give way to revival and prosperity. Repeal of the Sherman Act was, by any measure, an act of congressional repentance. Indeed, it was an open admission that the Silver Panic was the offspring of a profligate, overbearing, and irresponsible government. Historian Ernest Ludlow Bogart summarized the lessons of the Panic of 1893:

> It must be said that the net results of this experiment of a "managed currency," that is, one in which the government undertakes to provide the necessary money for the people, were disastrous. For the maintenance of a suitable supply the operation of normal economic forces is more reliable than the judgment of a legislative body. [117]

—*LWR, June 1978*

---

[115] Ibid, p. 138.

[116] "Need Buy No More Silver," *New York Times*, 2 November 1893, p. 1.

[117] Ernest Ludlow Bogart, *Economic History of the American People* (New York: Longmans, Green and Co., 1937), p. 693.

46

Chapter **Forty-Six**

Public Money for Private Charity

When President Bush announced his controversial "faith-based initiative" in 2001, it brought to mind something I learned years ago from readings on ancient Roman history.

After years of being shunned and even persecuted, Christians suddenly enjoyed the official blessing of the Roman state when Emperor Constantine came to power in 324 A.D. For the first time, imperial funds were used to subsidize priests and churches. Christians emerged from hiding in Rome's catacombs to partake of the state's largess. A faith that might have saved an empire was thus corrupted and in the end proved to be a futile safeguard against Rome's ultimate destruction at the hands of barbarians a century and a half later.

Indeed, before the barbarians arrived in 476, Emperor Julian launched a backlash against state-supported Christian influence in 361. He crippled the church by withdrawing the financial aid on which it had become dependent, and even forbade Christians from teaching in the schools. Because the Roman state was paying the Christian piper, it eventually called most of the tunes.

For the sake of both their faith and Roman society at large, the Christians of the fourth century should have remained pure and independent—advice expressed well 13 centuries later by the English poet John Dryden: "better shun the bait than struggle in the snare."

President Bush is right to recognize the fruitful role of America's private, faith-based "armies of compassion." For many reasons, such groups are far more effective in solving social problems—poverty, homelessness, illiteracy, to name a few—than are government programs and bureaucracies. They treat the whole person, which means they get to the root of problems that stem from spiritual, attitudinal, and behavioral deficiencies. They demand accountability, which means they don't simply hand over a check every two weeks without expecting the needy to do much in return or to change destructive patterns of behavior. And if they don't produce results, they wither; the parishioners or others who voluntarily support them will put their mites elsewhere.

When a government program fails to perform, its lobbyists make a case for more money and they usually get it. Literally tens of thousands of faith-based organizations, large and small, that demonstrate every day in America what management expert Peter Drucker once said of nonprofit agencies in the private sector: They "spend far less for results than governments spend for failure."

In a single pithy question, John Fund of *The Wall Street Journal* underscored the instinctive, gut-level regard that Americans have for private aid, no matter what they may say in public: "If you had a financial windfall and wanted to help the poor, would you even think about giving time or a check to the government?" Millions of Americans give to the Red Cross and the Salvation Army; almost nobody writes checks to the welfare department.

President Bush's initiative would "pioneer a new model of cooperation," in part through federal contracts with faith-based groups to provide a wide range of social services. The problem with it is not, as some critics argue, that it puts faith in a position to corrupt the government. All the ingredients necessary for corruption in government are already there: vast sums of other people's money and far more power than any government should ever have.

Government Corrupts

The real problem with the President's initiative is the same as was manifested painfully in ancient Rome—government will be in a position to corrupt faith. The fact that the modern American state is relentlessly secular is one reason, but not the primary one. Resting as it does on the compulsory tax power, government funding of any kind, by its nature, is at odds with the very thing that makes private faith-based programs work: impulses that are entirely voluntary and inner-motivated.

From start to finish, what private charities do is a manifestation of free will. No one is compelled to provide assistance. No one is coerced to pay for it. No one is required to accept it. All parties come together of their own individual volition. And that's the magic of it. The link connecting the giver, the provider, and the receiver is strong precisely because each knows he can walk away at the slightest hint of insincerity, broken promises, or poor performance. Because each party is giving of his own time or resources voluntarily, he tends to focus on the mission at hand and doesn't get bogged down or diverted by distant or secondary agendas, like filling out the proper paperwork or currying favor with the political powers that be.

Most people of faith—whether they be Christian, Jew, Muslim, or something else—would ordinarily be the first to argue that God doesn't need federal funds to do His work; just a change of heart will do, one heart at a time. Sadly, there are more than a few people of faith who have succumbed to temptation and are arguing that their organizations now must take advantage of the Bush proposal or else precious lives will not be turned around. That the mere offer of future funding is enough to turn some eyes to Washington that previously were aimed somewhat higher suggests a subtle corruption of faith has already begun.

The administration argues that it will scrupulously avoid any direct support of actual religious activities. It will fund the bed a homeless person sleeps in, not the Bible his Salvation Army mentor reads to him. But as government and private funds flow into the same pot, it may be very hard to follow what flows out of it and for what purpose, without a smothering paper burden to guarantee what the politicians call "accountability."

In Michigan, the Salvation Army accepts tax money to supplement the private donations it collects for taking care of the homeless. In 1995, the city of Detroit imposed a 25-page ordinance to make sure that shelters like those run by the Army are up to snuff. It requires, among other things, that all staffers be trained in resident complaint and grievance procedures and that all meal menus be approved by a dietitian registered with the American Dietetic Association—"minor" diversions from the spiritual mission of the Army, but all intended "for the public good," to be sure.

Advocates for the Bush proposal argue that this administration's people in government will not burden faith-based charities with that kind of do-gooder bureaucratic rigmarole. But its people will not always be there. Those Romans who thought they had a friend in Constantine were undoubtedly more than a little upset with Julian.

—LWR, August 2001

47

Chapter **Forty-Seven**

Equality, Markets, and Morality

The subject of "equality" is the source of much political debate. Ever since the founding era, free-market thinkers have argued for equality of opportunity in the economic order. Equality, in other words, is a framework, not a result. In modern terms the goal is a level playing field. Government is a referee that enforces property rights, laws, and contracts equally for all individuals.

What the free-market view means in policy terms is no (or few) tariffs for business, no subsidies for farmers, and no racism written into law. Also, successful businessmen will not be subject to special taxes or the seizure of property.

In America this view of equality is enshrined in the Declaration of Independence ("all men are created equal and are endowed by their creator with certain inalienable rights") and the Constitution ("imposts and excises shall be uniform throughout the United States" and "equal protection of the laws"). Much of America's first century as a nation was devoted to ending slavery, extending voting rights, and securing property and inheritance rights for women—fulfilling the Founders' goal of equal opportunity for all citizens.

Progressives and modern critics of equality of opportunity have launched two significant criticisms against the Founders' view. First, that equality of opportunity is impossible to achieve. Second, to the extent that equality of opportunity has been tried, it has resulted in a gigantic inequality of outcomes. Equality of *outcome*, in the Progressive view, is desirable and can only be achieved by massive government intervention. Let's study both of these objections.

To some extent, of course, the Progressives have a valid point—equality of opportunity is, at an individual level (as opposed to an institutional level) hard to achieve. We are all born with different family advantages (or disadvantages), with different abilities, and in different neighborhoods with varying levels of opportunity. As socialist playwright George Bernard Shaw said on the subject, "Give your son a fountain pen and a ream of paper and tell him that he now has an equal opportunity with me of writing plays and see what he says to you."

What the Progressives miss is that their cure is worse than the illness. Any attempt to correct imbalances in family, ability, and neighborhood will produce other inequalities that may be worse than the original ones. Thomas Sowell writes, "[A]ttempts to equalize *economic* results lead to greater—and more dangerous—inequality in *political* power." Or, as Milton Friedman concluded, "A society that puts equality—in the sense of equality of outcome—ahead of freedom will end up with neither equality nor freedom. The use of force to achieve equality will destroy freedom, and the force, introduced for good purposes, will end up in the hands of people who use it to promote their own interests."

Failure During the New Deal

Sowell's and Friedman's point is illuminated by the failed efforts of the federal government to reduce inequalities during the New Deal. In the early 1930s the United States had massive unemployment (sometimes over 20 percent). In 1932 President Herbert Hoover supported the nation's first relief program: $300 million was distributed to states. This was not a transfer from richer states to poorer states but a political grab by most state governors to secure all they could. Illinois played this game well and secured over $55 million, more than New York, California, and Texas combined.

Massachusetts, with almost as many people as Illinois, received zero federal money. Massachusetts had much poverty and distress, but Governor Joseph Ely believed states should try to supply their own needs and not rush to Washington to gain funds at someone else's expense. Ely therefore promoted a variety of fundraising events throughout his state to help those in need. "Whatever the justification for [federal] relief," Ely noted, "the fact remains that the way in which it has been used makes it the greatest political asset on the practical side of party politics ever held by any administration."

In 1935 President Franklin Roosevelt confirmed Ely's beliefs by turning the Works Progress Administration (WPA), which he had established, into a gigantic political machine to transfer money to key states and congressional districts to secure votes. Roosevelt and his cohorts used the rhetoric of removing inequalities as a political cover to gain power. Reporter Thomas Stokes won a Pulitzer Prize for his investigative research that exposed the WPA for using federal funds to buy votes.

The use of tax dollars, then, to mitigate inequality failed because—whatever the good intentions—the funds quickly became politicized.

Presidential (and congressional) authority to tax and to transfer funds from one group to another also proved to be a dangerous centralization of power. Taxation increased both in size and complexity. The IRS thus became a weapon a president could use against those who resisted him. "My father," Elliott Roosevelt observed of his famous parent, "may have been the originator of the concept of employing the IRS as a weapon of political retribution."

Sowell and Friedman indeed recognized that efforts to remove inequalities would create new inequalities, perhaps just as severe, and would also dangerously concentrate power in the hands of politicians and bureaucrats. But Sowell and Friedman have readily conceded that when markets are left free, the inequality of outcomes is not necessarily morally justified. In other words, some people—through luck or inheritance—become incredibly rich and others, who may have worked harder and more diligently, end up barely earning a living. Rewards, as F. A. Hayek, among others, has noted, are "based only partly on achievements and partly on mere chance." Societies are more prosperous under free markets, but individual success and failure can occur independently of ability and hard work.

Progressive Claims in Light of History

What the historical record does seem to demonstrate is that the richest men in American history have been creative entrepreneurs who have improved the lives of millions of Americans and have achieved remarkable upward mobility doing so. For example, the first American to be worth $10 million was John Jacob Astor, a German immigrant and a son of a butcher. Astor founded the largest fur company in the United States, transforming tastes and lowering costs in clothing for people all over the world.

John D. Rockefeller, the first American to be worth $1 billion, was the son of an itinerant peddler. Yet Rockefeller, with little education or training, went into the business of refining oil and did it better than anyone in the world. As a result, he sold the affordable kerosene that lit up most homes in the world. (He had a 60 percent world market share in the late 1800s.)

Henry Ford, the son of a struggling farmer, was the second American billionaire. He used the cheap oil sold by Rockefeller and cheap steel that was introduced by immigrant Andrew Carnegie to make cars affordable for most American families. The most recent wealthiest men in the United States—Sam Walton and Bill Gates—both came from middle-class households and both added much value for most American consumers.

Free markets may yield odd results and certainly unequal outcomes, but the greater opportunities and prosperity have made the tradeoff worthwhile for American society.

—BWF, September 2008

Part VII

Individuals Against Government Injustice

48

Chapter **Forty-Eight**

The Inspiring Story of Thomas Clarkson: A Student's Essay
that Changed the World

As a former university professor, I've read thousands of students'
essays through the years—sometimes joyously, but just as often
painfully. Occasionally, the process of researching and writing exerted a
significant influence on a student's future interests and behavior.

But of all the student essays ever written, I doubt that any had as
profound an effect on its author and on the world as one that was
penned 220 years ago at the University of Cambridge.

The university's annual Latin essay contest was known throughout
Britain, and the honor of winning it was highly prized. In 1785, the topic
for the competition was prompted by a horrific human tragedy a few
years before: Near the end of a long voyage from Britain to Africa to the
West Indies, the captain of the British slave ship *Zong* had ordered his
crew to throw 133 chained black Africans overboard to their deaths. He
reckoned that by falsely claiming the ship had run out of fresh water, he
could collect more for the "cargo" from the ship's insurer than he could
fetch at a slave auction in Jamaica.

No one in the *Zong* affair was prosecuted for murder. A London court ruled the matter a mere civil dispute between an insurance firm and a client. As for the Africans, the judge declared their drowning was "just as if horses were killed," which, as horrendous as it sounds today, was a view not far removed from the conventional wisdom that prevailed worldwide in 1785.

Slavery, after all, was an ancient institution. Even with our freedoms today, the number of people who have walked the earth in bondage far outnumbers those who have enjoyed even a modest measure of liberty.

Indeed, perhaps the luckiest of the people taken captive and bound for a life at the end of a lash were those who succumbed aboard ship, where mortality rates sometimes ran as high as 50 percent. Surviving the "Middle Passage" across the Atlantic from Africa was only the start of a hellish experience—endless and often excruciating toil, with death at an early age.

Moved by the fate of the *Zong*'s victims and the indifference of the court, the university vice chancellor in charge of selecting the topic for the 1785 contest at Cambridge chose this question: *Anne liceat invitos in servitutem dare?*—Is it lawful to make slaves of others against their will?

Enter Thomas Clarkson, a man who, with a handful of compatriots armed only with words, would clutch the public by the neck and not let go until it consigned slavery to the moral ash heap of history. The poet Samuel Taylor Coleridge would later call him a "moral steam engine" and "the Giant with one idea."

Clarkson, born in Wisbech in 1760, was a 25-year-old Cambridge student when he decided to try his luck in the essay contest. He hoped to be a minister, and slavery was not a topic that had previously interested him. Still, he plunged into his research with the vigor, meticulous care and mounting passion that would come to characterize nearly every day of his next 61 years. Drawing on the vivid testimony of those who had seen the unspeakable cruelty of the slave trade firsthand, Clarkson's essay won first prize.

What Clarkson had learned wrenched him to his very core. Shortly after claiming the prize, and while riding on horseback along a country road, his conscience gripped him. Slavery, he later wrote, "wholly engrossed" his thoughts. He could not complete the ride without frequent stops to dismount and walk, tortured by the awful visions of the traffic in human lives. At one point, falling to the ground in anguish, he determined that if what he had written in his essay were indeed true, it led to only one conclusion: "It was time some person should see these calamities to their end."

The significance of those few minutes in time is summed up in a splendid recent book by Adam Hochschild, *Bury the Chains: Prophets and Rebels in the Fight to Free an Empire's Slaves*:

> If there is a single moment at which the antislavery movement became inevitable, it was the day in 1785 when Thomas Clarkson sat down by the side of the road at Wades Mill. . . . For his Bible-conscious colleagues, it held echoes of Saul's conversion on the road to Damascus. For us today, it is a landmark on the long, tortuous path to the modern conception of universal human rights.

More than two centuries later, that very spot is marked by a monument, not far from London.

Thus began Clarkson's all-consuming focus on a moral ideal: No man can rightfully lay claim, moral or otherwise, to owning another. Casting aside his plans for a career as a man of the cloth, he mounted a bully pulpit and risked everything for the single cause of ending the evil of slavery.

At first, he sought out and befriended the one group—the Quakers—who had already embraced the issue. But the Quakers were few in number and were written off by British society as an odd fringe element. Quaker men even refused to remove their hats for any man, including the king, because they believed it offended an even higher authority. Clarkson knew that antislavery would have to become a mainstream, fashionable educational effort if it were to have any hope of success.

On May 22, 1787, Clarkson brought together 12 men, including a few of the leading Quakers, at a London print shop to plot the course. Alexis de Tocqueville would later describe the results of that meeting as "extraordinary" and "absolutely without precedent" in the history of the world. This tiny group, which named itself the Society for the Abolition of the African Slave Trade, was about to take on a firmly established institution in which a great deal of money was made and on which considerable political power depended.

Powered by an evangelical zeal, Clarkson's committee would become what might be described as the world's first think tank. Noble ideas and unassailable facts would be its weapons.[118]

"Looking back today," writes Hochschild, "what is more astonishing than the pervasiveness of slavery in the late 1700s is how swiftly it died. By the end of the following century, slavery was, at least on paper, outlawed almost everywhere." Thomas Clarkson was the prime architect of "the first, pioneering wave of that campaign"—the antislavery movement in Britain, which Hochschild properly describes as "one of the most ambitious and brilliantly organized citizens' movements of all time."

The credit for ending slavery in the British Empire is most often given to William Wilberforce. He was the longtime parliamentarian who never gave in to overwhelming odds, introducing bill after bill to abolish the trade in slaves, and later slavery itself.

Wilberforce was a hero in his own right—but Thomas Clarkson was prominent among those who first proposed to Wilberforce that he be the movement's man in Parliament. Moreover, it was the information Clarkson gathered crisscrossing the British countryside—logging 35,000 miles on horseback—that Wilberforce often used in parliamentary debate. Clarkson was the mobilizer, the energizer, the fact-finder and the very conscience of the movement.

In *Thomas Clarkson: Friend of Slaves*, biographer Earl Leslie Griggs writes that this man on fire was "second to no one in indefatigable

---

[118] Another memorable and pivotal figure in this great movement was John Newton. Newton is known today as the author of perhaps the most popular hymn in Christendom, "Amazing Grace," with its stirring first stanza:

Amazing grace, how sweet the sound, that saved a wretch like me; I once was lost, but now am found, was blind but now I see.

What is less well-known is that Newton's lyrics were autobiographical. He had been a slave ship captain given to incessant cursing and stonyhearted treatment of his captives, but had undergone a spiritual awakening and penned the song that moves congregations across the world to this day.

Newton served the cause against slavery more immediately during this seminal period through an entreaty to William Wilberforce. Early in Wilberforce's parliamentary career, before becoming involved in the antislavery effort, he had toyed with the notion of leaving government. John Newton convinced him to stay, advancing the view that God intended Wilberforce to fulfill a great purpose.

energy and unremitting devotion to an ideal," and that, "He inspired in his friends confidence in his ability to lead them."

In a diary entry for Wednesday, June 27, 1787, Clarkson tells of the moment he arrived in the slave ship port of Bristol. Genuine misgivings about his work gave way to a steely determination that served him well in the battles ahead:

> I began now to tremble, for the first time, at the arduous task I had undertaken, of attempting to subvert one of the branches of the commerce of the great place which was then before me. I began to think of the host of people I should have to encounter in it. I anticipated much persecution in it also; and I questioned whether I should even get out of it alive. But in journeying on, I became more calm and composed. My spirits began to return. In these latter moments I considered my first feelings as useful, inasmuch as they impressed upon me the necessity of extraordinary courage, and activity, and perseverance, and of watchfulness, also, over my own conduct, that I might not throw any stain upon the cause I had undertaken. When, therefore, I entered the city, I entered it with an undaunted spirit, determining that no labour should make me shrink, nor danger, nor even persecution, deter me from my pursuit.

Clarkson translated his prize-winning essay from Latin into English and supervised its distribution by the tens of thousands. He helped organize boycotts of the West Indian rum and sugar produced with slave labor. He gave lectures and sermons. He wrote many articles and at least two books. He helped British seamen escape from the slave-carrying ships they were pressed into against their will. He filed murder charges in courts to draw attention to the actions of fiendish slave ship captains. He convinced witnesses to speak. He gathered testimony, rustled up petition signatures by the thousands and smuggled evidence from under the very noses of his adversaries. His life was threatened many times, and once, surrounded by an angry mob, he very nearly lost it.

The long hours, the often thankless and seemingly fruitless forays to uncover evidence, the risks and the costs that came in every form, the many low points when it looked like the world was against him—all of that went on and on, year after year. None of it ever made the smallest dent in Thomas Clarkson's iron will.

When Britain went to war with France in 1793, Clarkson and his committee saw their early progress in winning converts evaporate. The opposition in Parliament argued that abandoning the slave trade would only hand a lucrative business to a formidable enemy. And the public saw winning the war as more important than freeing people of another color and another continent.

But Clarkson did not relent. He, Wilberforce and the committee kept spreading the message and looking for the best opportunities to advance it.

It was at Clarkson's instigation that a diagram of a slave ship became a tool in the debate. Depicting hundreds of slaves crammed like sardines in horrible conditions, it proved to be pivotal in winning the public.

Clarkson's committee also enlisted the help of famed pottery maker Josiah Wedgwood in producing a famous medallion with the image of a kneeling, chained black man, uttering the words, "Am I not a man and a brother?"

Indeed, Clarkson's imprint was on almost everything the committee did. It even produced one of the first newsletters and, as Hochschild suggests, one of the first direct-mail campaigns for the purpose of raising money.

The effort finally paid off. The tide of public opinion swung firmly to the abolitionists. The trade in slaves was outlawed by act of Parliament when it approved one of Wilberforce's bills in 1807, some 20 years after Clarkson formed his committee. Twenty-six more years of laborious effort by Clarkson, Wilberforce and others were required before Britain passed legislation in 1833 to free all slaves within its realm. The law took effect in 1834, 49 years after Clarkson's epiphany on a country road. It became a model for peaceful emancipation everywhere. Wilberforce died shortly afterwards, but his friend devoted much of the next 13 years to the movement to end the scourge of slavery and improve the lot of former slaves worldwide.

Clarkson died at the age of 86, in 1846. He had been the last living member of the committee he had gathered at the London print shop back in 1787. Hochschild tells us that the throngs of mourners "included many Quakers, and the men among them made an almost unprecedented departure from sacred custom" by removing their hats.

In *Thomas Clarkson: A Biography*, Ellen Gibson Wilson summed up her subject well when she wrote of this man from the little village of Wisbech, "Thomas Clarkson (1760–1846) was almost too good to be true—courageous, visionary, disciplined, self-sacrificing—a man who gave a long life almost entirely to the service of people he never met in lands he never saw."

An essay by a university student struck a spark, which lit a beacon, which saved millions of lives and changed the world. If you ever hear anyone dismiss the power of the pen, just tell them the story of Thomas Clarkson, his prize-winning essay and the astounding events they brought forth for humanity.

—LWR, May 2005

Afterword

Two years after the publication in 2005 of the first edition of this essay, a remarkable motion picture was released worldwide. 'Amazing Grace,' starring Ioan Gruffudd as William Wilberforce and Rufus Sewell as Thomas Clarkson, is a historically faithful, must-see movie for the entire family.

Sources and Recommended Readings

Bury the Chains: Prophets and Rebels in the Fight to Free an Empire's Slaves, By Adam Hochschild, Boston: Houghton Mifflin Company, 2005

Thomas Clarkson: Friend of Slaves, By Earl Leslie Griggs, Westport, Conn.: Negro Universities Press, 1970

Thomas Clarkson: A Biography, By Ellen Gibson White, New York: St. Martin's Press, 1990

Hero for Humanity: A Biography of William Wilberforce, By Kevin Belmonte, Colorado Springs, Colo.: NavPress, 2002

The Slave Trade, By Hugh Thomas, New York: Simon & Schuster, 1997

49

Chapter **Forty-Nine**

The Liberty Tradition Among Black Americans

Slavery and free institutions can never live peaceably together," Frederick Douglass observed. "Liberty . . . must either overthrow slavery, or be itself overthrown by slavery."

Douglass, black America's most renowned spokesman, made this argument during the Civil War. But what about after the war? Was it proper for the government afterward to intervene and assist blacks in overcoming centuries of bondage? Many black leaders today promote affirmative action, which gives racial preferences in hiring to black Americans. But that was not the thinking of Douglass and other black leaders, such as Booker T. Washington, after the Civil War.

Douglass, for example, in a major speech given in April 1865, expressed a desire for liberty alone. When the war ended, some whites and blacks wanted freed slaves to have special land grants or extensive federal aid. Douglass, a former slave himself, favored the later Civil Rights Bill of 1875, but shunned special privileges. "Everybody has asked the question . . . , 'What shall we do with the Negro?' I have had but one answer from the beginning. Do nothing with us!"

Douglass used the metaphor of an apple tree to drive his point home. "If the apples will not remain on the tree of their own strength, . . . let them fall! . . . And if the Negro cannot stand on his own legs, let him fall also. All I ask is, give him a chance to stand on his own legs! Let him alone! . . .[Y]our interference is doing him a positive injury."

Finally, Douglass concluded, "If the Negro cannot live by the line of eternal justice, . . . the fault will not be yours. . . . If you will only untie his hands, and give him a chance, I think he will live."

Douglass knew much about rising and falling on his own merits. A fugitive slave, he fled northward and joined the antislavery movement in Massachusetts in 1841. He wrote an autobiography and edited the *North Star*, a newspaper promoting freedom for all blacks. Douglass was tall with a mass of hair, penetrating eyes, and a firm chin. Stubborn and principled, he was a captivating orator and spoke all over the United States before and after the Civil War. He was even appointed U.S. minister to Haiti in 1889.

Douglass was especially comfortable speaking before audiences committed to freedom of opportunity for blacks. Not surprisingly, therefore, he came to Michigan in the middle of the Civil War to speak at Hillsdale College, founded in 1844 as only the second integrated college in the nation. The college was somewhat depleted because most of the male students had enlisted in the Union army, which would ultimately win the war and secure the freedom that Douglass had been promoting for over 20 years.

When Douglass died in 1895, Booker T. Washington, founder of the Tuskegee Institute in Alabama, became the most prominent spokesman for black Americans. Like Douglass, Washington was born into slavery, and also like Douglass, he became a forceful writer and orator. In fact, Washington researched and published a biography of Douglass to promote their mutual ideas.

For example, Washington shared Douglass's belief that equal opportunity, not special privileges, was the recipe for success for blacks. Two years after Douglass's death, Washington also made the pilgrimage to Hillsdale College and spoke to the students about promoting in the black community "efficiency and ability, especially in practical living."

He elaborated on this idea in his 1901 book *Up From Slavery*. "I believe," Washington insisted, "that my race will succeed in proportion as it learns to do a common thing in an uncommon manner; learns to do a thing so thoroughly that no one can improve upon what it has done; learns to make its services of indispensable value."

What about discrimination—say, when a white employer uses his freedom to refuse to hire a black or to force him into segregated facilities? In such cases Washington sometimes argued for direct action. In 1894 he endorsed the blacks who boycotted newly segregated streetcars in Atlanta. In 1899 and 1900 he publicly opposed efforts by the states of Georgia and Louisiana to disfranchise blacks. Washington insisted, "I do not favor the Negro's giving up anything which is fundamental and which has been guaranteed to him by the Constitution."

More often than not, however, Washington thought that trying to use the force of government to advance the black cause was not as effective as improving the race over time and making blacks indispensable to the American economy. He observed, "No man who continues to add something to the material, intellectual, and moral well-being of the place in which he lives is long left without proper reward. This is a great human law which cannot be permanently nullified." Put another way, Washington declared, "An inch of progress is worth more than a yard of complaint."

Thus when white racists used their freedom to discriminate against blacks, blacks needed to use their freedom to build factories, invent products, and grow crops to make themselves indispensable to economic progress in America. To Washington, that meant two courses of action.

National Negro Business League

First, he founded the National Negro Business League to bring together hundreds of black businessmen and inventors to share ideas and promote economic development. After some initial reluctance, Washington even used this forum to champion black businesswomen, such as hair-care entrepreneur Madam C. J. Walker, the first black female millionaire.

Second, Washington promoted more education for blacks. Education to Washington, especially industrial education that stressed manual labor as well as literary skill, was the means to producing future entrepreneurs, inventors, and teachers that would expand the foundation of black achievement and make racial progress inevitable.

Tuskegee Institute was Washington's main focus, but he encouraged the various black schools and colleges that sprang up all around the nation. While only one black college existed before the Civil War, an average of more than one each year was created in the decades after the war.

What was the result of the emphasis on liberty, self-help, and education stressed by Douglass and Washington? Some black leaders, such as W. E. B. DuBois, criticized the slow and uneven progress, but in truth, black advancement was visible and compelling. Black literacy rates (age 10 and over) went from 20 percent in 1870 to 84 percent by 1930. That meant that in 1930—in sharp contrast to 1870—any honestly administered literacy test for voting would disfranchise almost as many whites as blacks.

During these 60 years black inventors came forth with dozens of major inventions: lubricating systems for train engines, ventilator screens to protect passengers on those trains, the traffic light, and hundreds of uses for the lowly peanut.

These advances slowly helped break down the stereotypes of blacks as illiterate and unskilled. Some of the evidence for change in attitude was symbolic. For example, Booker T. Washington, who had been the first black invited to the White House, became the first black to be honored on an American coin in 1946. The next year major league baseball was integrated; 12 years later all major league teams were integrated, and it was accomplished Booker T. Washington-style, without government interference or mandates.

As black Americans increasingly showed themselves to be educated and contributing parts of the American economy, racist arguments broke down and public support for integration and voting rights began to increase. Change was not always steady or peaceful, but it did come. Douglass and Washington were its forerunners. Douglass said it best 140 years ago: "All I ask is, give him [the black American] a chance to stand on his own legs."

—BWF, May 2005

50

Chapter **Fifty**

The Costs of Segregation to the Detroit Tigers

Many people know the remarkable and inspiring story of Jackie Robinson and how he endured racial insults to integrate major league baseball in 1947. In Robinson's first year alone he won the rookie-of-the-year award and led his Brooklyn Dodgers to the National League pennant.

But Robinson was only part of the integration story. What about those teams that refused to hire blacks, that insisted on following racist policies? What made them finally decide to integrate?

To answer these questions, it is useful to focus on the Detroit Tigers. While other major league teams were signing Satchel Paige, Willie Mays, Hank Aaron, and other black stars, the Detroit Tigers, under owner Walter Briggs, refused to hire any blacks. Wendell Smith, a black athlete and sportswriter, called Briggs "very prejudiced. He's the major league combination of Simon Legree and Adolf Hitler." Smith was no doubt exaggerating. However, the Tigers were indeed the next-to-last team in the major leagues to integrate (in 1958)—and only did so after Briggs had died.

Let's look at the results of Detroit's decision to avoid hiring blacks. Before baseball integrated, Detroit was a top team in the major leagues. Led by ace pitcher Hal Newhouser and sluggers Hank Greenberg and Rudy York, the Tigers won the American League pennant in 1945. During each of the next two years, they finished in second place, clearly among the best teams in baseball.

The next year, 1948, the Cleveland Indians signed two outstanding black players: Larry Doby, a power-hitting outfielder, and Satchel Paige, possibly the greatest pitcher of his generation. The result was that Indians won the pennant by one game, and then, with seven key hits from Doby, they won the World Series. What's more, Cleveland set a major league record for attendance—2.7 million fans bought tickets to watch the integrated team play.

The examples of Brooklyn and Cleveland gave the other teams something to ponder. They could continue to ignore black talent, but there would be a cost: fewer wins and fewer fans.

The Detroit Tigers learned this lesson the hard way. In 1948 the Tigers dropped from second to fifth place in the American League—and during the next ten years they would finish among the top three teams only once. In 1952 they wound up in last place in the American League, winning only 50 games and losing 104. No batter on the team hit higher than .284.

From 1945 to 1952, the Tigers had plunged from world champions to cellar dwellers, yet Walter Briggs still refused to sign a black player or develop any blacks in Detroit's minor-league system. The Tigers did bring up Al Kaline and Harvey Kuenn, two excellent white players, who both won batting titles in the 1950s. But their talents were wasted without a quality supporting cast that included talented blacks.

With Detroit in a tailspin, Walter Briggs died and the Briggs family sold the Tigers in 1956 to Fred Knorr, a Michigan man who was very different from Briggs. During the 1930s, while Briggs was enjoying segregated baseball in Detroit, Knorr was 100 miles west, graduating from Hillsdale College, the second oldest campus in the United States to have an integrated student body. Knorr believed in integration on principle and soon helped contribute $75,000 to develop 17 black players in Detroit's minor-league system.

Knorr was killed in an accident in 1960, but his policy of integration was paying off, and the Tigers made a splendid comeback during the

1960s. They signed Willie Horton, a power-hitting outfielder, and Earl Wilson, a veteran pitcher who won 22 games in his first season as a Tiger. In 1968 Wilson, along with Denny McLain, was a mainstay of the Tiger pitching staff. Horton hit 36 home runs and was fourth in the league in batting average. The Tigers that year, after a long drought, went on to win the pennant and the World Series.

Lessons Learned

What lessons can we learn from Detroit's experience with segregation? First, as baseball expert Steve Sailer has noted, "competitive markets make irrational bigotry expensive—not impossible, but costly." In the 1950s Detroit could continue to field segregated teams, but only at a price. Joseph Bibb, a black sportswriter, said it well: "The white man wants money and color pays off."

The Boston Red Sox learned this lesson the hard way, too. In 1959, one year after Detroit, Boston became the last team in major league baseball to integrate. The Red Sox, like the Tigers, paid their price for segregation in the won-lost column. More specifically, in 1946, Boston won the American League pennant (with Detroit finishing second). From 1947 to 1951, with integration still slow, Boston never finished lower than third place in the American League. But they never finished higher than third place from 1952 to 1959, the year they finally integrated. During those bleak years, Boston manager Pinky Higgins, a native of Red Oak, Texas, insisted, "There'll be no niggers on this ball club as long as I have anything to say about it." No pennants either. Boston's superstar Ted Williams was the greatest hitter in baseball during the 1950s, but without roles for black players his Red Sox languished during that decade.

There is an economics lesson to learn here, too. The integration of baseball was a triumph of the free market. No government mandate forced Branch Rickey, the Dodgers' general manager, to sign Jackie Robinson. Self-interest, in the form of economic gain, was the key to integrating not just one team, but, within 12 years, all teams in the major leagues. Quotas and affirmative action were unnecessary and would have been counterproductive. When the baseball commissioner finally allowed open competition, some owners quickly wanted to hire black players—and soon after they did so, all teams voluntarily followed suit. Nobody forced anyone to do anything he didn't want to do.

One final point is that free markets in baseball provided black heroes to all Americans during the 1940s and 1950s. Whites all over Brooklyn cheered mightily for Jackie Robinson to clobber white pitchers, and for his black teammate, Don Newcombe, to strike out white hitters. After winning the 1948 World Series, Cleveland teammates Larry Doby and Steve Gromek, one black and the other white, were photographed in a spontaneous embrace. Racial barriers receded and sports became the entering wedge that helped make the revolution in race relations possible.

—BWF, December 2003

51

Chapter **Fifty-One**

Elijah McCoy and Berry Gordy: Ingenuity Overcomes

Part of the tragedy of affirmative action is its implied premise that intended beneficiaries can't succeed in business unless government grants them special privileges. But history shows that when people have the freedom to succeed, remarkable entrepreneurs and innovators emerge. Two examples separated by a century—Elijah McCoy and Berry Gordy—show how black innovators changed American life before the existence of affirmative action.

Railroads were one of the greatest inventions of the nineteenth century. One man who was indispensable in helping the railroads run efficiently and on time was Elijah McCoy. He was born in 1843 in Canada, where his parents had fled from Kentucky to escape slavery. In Canada, the McCoys learned that individual freedom and training in the marketplace were keys to opening opportunities for blacks.

On reaching manhood, Elijah McCoy went to Scotland for training in mechanical engineering. When it came time to apply his industrial skills, the Civil War had ended and blacks were legally free. McCoy came back to the United States and settled in Ypsilanti, Michigan, where he began working for the Michigan Central Railroad.

Determined to Achieve

Despite his training, McCoy was offered the lowly job of locomotive fireman. He accepted it with a determination to show the railroad that he could accomplish more.

He immediately applied his skills to a major problem: the dangerous overheating of locomotives. Trains had to stop regularly so that their engines could be oiled to reduce friction. If trains stopped infrequently, the overheating could damage parts or start fires. If they stopped too often, freight and passengers would be delayed. McCoy invented a lubricating cup that oiled engine parts as the train was moving. He secured a patent for it in 1872 and steadily improved it.

Others tried to imitate McCoy's invention, but he kept ahead of them with his superior engineering skills. His standard of quality was so high that the cup became known as "the real McCoy," which many believe to be the origin of the famous phrase.

The invention helped the Michigan Central run safer and quicker across the state. It was also put to use in stationary engines and even in steamship engines. The grateful management of the Michigan Central promoted McCoy and honored him as a teacher and innovator for the railroad.

McCoy showed remarkable creative energy during the next 50 years. He received 51 more patents, mostly for lubricating devices. Not even old age dimmed his creative light. When he was 77, he patented an improved airbrake lubricator; when he was 80, he patented a vehicle wheel tire. He founded the Elijah McCoy Manufacturing Company in Detroit in 1920 to make and sell his inventions.

Elijah McCoy was one of many black Americans who after the Civil War improved the American workplace and showed skeptical whites what free, enterprising blacks could accomplish. In the late 1950s, 30 years after his death, another black American from Detroit, Berry Gordy, was using the free market to transform American music.

The Motown Sound

Forty years ago, many blacks enjoyed rhythm and blues music, but it was routinely unprofitable and often performed in shabby venues. Berry Gordy, a songwriter and assembly-line worker, had a vision of taking black-inspired music out of the slums and giving it broad, national appeal as a respectable art form. In 1959, Gordy borrowed $800 from his family and risked it to start Motown Record Corporation, named for the "motor town" of Detroit.

Once in business, Gordy hustled musical talent from the streets of the city and pinched pennies to survive. He set up a used two-track recorder in his small house at 2648 West Grand Boulevard that became Motown headquarters. His father did the plastering and repairs, and his sister did the bookkeeping. His vocal studio was in the hallway, and his echo chamber was the downstairs bathroom. "We had to post a guard outside the door," Gordy says, "to make sure no one flushed the toilet while we were recording."

The fact that Gordy started Motown out of his home is more than a quaint historical footnote. Doing that today in Detroit's residential areas would violate the city's repressive ban on home-based businesses—a sad comment on how stifling Detroit's regulations and taxes have become since the 1950s.

Gordy's success is sometimes ascribed to his knack for writing and producing hit songs. But there was more than that. As actor Sidney Poitier observed, "Berry Gordy . . . set out to make music for all people, whatever their color or place of origin." In doing so, Gordy made black music—the Motown sound—part of the mainstream popular culture in America.

What an achievement! Gordy had white teens all over America humming the catchy tunes of the Four Tops, the Miracles, and the Temptations. After that he promoted a flurry of black stars including Diana Ross, Michael Jackson, and Stevie Wonder. Gordy so much wanted their music, and that of other Motown singers, to reach the larger white audience in America that the sign on his headquarters read, "Hitsville, U.S.A."

The impact of Gordy's remarkable achievement is worth pondering. At one level, he created more opportunities for blacks everywhere in the music business—production, nightclubs, recording, and marketing. Beyond that, in an era of racial tensions, Gordy's music bonded blacks and whites. In 1964 and 1965, some whites attacked blacks in Oxford, Mississippi, and Selma, Alabama. But during this time, many white fans everywhere were making number-one hits for Gordy out of the first three songs by the Supremes: "Where Did Our Love Go?," "Baby Love," and "Come See About Me."

The Motown sound became mainstream American music not by law or force, but by choice. It was clever entrepreneurship, not affirmative action, that persuaded whites to integrate black musicians into their record collections. Gordy used well-crafted songs to capture not just first place on *Billboard*'s Top 100, but the number two and three slots as well for the whole last month of 1968.

America's system of private enterprise gave Gordy the chance to air his records on radio stations and have them compete for sales in record stores all over America. But when Gordy tried to expand the Motown sound into England, he found government standing in his way. The government stations, especially the British Broadcasting Company, refused to play Motown records and give Gordy the chance that private enterprise gave him in the United States. "Because we couldn't get our records on the government stations," Gordy said, "our earliest airplay had come from *Radio Veronica* and *Radio Caroline*, 'pirate ships' anchored a few miles off the coasts of England and Holland."

The Motown music broadcast from those pirate ships captivated British listeners. Soon the demand for Gordy's records swamped record stores from Liverpool to London and forced the bureaucrats to permit the music to be heard on government stations. When Radio Free Europe and The Voice of America began playing Gordy's records, his empire penetrated the Iron Curtain and truly became an international force.

Success, Gordy explains to this day, starts with a dream. "That's what's wrong with people," Gordy said when he started Motown. "They give up their dreams too soon. I'm never going to give up mine." And because he didn't give up, black Americans have more opportunities today and American music has changed forever.

Throughout much of American history, black entrepreneurs and innovators have been objects of discrimination. But, as the stories of Elijah McCoy and Berry Gordy suggest, the remedy for discrimination in the past is not reverse discrimination in the present, but the freedom to invent, create, and produce in a free market.

—BWF, January 1999

52

Chapter **Fifty-Two**

The Difference One Can Make

The truest hero does not think of himself as one, never advertises himself as such and does not perform the acts that make him a hero for either fame or fortune. He does not wait for government to act if he senses an opportunity to fix a problem himself. On July 27, 2006 in the quiet countryside of Maidenhead, England, we spent several hours with a true hero: Sir Nicholas Winton. His friends call him "Nicky."

In the fall of 1938, many Europeans were lulled into complacency by British Prime Minister Neville Chamberlain, who thought he had pacified Adolf Hitler by handing him a large chunk of Czechoslovakia at Munich in late September. Winston Churchill, who would succeed Chamberlain in 1940, was among the wise and prescient who believed otherwise. So was Nicholas Winton, then a 29-year-old London stockbroker.

Having made many business trips to Germany in previous years, Winton was well aware of Jews being arrested, harassed and beaten. The infamous *Kristallnacht* of November 9, 1938—in which Nazi thugs destroyed Jewish synagogues, homes and businesses while murdering scores of Jews across Germany—laid to rest any doubts about Hitler's deadly intentions. His increasingly aggressive anti-Semitism and Germany's occupation of the Sudetenland in October 1938 spurred a tide of predominately Jewish refugees. Thousands fled to as-yet unoccupied Czechoslovakia, especially to Prague. Some had relatives and friends to move in with, but many settled into makeshift refugee camps in appalling conditions in the midst of winter.

Winton had planned a year-end ski trip to Switzerland with a friend, but was later convinced by him at the last moment to come to Prague instead because he had "something urgent to show him"—namely, the refugee problem. Near Prague, Winton visited the freezing camps. What he saw aroused deep feelings of compassion within him: orphans and children whose parents had already been arrested, and families desperate to somehow get at least their children out of harm's way. Jewish parents who were lifetime residents and citizens in the country were also anxious to send their children to safety, hoping in vain that the storm would blow over. They, like Winton, sensed that the Nazis wouldn't rest until they took the rest of the country, and perhaps all of Europe as well. The thought of what could happen to them if the Nazis devoured the rest of Czechoslovakia was enough to inspire this good man into action.

It would have been easy to assume there was nothing a lone foreigner could do to assist so many trapped families. Winton could have ignored the situation and resumed his vacation in Switzerland, stepping back into the comfortable life he left behind. Surely, most other people in his shoes would have walked away. Despite the talk of "peace in our time," Winton knew the clock was ticking. If any help could be mustered, it needed to come quickly. The next steps he took ultimately saved 669 children from death in Nazi concentration camps.

Getting all the children who sought safety to a country that would accept them seemed an impossible challenge. Back in London, he wrote to governments around the world, pleading for an open door, only to be rejected by every one (including the United States) but two: Sweden and Great Britain. He assembled a small group of volunteers to assist with the effort. Even his mother pitched in.

The London team's counterpart in Prague was a Brit named Trevor Chadwick. He gathered information from parents who wanted their children out, then forwarded the details to Winton, who used every possible channel in his search for foster homes. There were 5,000 children on his lists. At no charge, British newspapers published

Winton's advertisements to stir interest and highlight the urgent need for foster parents. When enough homes could be found for a group of children, Winton submitted the necessary paperwork to the Home Office. He assisted Chadwick in organizing the rail and ship transportation needed to get them to Britain.

Winton also took the lead in raising the funds to pay for the operation. The expenses included the 50 British pounds the Home Office required for each child (the equivalent of $3,500 per child in today's dollars) to cover any future costs of repatriation. Hopes that the danger would pass and the children could be returned evaporated as war clouds gathered in the spring and summer of 1939.

Picture in your mind the unimaginable: the railway station in Prague when anguished parents and relatives loaded the children onto the trains and said what would be for most, their final goodbyes. Boys and girls, many younger than five, peered out the windows of the steaming trains wondering about their uncertain future. No one knew if they would ever be reunited with their families again.

The first 20 of "Winton's children" left Prague on March 14, 1939. Hitler's troops overran all of Czechoslovakia the very next day, but the volunteers kept working, sometimes forging documents to slip the children past the Germans. By the time World War II broke out on September 1, the rescue effort had transported 669 children out of the country in eight separate groups by rail. A ninth batch of 250 more children would have been the largest of all, but war prompted the Nazis to stop all departures. Sadly, none of those children lived to see the Allied victory less than six years later. Pitifully few of the parents did either.

Vera Gissing, one of the children Winton saved, and now in her late 70s, puts the rescue mission in perspective: "Of the 15,000 Czech Jewish children taken to the camps, only a handful survived. Winton had saved a major part of my generation of Czech Jews."

Vera's story is an especially poignant one. She was 10 years old when she left Prague on the fifth train on June 30, 1939. Two of her cousins were on the ninth train that never made it to freedom. Her mother died of typhus two days after liberation of the Bergen-Belsen concentration camp to which she was sent. Her father was shot in a Nazi death march in December 1944. Vera has no doubt about her own fate had it not been for Nicholas Winton.

Why did he do it? It certainly was not for the plaudits it might bring him. Indeed, he never told anyone about his achievement for half a century. Not until 1988, when his wife stumbled across a musty box of records and a scrapbook while cleaning their attic, did the public learn of Winton's story. The scrapbook, a memento put together by his volunteers when the operation shut down, was filled with documents and pictures of Czech children. For all those decades, the children and the families who took them in knew little more than the fact that some kind soul, some guardian angel, had saved their lives.

What compelled this man to take on a challenge ignored by almost everyone else? We sat down with Vera and Nicky at the latter's home in late July to ask this very question. One would hardly guess that Nicky is 97; he looks and speaks with the vigor of someone years younger. He greeted us heartily, escorting us through his living room and into the backyard where he picked some fresh mulberries for us. He still tends to the gardens around his house.

This is a quiet man. In some ways he is a reminder of Aristotle's *magnanimous* man (from his *Nicomachean Ethics*). Aristotle said the good-souled man is ashamed to receive benefits, and always repays more than he has received. "It is the characteristic of the magnanimous man to ask no favor but to be ready to do kindness to others," he wrote in his *Ethics*. You hear no boasting from Nicky, no words designed to put any special focus on what he did. In a matter-of-fact fashion, he told us, "Because it was the thing to do and I thought I could help." One can't help feeling drawn to a man for whom doing good for its own sake seems to come so naturally.

In *The Power of Good*, a recent International Emmy Award-winning documentary from Czech producer Matej Minac, Nicky says he kept quiet about the rescue mission because "it was such a small part of my life." Indeed, the operation spanned only eight months, while he was still working at the stock exchange, and it was prior to his marriage. Still, to us, the explanation seemed inadequate. We pressed him on the point.

"When the war started and the transports stopped, I immediately went into the RAF (Royal Air Force), where I stayed for the next five years. When peace came, what was a 35-year-old man to do, traverse the country looking for boys and girls?" At the end of the war, Nicky Winton was busy re-starting his own life. What he did to save so many others just six years earlier was behind him, and over. For all that he knew, the children might have returned to their homeland (as indeed, some did). "Wherever they were, I had good reason to assume they were safe and cared for," he said. Indeed, among their ranks in later life would be doctors, nurses, therapists, teachers, musicians, artists, writers, pilots, ministers, scientists, engineers, entrepreneurs and even a Member of the British Parliament. Today they and their children, grandchildren and great-grandchildren number about 5,000.

Recent interviews with many of the adult "Winton Children" reveal not only a deep appreciation for the man whose initiative saved them, but also for living life to its fullest. Many express a lifelong desire to help others as a way of honoring the loved ones who made the painful choice to trust the young stockbroker from Britain. "We understand how precious life is," Vera told us. "We wanted to give something back to our natural parents so their memory would live on."

Years after coming to Britain, Vera asked her foster father, "Why did you choose me?" His reply sums up the spirit of the good people who gave homes to the 669: "I knew I could not save the world and I knew I could not stop war from coming, but I knew I could save one human soul."

So humble is Nicky Winton that others have to *tell* him, over his own objections, just what an uncommon man he is. Like the other "Winton Children" who have come to know him now, Vera reminds him frequently that she owes her very life to him.

In our effort to add to the chorus of friends and admirers who want Nicky Winton to understand just how we feel about him, we told him this: "You did not save only 669 children. Your story will elevate the moral eloquence of lending a loving hand when lives are at stake. Some day, somewhere, perhaps another man or woman will confront a similar situation and will rise to the occasion because of your example. This is why the world must know what you did and why we think of you as a hero even if you do not."

In 1988, a television show seen across Britain, *That's Life*, told the Winton story to a large audience and brought Nicky together with many of his "children" for the first time since those horrific, fateful days of 1939. He is in regular correspondence with, and often visited by, many of them—a source of joy and comfort since his wife Grete passed away in 1999. Vera, who lives just a few miles from Nicky, sees him regularly. She has co-authored a book which tells the full story, *Nicholas Winton and the Rescued Generation: Save One Life, Save the World*.

Governments have honored Nicky with awards and the recognition he never sought. In 1999 he was granted the Honorary Freedom of the Royal Borough of Windsor and Maidenhead for a lifetime dedicated to humanitarian activities. This award makes Nicky a member of a small elite group, which includes Queen Elizabeth, the Duke of Edinburgh and Prince Charles. The Queen has conferred a knighthood upon him. President George W. Bush wrote him earlier this year, expressing gratitude for his "courage and compassion." The documentary, *The Power of Good*, is slowly spreading the Winton story around the world, as are an earlier, superb dramatization called *All My Loved Ones* and, of course, Vera's book.

In a world wracked by violence and cruelty, Nicky Winton's selfless actions nearly seven decades ago should give us all hope. Edmund Burke once said, "All that is necessary for the triumph of evil is for good men to do nothing." It's more than a little comfort to know that in our midst are men and women like Nicky Winton whose essential decency can, and did, triumph over evil.

—LWR and Benjamin D. Stafford, August 2006

Authors' postscript: Three weeks after meeting Nicky in England, we learned another remarkable fact about him that never came up during our visit. On his 94th birthday in May 2003, he became the oldest man to fly in an ultralight aircraft (known in the U.K. as a "microlight"). He did it to raise money for one of his favorite charities, Abbeyfield Houses for the aged. His pilot in the two-seater was Judy Leden, a world champion microlight flyer and daughter of one of the children Nicky saved in 1939.

Part VIII

The Big Government Warfare State

53

Chapter **Fifty-Three**

James Madison: The Constitutional War President

Is it possible for a president to run a war effectively and obey the Constitution at the same time? Most historians would say no; after all, they persistently rank Abraham Lincoln and Franklin Roosevelt as two of the nation's greatest presidents. Lincoln and Roosevelt, as war presidents, centralized power, restricted liberty, and suspended key parts of the Constitution during their stints in office. Historians like men of action, especially when these actions seemingly help win wars.

However, James Madison, the first war president in U.S. history, did not set such a precedent. War emergencies, he argued, were tests to obey the Constitution, not ignore it. His conduct in the War of 1812 is illuminating, and worth reviewing.

The War of 1812 was peculiar in that the United States was not under attack, or even the threat of attack. Many, therefore, have argued that the war was avoidable. American commerce, however, was being restricted by the Napoleonic Wars between France and Great Britain. Furthermore, Britain was seizing American ships, kidnapping ("impressing" as it was called) sailors, and stirring Indians in the Northwest to launch raids on American soil.

In the diplomacy that led to war, Madison did not hold press conferences or buttonhole senators. He let Congress debate the problem and pass laws to deal with it. Macon's Bill No. 2, which Congress passed and Madison decided to sign, guided our policy in the two years before war. It offered peace and trade to either France or Britain if either would leave our trade unhampered.

When Britain persisted in halting American ships and seizing the sailors, Madison believed the United States should go to war. But he did not act on this belief until Henry Clay, leading a delegation of congressmen, urged him to support the war publicly before Congress voted on it. This Madison did, and Congress voted (79–49 in the House and 19–13 in the Senate) to go to war.

Once war was declared, it had to be funded. The previous year, Congress had refused to re-charter the Bank of the United States, and so the nation had no central bank to borrow from. Direct taxes were another possibility for raising money, but Madison avoided them during much of the war.

Instead, Madison, as commander-in-chief, worked with Congress to finance the war in part by privatizing it. The navy, for example, lagged far behind Britain in ships and manpower. Therefore, Madison urged private shippers to attack Britain, from the American coast to the British Isles. An estimated 526 merchants-turned-hunters stalked and attacked vulnerable British ships, commercial or naval. Any profits, from cargo or ransom, were split among captains and crew.

Some of these private ships were sunk quickly by the British, but others pestered and perplexed their enemies. The *Yankee*, from Bristol, Rhode Island, and the *American*, from Salem, Massachusetts, each won over $1 million in booty. Thomas Boyle, of Baltimore, took his *Comet* into British waters and won 40 hit-and-run skirmishes, and then outrageously declared Britain to be blockaded. America's mosquito fleet demoralized the Royal Navy and forced Britain to convoy all of their trade in the Atlantic Ocean.

The U.S. army, of course, needed cash for troops and arms. Madison, as co-author of *The Federalist Papers*, was suspicious of centralized power and argued persuasively for limited government at the constitutional convention. He tried to avoid taxing to support the war, calling it a dangerous precedent and a recipe for waste and a permanent bureaucracy. Instead, he worked with Congress and the Treasury to float about $80 million in government bonds; he urged private citizens to invest in their troops, and he funded most of the war doing that.

In an emergency bond drive in 1813, after a series of U.S. military defeats, four immigrants stepped up with over $9 million in cash to keep their adopted country in the fight. These men—German-born John Jacob Astor and David Parish, French-born Stephen Girard, and English-born Alexander Dallas—risked their wealth to defend the liberty they had used in building their fortunes.

White House Burned

During the war the army lost many battles, and some critics have faulted Madison for appointing weak generals. It's true that the Canadians captured Detroit, defended Niagara, and repelled American advances on Canadian soil. Then British troops, fresh from defeating Napoleon, invaded America, burned the White House, and chased officials out of Washington, D. C.

But Madison recovered well. He had at first appointed veterans of the Revolutionary War, men who were senior officers. They did poorly. But by the summer of 1814, he had younger men in charge, and the United States lost no major battle after that.

Madison handled adversity in a way that preserved individual liberty. When political opponents attacked him for military setbacks, he never jailed them, deported them, or shut down their newspapers—as did future war presidents. Even when hostile Federalists met to consider secession, Madison never interfered with their civil liberties, or those of anyone else. He asked aliens to register, and that was it.

Fighting a constitutional war was sometimes awkward and disjointed, but it ultimately succeeded. Madison, who had been second-guessed during the fighting, was commended afterward. His decision to conduct the war in an atmosphere of liberty had helped unify the nation and it proved popular at the polls. His Republican Party gained seats on the Federalists in the off-year elections in 1814. Two years later, James Monroe, Madison's loyal secretary of state, won the presidency in a landslide that caused the embarrassed Federalists to virtually disband as a political party.

In Madison's last year in office, he supported a revenue tariff, not direct taxes, to help pay back the loyal immigrant bondholders. Within

20 years, not only was the war paid off but so was the entire national debt. The federal government was returning a surplus to the states.

Marshall Smelser, a historian of the early Republic, ably summarized Madison's war presidency this way: "Madison's conduct has brought him condemnation as a weakling. Actually, the father of the Constitution was following his conviction that policy must rise from the people through their branch of government. . . . It is hardly a mark of weakness to take a firm view of the nature of the Constitution and to operate from it as a principle."

—BWF, February 2003

54

Chapter **Fifty-Four**

The Economic Costs of the Civil War

Even after 150 years, the Civil War evokes memories of great men and great battles. Certainly that war was a milestone in U.S. history, and on the plus side it reunited the nation and freed the slaves.

Few historians, however, describe the costs of the war. Not just the 620,000 individuals who died, or the devastation to southern states, but the economic costs of waging total war. What was the economic impact of the Civil War on American life?

The first and most important point is that the Civil War was expensive. In 1860 the U.S. national debt was $65 million. To put that in perspective, the national debt in 1789, the year George Washington took office, was $77 million. In other words, from 1789 to 1860, the United States spanned the continent, fought two major wars, and began its industrial growth—all the while reducing its national debt.

We had limited government, few federal expenses, and low taxes. In 1860, on the eve of war, almost all federal revenue derived from the tariff. We had no income tax, no estate tax, and no excise taxes. Even the hated whiskey tax was gone. We had seemingly fulfilled Thomas

Jefferson's vision: "What farmer, what mechanic, what laborer ever sees a tax-gatherer of the United States?"

Four years of civil war changed all that forever. In 1865 the national debt stood at $2.7 billion. Just the annual interest on that debt was more than twice our entire national budget in 1860. In fact, that Civil War debt is almost twice what the federal government spent before 1860.

What's worse, Jefferson's vision had become a nightmare. The United States had a progressive income tax, an estate tax, and excise taxes as well. The revenue department had greatly expanded, and tax-gatherers were a big part of the federal bureaucracy.

Furthermore, our currency was tainted. The Union government had issued more than $430 million in paper money (greenbacks) and demanded it be legal tender for all debts. No gold backed the notes.

The military side of the Civil War ended when Generals Ulysses S. Grant and Robert E. Lee shook hands at Appomattox Court House. But the economic side of the war endured for generations. The change is seen in the annual budgets before and after the war. The 1860 federal budget was $63 million, but after the war, annual budgets regularly exceeded $300 million. Why the sharp increase?

First, the aftermath of war was expensive. Reconstruction governments brought bureaucrats to the South to spend money on reunion. More than that, federal pensions to Union veterans became by far the largest item in the federal budget (except for the interest payment on the Civil War debt itself). Pensions are part of the costs of war, but the payments are imposed on future generations. In the case of the Civil War, veterans received pensions only if they sustained injuries severe enough to keep them from holding a job. Also, widows received pensions if they remained unmarried, as did their children until they became adults. Confederates, of course, received no federal pensions.

Pensions and Tensions

The Civil War pensions shaped political life in America for the rest of the century. First, northern states benefited from pension dollars at the expense of southern states. That kept sectional tensions high. Second, Republicans "waved the bloody shirt" and blamed Democrats for the war. Republican presidents had incentives to keep the pension system strong, and the Grand Army of the Republic (GAR) lobbied to get as much money for veterans as possible.

The federal government established pension boards to determine whether injuries to veterans warranted a pension. But the issue was complex. Sometimes, veterans created or faked injuries; others argued that injuries received after the war—for example, falling off of a ladder while fixing a roof—were really war injuries. If the pension board turned down an application, the veteran sometimes pleaded to his congressman—who was often able to get a special pension for his constituent through Congress. The corrupt pension system corroded politics for the whole 1865–1900 period.

President Grover Cleveland tried to stop congressmen from voting pensions to constituents with bogus injuries by vetoing bill after bill. His successor, Benjamin Harrison, "solved" the problem by signing the Blair bill, which liberalized pensions to the point that even old age made a veteran eligible for a pension. During the 1890s, after most veterans had died, pension payments remained a huge and corrupting item in the federal budget.

The economic impact of the Civil War extended beyond pensions. One argument made during the war was that transportation needed to be improved to connect California with the other Union states. President Lincoln signed a bill establishing federal subsidies for building two transcontinental railroads.

Lincoln was a gifted writer and an able defender of natural rights, but on railroad subsidies he had a reverse Midas touch. During the 1830s, for example, when Lincoln was in the Illinois legislature, he helped lead the charge for a $12 million subsidy to bring railroads to the major cities of Illinois. Unfortunately for Lincoln, the money was wasted and the railroads largely went unbuilt. According to William Herndon, Lincoln's law partner, "[T]he internal improvement system, the adoption of which Lincoln had played such a prominent part, had collapsed, with the result that Illinois was left with an enormous debt and an empty treasury."

Bribes Across America

When Lincoln signed the transcontinental railroad bill in 1862, he was creating an even larger boondoggle. The Union Pacific and Central Pacific Railroads were to be paid by the mile to lay track from Omaha to Sacramento. Thus, the UP and CP had incentives to create mileage, but not quality mileage. Their railroads were sometimes not straight, and other times went over hilly terrain that was impossible for a train to surmount. When finished, parts of what they had built were unusable, but both lines had paid off politicians (with some of their subsidy money) to continue the subsidies and not inquire closely on how they were being spent.

Lincoln is not responsible for the corruption that occurred after he died, but the Republican leaders during the war committed themselves to many federal interventions other than the constructive one of ending slavery. The National Banking Act of 1863, and amendments to it, brought greater federal control to banking and imposed a 10 percent tax on state bank notes.

The Morrill Act of 1862 gave 17.4 million acres of federal land to states to build land-grant colleges to teach citizens agriculture and science. Gifts of land and statements of educational focus seem like minor interventions, but the Constitution gave no role to the federal government in subsidizing education or creating universities. The Morrill Act became an entering wedge for later interventions (the Hatch Act of 1887 and the Smith Lever Act of 1914) that established direct federal subsidies to those same land-grant colleges.

Once the federal government intervenes in an area, it's hard to remove the controls and easy to expand them. The Gilded Age generation did, however, halt some of those Civil War interventions. Those moves back to freer markets in the late 1800s help account for the tremendous economic growth during that time.

Some Rollbacks

The starting point here is the decision after the Civil War to reduce the $2.7 billion national debt. From 1866 to 1893, the U.S. government had budget surpluses each year and slashed the national debt to $961 million. Annual revenue during these years was about $350 million and expenses were about $270 million—most of which consisted of Civil War pensions and interest on the national debt.

One reason the federal budgets tended to be lower in the 1880s than in the 1860s and 1870s was that interest payments on the debt declined sharply as the debt disappeared. For example, the annual interest on the national debt dropped from $146 million in 1866 to only $23 million in 1893. The generation that fought the Civil War became the politicians of the Gilded Age, and they had the fortitude to wipe out almost two-thirds of the Civil War debt.

Speaking of Civil War politicians, those in the Grant administration—long maligned by historians—established many of the conditions for the freedom and prosperity of the Gilded Age. For example, Grant helped make sure the U.S. government had budget surpluses by winning $15.5 million from Britain for damages done to Union ships by the *Alabama* and other ships the British built for the Confederates. In 1875 Grant also signed the Specie Resumption Act, which promised to redeem the Civil War greenbacks for gold. Grant committed the United States to a sound currency and fiscal restraint.

Also under Grant, the income and estate taxes were abolished in 1872. He committed the U.S. government to budget surpluses with revenue almost exclusively drawn from tariff duties and excise taxes on alcohol and tobacco. Even before Grant was able to abolish the income tax, he had it changed from a progressive to a flat tax.

The income tax during the Civil War—the first in U.S. history—was not onerous by today's standards. Early in the Civil War, Congress passed a flat 3 percent tax on all income over $800 (which was much more than most families earned). Then Congress made the tax progressive and raised the top marginal rate to 10 percent.

When Grant had the income tax abolished, he returned the nation to the tax system envisioned by the Founders. In Federalist 21, for example, Alexander Hamilton defended a system of consumption taxes (tariffs and excises) against income taxes—which can be more divisive and more easily manipulated by politicians. Under consumption taxes, Hamilton argued, "The amount to be contributed by each citizen will in a degree be at his own option, and can be regulated by an attention to his resources." He added, "If duties are too high, they lessen the consumption. . . . This forms a complete barrier against any material oppression of the citizens by taxes of this class, and is itself a natural limitation of the power of imposing them."

After the Civil War, Americans chose to consume alcohol and tobacco in sufficient quantities to help pay down the debt each year for most of the rest of the century. American industry recovered under such limited government, and the Civil War generation paved the way for economic greatness. They overcame much of the financial damage from the Civil War.

—BWF, April 2011

55

Chapter **Fifty-Five**

Spanish-American War: Death, Taxes, and Incompetence

"Remember the *Maine!*" was the battle cry that led America into the Spanish-American War in 1898. The mysterious explosion of the U.S.S. *Maine* in Havana harbor killed 260 Americans and triggered hostility toward Spain, the suspected culprit. Spain was no threat to U.S. interests, but some Americans wanted to help the Cubans, who were struggling under Spanish rule, and others had visions of creating an American empire.

Exactly one hundred years ago, on December 10, 1898, the United States signed the peace treaty ending its short and victorious war with Spain. What is not widely known is, first, how inept the U.S. government was in organizing the war, and second, how the tax code changed as a result of the war. Those changes—higher taxes—became part of American life ever after.

The war was expensive, and taxpayers were squeezed. Congress hiked taxes on tobacco and alcohol, and also passed the first inheritance tax in American history. Those higher *taxes remained in place after the war* (except for a brief repeal of the inheritance tax). Internal revenue collections never exceeded $162 million in any year from the Civil War era to 1897. After the Spanish-American War, annual internal revenue collections never fell below $230 million. During the conflict, the United States also recorded its largest deficit since the Civil War years.

Government Ineptitude

The man in charge of organizing an army to fight Spain was the secretary of war, Russell Alger—a Detroit lumber baron and former governor of Michigan. Most historians of the Spanish-American War say that Alger did a dismal job. At one level, he was weak and unprepared. On March 9, 1898, six weeks before the U.S. declared war on Spain, Congress allocated $50 million "for national defense and for each and every purpose connected therewith." But Alger never insisted that any of it be used to prepare an army to fight.

In April, when the war began, Alger desperately struggled to equip the Army for battles in Cuba. Disaster followed disaster. For example, the soldiers were issued wool uniforms for a summer war in a tropical climate. The mess pans were leftovers from the Civil War. Few soldiers received modern rifles; most ended up with outdated Springfields, and some, like Michigan's 32nd regiment, had no rifles at all and never made it overseas. Those who did make it to Cuba ate food so sickening that soldiers called it "embalmed beef," and a special war commission later investigated what was in it.

Alger, of course, blamed the slow-moving bureaucracy, including the legions of political appointees in the War Department, for his problems. Alger himself, however, had to take full responsibility for appointing William R. Shafter as chief general for the Cuban campaign. Shafter, from Galesburg, Michigan, was 62 years old when the war broke out. He moved slowly because he weighed almost 300 pounds. He was ill during most of the fighting, and many questioned his abilities. Teddy Roosevelt, who led the charge up San Juan Hill, said that "not since the campaign of Crassus against the Parthians [over 2,000 years ago] has there been so criminally incompetent a general as Shafter."

Yet in spite of the snafus and bungling, the United States won the war. The Navy, which was well prepared, joined the Army to force a Spanish surrender at Santiago, Cuba. When the war ended, many Americans demanded a formal investigation of why the war department was so inefficient. Secretary Alger resigned in 1899 under heavy criticism and without clear support from President McKinley. In temporary retirement, Alger wrote a book, *The Spanish-American War*, to try to explain why so much went so wrong.

Those who are too critical of Alger miss a larger point. Incompetent generals, lazy bureaucrats, and a confused secretary of war are the stuff of most wars. That's one reason why wars should be avoided, if possible. What offsets the ineptitude is that America has had a free people eager to preserve their way of life and willing to overcome military hardships to do so.

Within four months and one week after Congress declared war, over 274,000 men had volunteered to put on wool uniforms, endure a disease-ridden tropical climate, eat bad food, and risk their lives shooting antique guns at menacing Spanish soldiers. Not all of these men made it to Cuba, but M.B. Stewart, one who did, said it best this way: "We were doing the best we knew and our lack of knowledge was more than outweighed by the magnificent spirit and discipline of both officers and men."

We have two groups, then: the American soldiers, raised in a culture of freedom and willing to preserve it if called upon; and the politicians, who seemed to care more about protecting their careers or building an overseas empire than they did about the lives of soldiers or the taxes on civilians. Even after the Spanish-American War, politicians missed their chance to balance the scales of justice. In 1902, the Michigan legislators selected Russell Alger to be a U.S. senator, and shortly thereafter they built a bronze bust of General Shafter in his hometown of Galesburg.

—*BWF, December 1998*

56

Chapter **Fifty-Six**

Don't Expect Much From Politics

The older I get and the more I learn from observing politics, the more obvious it is that it's no way to run a business—or almost anything else, for that matter. The deficiencies, absurdities, and perverse incentives inherent in the political process are powerful enough to frustrate anyone with the best of intentions. It frequently exalts ignorance and panders to it. And a few notable exceptions aside, it tends to attract the most mediocre talent with motives that are questionable at best.

In 2001 Max Kennedy, the ninth child of Robert and Ethel Kennedy, flirted with the idea of running for political office. A story in the July 15 *New York Times Magazine*, recounted his ill-fated attempt at a stump speech riddled with trite one-liners like these: "I want to fight for all of you. I'll commit myself heart and soul to be the kind of congressman who cares about you. I'll dedicate myself to fighting for working families to have a fair chance. I make you this one pledge: I will always be there for you."

Kennedy's handler pressed him repeatedly for a "take-away message," something of substance that his audience would remember. "What do you want people to take away from it?" he asked several different ways. The would-be candidate stammered and couldn't think of much other than "I'm a nice guy" until finally he admitted, "I don't know. Whatever it has to be."

Eligible for public office? Certainly, though in this case the subject fizzled out before his campaign was ever lit, and he has presumably found useful work elsewhere. Hundreds just like Max Kennedy get elected every year. But would it ever occur to you to put someone who talks this way in charge of your business? Outside of politics, is there any other endeavor in which such nonsense is as epidemic?

Welcome to the silly side of politics. It's characterized by no-speak, doublespeak, and stupidspeak—the use of one's tongue, lips, and other speechmaking body parts to sway minds without ever educating them, and deceiving them if necessary. The serious side of politics comes afterwards when the elected actually do something, even if—as is often the case—it bears little resemblance to what they promised. It's serious business in any case because it's the part where coercion puts flesh on the rhetorical bones. What makes a politician a politician, and differentiates politics from all other walks of life, is that the politician's words are backed up by his ability to deploy legal force.

This is not a trivial point. After all, in the grand scheme of life there are ultimately only two ways to get what you want. You can rely on voluntary action (work, production, trade, persuasion, and charity) or you can swipe. Exemplars of voluntary action are Mother Teresa, Henry Ford, Bill Gates, J.K. Rowling, and the kid who delivers your newspaper. When someone who isn't elected or appointed to any post in government swipes something, he's a thief.

If acting in his capacity as a government official, one who might otherwise be thought of as a thief is considered at least by many to be a "public servant." And he's not swiping, he's "appropriating."

Neither Reason Nor Eloquence

No generation ever grasped the meaning of this better than that of America's Founders. George Washington is credited with having declared that "Government is not reason. It is not eloquence. It is force. Like fire, it is a dangerous servant and a fearful master." In other words, even when government is no larger than what Washington wanted and does its job so well as to be a true "servant," it's still "dangerous."

Indeed, it's on this point that all the difference in the world is made. Things that rely on the regular affirmation of voluntary consent don't look at all like those that rest on force. Whereas mutual consent encourages actual results and accountability, the political process puts a higher premium on the mere promise or claim of results and the shifting of blame to other parties.

To win or keep your patronage and support, a provider of goods or services must manufacture something of real value. A business that doesn't produce or a charity that doesn't meet a need will quickly disappear. To get your vote, one politician only has to look or sound better than the next, even if both of them would renege on more pledges than they would keep. In the free marketplace, you almost always get what you pay for and pay for what you get. As a potential customer, you can say, "No, thanks," and take a walk. In politics the connection between what you pay for and what you actually get is problematic at best.

This is another way of asserting that your vote in the marketplace counts for so much more than your vote in the polling booth. Cast your dollars for the washing machine of your choice and that's what you get—nothing more and nothing less. Pull the lever for the politician of your choice and most of the time, if you're lucky, you'll get some of what you do want and much of what you don't. And the votes of a special-interest lobby may ultimately cancel yours out.

Some politicians like to rail against a practice in the private sector they call "bundling." If you want to buy a company's computer operating system, for example, you may also have to buy his Internet browser. That's not much different from what happens at your local bookstore: you may only want chapter one, but you've got to buy the whole book. But if "bundling" is a crime, then politics is Public Enemy No. 1. In some elections the options range from Scarface to Machine Gun Kelly. Politics may not be the oldest profession, but the results are often the same.

These important distinctions between voluntary, civil society and coercion-based government explain why in politics the Max Kennedy-types are the rule rather than the exception. Say little or nothing, or say silly things, or say one thing and do another—and your prospects of success may only be enhanced. When the customers are captives, the seller may just as easily be the one who whispers seductive nonsense in their ears as the one who puts something real on their plates.

Like it or not, people judge private, voluntary activities by a higher standard than they do public acts of the political process. That's all the more reason to keep politics a small and isolated corner of our lives. We all have so many more productive things to tend to.

—LWR, December 2001

About the Authors

Lawrence W. Reed has served as president of the Foundation for Economic Education since September 1, 2008. Prior to that, he was president for twenty years of the Mackinac Center for Public Policy in Midland, Michigan. Reed has authored over 1,000 columns and articles in dozens of newspapers, magazines and journals in the U. S. and abroad, as well as five books. He has lectured in dozens of nations.

Reed's articles have appeared in *The Wall Street Journal*, *Christian Science Monitor*, *USA Today*, *Baltimore Sun*, *Detroit News* and *Detroit Free Press*, among many others. His interests in political and economic affairs have taken him to 78 countries on six continents. He holds a B.A. degree in Economics from Grove City College (1975) and an M.A. degree in History from Slippery Rock State University (1978), both in Pennsylvania. He holds two honorary doctorates from Central Michigan University (Public Administration, 1993) and Northwood University (Laws, 2008). He is a member of the Mont Pelerin Society and is an advisor to numerous organizations around the world. A full bio is available at FEE.org and on Wikipedia.

Burton Folsom is the Charles Kline Professor of History and Management at Hillsdale College and senior historian for the Foundation for Economic Education. He holds a Ph.D from the University of Pittsburgh. He lectures widely throughout the U.S. and is a regular speaker at FEE's summer seminars for college students.

Folsom has publshed seven books, including the widely acclaimed *The Myth of the Robber Barons*, now in its sixth edition. His work on the first two terms of Franklin Roosevelt, *New Deal or Raw Deal?*, is considered a ground-breaking revision of the FDR myth. The sequel, co-authored with his wife Anita, is *FDR Goes to War* (Simon & Schuster, 2011). He and his wife write for their blog at www.BurtFolsom.com.